D1000664

Z.R

The Philosophy
of
Anaxagoras

The Philosophy

of

Anaxagoras

As reconstructed by

FELIX M. CLEVE

MARTINUS NIJHOFF / THE HAGUE / 1973

ALBRIGHT COLLEGE LIBRARY

© *1973 by Martinus Nijhoff, The Hague, Netherlands*
All rights reserved, including the right to translate or to
reproduce this book or parts thereof in any form

ISBN 90 247 1573 3

PRINTED IN THE NETHERLANDS

182.8
C635
P

147725

TABLE OF CONTENTS

INFINITY IN SPACE AND TIME

One Cosmos or Many Cosmoi?

The Ostensible Beginning in Time

ANAXAGORAS AND POSTERITY

The Elements – Aristotelian and Otherwise

Nous – Aristotelian and Otherwise

FOREWORD

Philosophia facta est,
Quae philologia fuit.

"It is indeed disastrous that of those earlier philosophic masters so little has remained, and that we have been deprived of anything complete. Because of that loss, we unintentionally measure them in wrong proportions and allow ourselves to be influenced against them by the merely accidental fact that Plato and Aristotle have never been short of praisers and copyists. ... Probably the grandest part of Greek thought, and of its expression in words, has got lost."

Friedrich Nietzsche, who wrote these sentences in 1873,* is quite right (save that he takes for an accident what certainly was not one). Plato, our great Plato, is really but an imposing synthesis, the admirable architect of a grand building, practically none of the stones of which come from himself. And Aristotle, as far as his philosophy is concerned, is apparently little else but a Plato deprived of his poetical make-up, those ostensible differences notwithstanding which Aristotle himself is given to emphasizing. The truly great ones, the giants, the really original thinkers, the pure philosopher types, these are in the time before Plato. Again: Nietzsche is right.

But – his plaint is not quite justified. Those grand constructions are not hopelessly lost. We have been "deprived of anything complete," but there have been left to us large numbers of fragments. It is doubtless true that works complete in a literary sense cannot be joined together from these remains. On the basis of the extant fragments, at any rate, a philological reconstruction is not feasible. However, we

---

* *Die Philosophie im tragischen Zeitalter der Griechen* ("Es ist ein wahres Unglück, dass wir so wenig von jenen älteren philosophischen Meistern übrighaben und dass uns alles Vollständige entzogen ist. Unwillkürlich messen wir sie, jenes Verlustes wegen, nach falschen Maassen und lassen uns durch die rein zufällige Tatsache, dass es Plato und Aristoteles nie an Schätzern und Abschreibern gefehlt hat, zuungunsten der Früheren einnehmen. ... Wahrscheinlich ist uns der grossartigste Teil des griechischen Denkens und seines Ausdruckes in Worten verloren gegangen".)

might attempt something rather different: reconstruction in a *philo-sophical* sense. This should not be a total impossibility.

I am well aware of the official dogma concerning the pre-Socratic philosophers: "Versuche, ihre Systeme auf abstrakt begrifflichem Wege zu rekonstruieren, sind aussichtslos."* And likewise: "The early Greek period is more a field for fancy than for fact."**

But we are hardly compelled to agree.

In principle, a philosophic reconstruction is not impossible. It is impossible only to the old-fashioned nothing-but-philologist, just as it would be impossible to the mere philologist to reconstruct a whole from fragments of an ancient mathematician's work.

Cognition of like by like – it is here, if anywhere, that that old rule applies. *Command of the Greek language, though indispensable for this task, is not enought for grasping, let alone for judging, Greek philosophy.* In those olden times, all people in Greece spoke Greek, after all...

What is to be accomplished by philosophic reconstruction is not to fit togéther, like pieces of a jig-saw puzzle, stray fragments into a literary whole; but *to construct a philosophic building in such a way that all the authentic material handed down can be fitted in.*

* Ueberweg-Praechter, *Geschichte der Philosophie*, I¹², p. 42.
** T. V. Smith, *Philosophers Speak for Themselves*, p. XI.

PROLOGUE

Blessed is the man who holds in his mind
    Knowledge of science and neither for damage
Of his fellow-men nor wrongful deeds
                      Intends to go,
But looks at immortal Nature's rule
    Lasting for ever, Nature's beginning
                      And where and how.
    People of this kind never are worried
With grief over shameful commissions.

    Ὄλβιος ὅστις τῆς ἱστορίας
ἔσχε μάθησιν, μήτε πολιτῶν
    ἐπὶ πημοσύνην μήτ' εἰς ἀδίκους
              πράξεις ὁρμῶν,
ἀλλ' ἀθανάτου καθορῶν φύσεως
    κόσμον ἀγήρων, ἥ τε συνέστη
             χὥπῃ χὥπως.
    τοῖς δέ τοιούτοις οὐδέποτ' αἰσχρῶν
ἔργων μελέδημα προσίζει.

Euripides (fragm. 910 N.)

Anaxagoras of Klazomenai,
Master of Euripides and Pericles of Athens,
was a beholder and an artist.

A beholder:
His eyes were groping for the jointlines
of this fragment of a world.

And he was an artist,
for this fragmentary world enticed him
to restoring it, according to its style,
in space and time.

Beholding
and, then, moulding what he had beheld
meant life itself to him.

He brooded on a building problem.
His work is dedicated to detail
How he,
The son of Hegesibulos,
Anaxagoras of Klazomenai,
Were he the world's construction engineer,
Would build this grand and beauteous cosmos
Out of a pile of particles
Minute and ultimate.

ANAXAGORAS OF KLAZOMENAI

(533–461/61 B.C.)

> "All has been arranged by Mind."
> *Anaxagoras*

INTRODUCTION

For quite a few decades, I have been attempting to reconstruct, in all its foundations, branches, and ramifications, the genuine system of one of the most gigantic of those giants: the system of Anaxagoras.[1]

The fundamental condition that all the authentic material must fit into the reconstruction has been fulfilled. Thus, if I may venture the claim, this *hypothetical* reconstruction, not of Anaxagoras' writing but of his philosophical system, seems to be fairly well substantiated.

The presentation of the doctrine of Anaxagoras as given in the following might appear somewhat surprising. It is in opposition to nearly all of the "established facts."

Sometimes, however, established facts turn out to be established, but not facts. And sometimes even several contrasting "facts" about one and the same thing may claim to be "established."

Three Different Biographies

Take, for instance, the mere dates of the main items in Anaxagoras' biography. Strange as it may seem, there are no less than three versions.

Common to all of them is the statement that Anaxagoras was born

---

[1] The first results of this attempt appeared 1917 in Vienna under the title *Die Philosophie des Anaxagoras. Versuch einer Rekonstruktion.* The final results were given in the book *The Philosophy of Anaxagoras – An Attempt at Reconstruction,* published 1949 in New York. The following presentation is meant as a revised form of the latter publication. It is now part of *The Giants of Pre-Sophistic Greek Philosophy* (2 vols., The Hague 1965; third edition 1973).

in Klazomenai in Asia Minor, came to Athens, and taught there for thirty years; that he was finally indicted and sentenced to death "for impiety and Persian leanings"; that Pericles helped him to escape; that then he fled to Lampsakos in Asia Minor where he died.

But as to everything else, there is disagreement, even concerning the dates of birth and death and the date of his trial.

Version Number One. Anaxagoras was born in 500 B.C., lived and taught in Athens from 461 to 432, was accused and sentenced in 432 and, having been rescued by his *friend* Pericles, left for Lampsakos where he died in 428.

This is the current, "orthodox" version, based on Apollodorus' somewhat schematic statements and backed by authorities such as Diels; which is to say that it is accepted by the majority.

Version Number Two. Lifetime: 500–428 (as above); residence in Athens: 480–450; date of the trial: 450; then residence in Lampsakos where he conducts a flourishing and influential school of philosophy for the last two decades of his life.

This version was proposed, and supported with some impressive arguments, by A. E. Taylor in a clever essay, "On the Date of the Trial of Anaxagoras." [1]

Version Number Three. Already more than a hundred years ago, the great philologist K. F. Hermann contended that 534 B.C. (Olymp. 61/3) was the year of the birth of Anaxagoras.[2] And according to another German philologist, Georg Friedrich Unger, the main dates would be as follows: Anaxagoras was born in 533, came to Athens in 494 (after the fall of Miletus), and taught there for thirty years. Among his pupils were some of the afterwards most famous Athenians, such as Themistocles,[3] Pericles, and Euripides. After the fall of the meteoric stone of Aigospotamoi in 467/6 [4] – to him a confirmation of his astrophysical theories – he made up his mind to put his doctrine down in writing, published his book in 466 and, thereupon, was indicted and sentenced – "for impiety and Persian leanings" – in 465. Rescued by his *pupil* Pericles, who was just successfully beginning his career at that time (after the death of Aristides in 467), he left for Lampsakos (then still under Persian rule) where he died some years later, in 462 or 461.

---

[1] *The Classical Quarterly*, II (1917), 81–87.
[2] *De philos. Ionic. aetatibus*, Göttingen, 1849, p. 10 ff.
[3] according to Stesimbrotos. Cf. Plutarch. Them. 2.
[4] according to more recent estimates, in 468/7.

This version has been presented by Unger in 1884 in a brilliant, detailed research on *"Die Zeitverhältnisse des Anaxagoras und Empedokles"* [1] in which he accounts for all his statements with convincing arguments. To quote just one of them: Aside from the fact that in none of the Platonic dialogues is Anaxagoras introduced as a living person, Socrates who was born in 469 attended lectures by Archelaos, a disciple of Anaxagoras'. Would Socrates have become a hearer of the disciple if the master himself had taught in Athens until 432?

Topic for an Historical Novel ...

On the basis of the usual chronology, the indictment of Anaxagoras not only "for impiety," but also "for Persian leanings" has been considered completely senseless, and rightly so. By the Hermann and Unger version, however, such indictment is given a certain appearance of justification. And without at least a seeming justification such an inculpation would have been ineffective, needless to say:

It was from a Persian province that in 494, after the destruction of Miletus, Anaxagoras came to Athens. And when finally fleeing to Lampsakos, he went to a town still under Persian rule at that time. And besides, exactly then this town was a personal estate of Anaxagoras' former pupil Themistocles to whom shortly before, when from ungrateful Athens he came to Persia as a refugee, the three cities, Magnesia, Lampsakos, and Myus, were presented as a gift by King Artaxerxes I (465–424 B.C.). Themistocles himself died in Magnesia in 460 B.C.

Time Is Not Reversible ...

There are, then, no less than three sets of greatly differing "established facts." For inner reasons, I for one prefer version number three.

Quite generally, therefore, reproachful pointing at contradictions of "established facts" is not enough to cause me worry if I can point, in turn, at some of Anaxagoras' own words contrary to such alleged "facts" as "established" by later authorities – whatever their names may be.

There are those who would like not only "facts," but also estimates to be "established" once and for all. And so someone has indeed

[1] *Philologus*, IV (1884) Suppl., 511–550.

3

produced the objection that I have "over-emphasized Anaxagoras' place in the philosophy of the era."

Such an objection is tantamount to taking for granted and established what precisely is the question:

The place Anaxagoras has held so far had been given him on the basis of the old opinions and interpretations – those interpretations and opinions which now are being questioned and contested. It is not that I started by "over-emphasizing the place of Anaxagoras" and then, on this presupposition, undertook to reconstruct his philosophy. It is exactly the other way round: On the basis of the results of more than thirty years of research, I am now suggesting some change in the estimate of the place due to Anaxagoras in the philosophy of mankind (not: "of the era"!).

The only presuppositions on which I venture to base my reconstruction are as follows:

1. that Anaxagoras was a real philosopher, and not a babbler;

2. that, as after all a human being, Anaxagoras must not be expected to have foreseen what would happen even a single day after his death, let alone some decades or centuries later; and, consequently,

3. that Anaxagoras cannot justly be blamed for not having paid his world-renowned successors enough reverence to harmonize his philosophy with their interpretations.[1]

Time is not reversible. Therefore, if we want to arrive at an understanding of what the genuine Anaxagoras thought and taught, we may, in fact we must, presuppose all that he could have learned from his philosophic predecessors and contemporaries. But on the other hand, while attempting to reconstruct his philosophy, all of our knowledge, and even notions, that arose from later periods of human thought must be silenced and forgotten.

A difficult task, indeed, but as thrilling as an actor's! To impersonate Orestes in a tuxedo would hardly be proper, would it? And so, too, in the historic theatre of mental evolution, true style is pertinent.

Yet, it is not as wearers of their costumes that the heroes of Greek tragedy have become eternal human models, but because they are

---

[1] Exactly the reverse is F. M. Cornford's opinion. To him "Anaxagoras' own language is very vague and ambiguous." Cornford deems it "safer ... to rely on the definite testimony of those who had certainly read his book (Aristotle, Theophrastus, Simplicius) and afterwards to consider whether the fragments can be fairly interpreted accordingly." ("Anaxagoras' Theory of Matter," *Classical Quarterly*, XXIV [1930] p. 22.)

embodiments of eternal types of human character, engaged in eternal human conflicts.

Likewise, beyond its mental costume, so interesting historically, the philosophy of Anaxagoras – in its very essence, its primary and prime conception – has come to be an eternal answer to an eternal question.

THE CONSTITUENTS OF THE UNIVERSE

Anaxagoras of Klazomenai, master of Euripides and Pericles of Athens, was a beholder and an artist.

A beholder: His eyes were groping for the jointlines of this fragment of a world.

And he was an artist. For this fragmentary world enticed him to restoring it, according to its style, in space and time.

Beholding and, then, moulding what he had beheld meant life itself to him.

He brooded on a building problem. His work is dedicated to detail how he, the son of Hegesibulos, Anaxagoras of Klazomenai, were he the world's construction engineer, would build this grand and beauteous cosmos out of a pile of particles minute and ultimate.

The Elements and Their Moiras

What are those ultimate units which, by their variously changing aggregation and combination, make the world's perceptible objects emerge and vanish and, in the past, effected the formation of this whole?

Aristotelian Reports

Concerning the stones with which Anaxagoras built up his universe, there is present a wide and significant divergence between the expositions of Aristotle and the words of Anaxagoras himself (as handed down by Simplikios).

Aristotle appears to designate the ultimate units of Anaxagoras by the term *homoiomereses* and usually cites as examples flesh, bone, and other parts of organisms:

> Anaxagoras ... (holds) the *homoiomereses* to be the elements, I mean such as flesh and bone and everything of that kind.
>
> Ἀναξαγόρας ... τὰ ... ὁμοιομερῆ στοιχεῖα (φησὶν εἶναι), λέγω δ' οἶον σάρκα καὶ ὀστοῦν καὶ τῶν τοιούτων ἕκαστον.
>
> *Arist. de caelo III 3. 302a31; A43.*

5

He, namely (sc., Anaxagoras), holds up as elements the *homoiomereses*, such as bone and flesh and marrow and all the others, of which the parts have the same names (sc., as the respective wholes).

ὁ μὲν γὰρ τὰ ὁμοιομερῆ στοιχεῖα τίθησιν οἷον ὀστοῦν καὶ σάρκα καὶ μυελὸν καὶ τῶν ἄλλων ὧν ἑκάστου συνώνυμον τὸ μέρος ἐστίν.

Arist. de gen. et corr. I 1. 314a18; A46.

In the extant fragments of Anaxagoras' work, however, the *seeds of things* are exemplified, instead, by *the bright* and *the dark, the rare* and *the dense, the dry* and *the moist, the warm* and *the cold.* The passages read as follows:

... the mixture of all things: of the moist and the dry, of the warm and the cold, of the bright and the dark (since also much earth was therein [1]), and, generally, of seeds infinite in quantity, in no way like each other.

... ἡ σύμμιξις πάντων χρημάτων, τοῦ τε διεροῦ καὶ τοῦ ξηροῦ καὶ τοῦ θερμοῦ καὶ τοῦ ψυχροῦ καὶ τοῦ λαμπροῦ καὶ τοῦ ζοφεροῦ (καὶ γῆς πολλῆς ἐνεούσης [1]) καὶ σπερμάτων ἀπείρων πλῆθος οὐδὲν ἐοικότων ἀλλήλοις.

fr. 4 (Simpl. phys. 156, 1 ff.).

... the dense is severed from the rare, the warm from the cold, the bright from the dark, and the dry from the moist.

... ἀποκρίνεται ἀπό τε τοῦ ἀραιοῦ τὸ πυκνὸν καὶ ἀπὸ τοῦ ψυχροῦ τὸ θερμὸν καὶ ἀπὸ τοῦ ζοφεροῦ τὸ λαμπρὸν καὶ ἀπὸ τοῦ διεροῦ τὸ ξηρόν.

fr. 12 (Simpl. phys. 156, 29–157, 1).

How is it that such strange elements are not mentioned by Aristotle in those passages, and that, instead, the aforesaid substances are referred to as kinds of *homoiomereses?* Or should perhaps the *homoiomereses* be something different from the *seeds* (σπέρματα) or *particles* (μοῖραι) of Anaxagoras?

Yet, in the lines following the first of the passages quoted, the term

---

[1] The intercalated *genetivus absolutus* καὶ γῆς πολλῆς ἐνεούσης ("since also much earth was [potentially] therein") is understood as an illustration of the second, the fourth, and the sixth of the preceding genitives. As to this reconstruction of the system, it does not matter whether we attribute these words of comment to Anaxagoras himself or consider them a marginal note by Simplikios, slipped into the text later on. I, for one, prefer the second opinion, even in spite of the Ionic form ἐνεούσης (cf. p. 202).

σπέρμα (seed) is used by Aristotle in exactly the same sense as the preceding ὁμοιομερές (*homoiomeres* [1]). He continues with the statement that in Anaxagoras' opinion

> air and ether [2] are mixtures of these (sc., flesh and bone) and all the other seeds.
>
> ἀέρα δὲ καὶ πῦρ [2] μείγματα τούτων καὶ τῶν ἄλλων σπερμάτων πάντων.
>
> *Arist. de caelo III 3. 302b1; A43.*

And once more, one cannot but doubt the Aristotelian presentation. According to Aristotle, Anaxagoras considered air and ether "mixtures of these (*i.e.*, flesh and bone) and all the other seeds" (cf. also Arist. de gen. et corr. 314a28–b1). But in Anaxagoras' own opinion, ether is a mixture of *the rare* and *the warm* and *the dry* and *the bright:*

> ... but the rare and the warm and the dry (and the bright) moved outward to the remoteness of the ether.
>
> ... τὸ δὲ ἀραιὸν καὶ τὸ θερμὸν καὶ τὸ ξηρὸν (we may safely complete: καὶ τὸ λαμπρὸν [3]) ἐξεχώρησεν εἰς τὸ πρόσω τοῦ αἰθέρος.
>
> *fr. 15 (Simpl. phys. 179, 3).*

It will be best, therefore, to use the reports of Aristotle, and later authors he influenced, with utmost care. In this hypothetical reconstruction of the foundations of the Anaxagorean system, I prefer to be guided rather *by the philosopher's own words and by reasons of inner consistency based on the technique of composition.*

An Old Question And a New Answer

How to develop the present state of the universe, in its differentiation and orderly movement, from a phase as undifferentiated as possible – the solution of this problem had been attempted by the Natural

---

[1] I am purposely not translating this term for the time being.

[2] πῦρ, usually "fire," is here the same as αἰθήρ, "ether," because, as Aristotle reports after some lines, "he (sc., Anaxagoras) calls fire and ether the same," τὸ πῦρ καὶ τὸν αἰθέρα προσαγορεύει ταὐτό (Arist. de caelo III 3. 302b4 [cf. also: de caelo I 3. 270b25 and Meteor. II 9. 369b14; likewise Hippol. Refut. I, 8 ff.[).

[3] We may do so on the basis of this passage in Hippolytus:
> ... but the opposites to these, the warm *and the bright* and the dry and the light, to move out toward the remoteness of the ether.
>
> ... τὰ δ' ἀντικείμενα τούτοις τὸ θερμὸν καὶ τὸ λαμπρὸν καὶ τὸ ξηρὸν καὶ τὸ κοῦφον εἰς τὸ πρόσω τοῦ αἰθέρος ὁρμῆσαι.
>
> *Hippol. refut. I 8, 2; A42.*

The same was done by Schorn as early as 1829.

Philosophers before Anaxagoras. Why was Anaxagoras induced to take up that problem once more and look for another solution?

The ancient Ionian philosophers had an ideal of construction: For them the whole variety of the universe was to originate from a single primary substance. And they believed they had really succeeded in finding a unique homogeneous substance, through the transformations of which the whole world must have emerged.

Thales considered water to be such a homogeneous principle. But how could it happen that he failed to notice that water was not at all a homogeneous substance? How could he fail to see that, on the contrary, the term "water" was a designation for a mixture, a mixture of a good many substances of quite different kinds, such as the moist, the cold, the dark, to mention only a few?

Heraclitus – I am speaking here as if I were Anaxagoras; that is why I am taking Heraclitus, in this connection, as a natural philosopher only – Heraclitus erroneously thought he had discovered that ether (πῦρ) was the homogeneous primary substance and did not perceive that what men call ether is a mixture of the bright, the warm, the dry, the light, and some other elements.

Anaximander had avoided, it is true, the mistakes of the others. In his opinion, the primary substance, having changed into the numerous substances of the universe, on this very account no longer existed and, therefore, was indeterminable (ἄπειρον, cf. p. 150). But to think that substances so utterly dissimilar as the warm, the moist, the bright, etc., have sprung from a single primary substance is certainly as impossible as to believe they have originated from one another, for instance the light from the warm, the bright from the light, or the moist from the bright.

In other words, for Anaxagoras the elements of his predecessors were not elementary enough. He understood their "elements" as mixtures of still simpler things.[1]

---

[1] There is a striking analogy in India where the Sâmkhya philosophers' approach to the same problem is very similar. Of their five basic substances ether alone is considered strictly pure since it is only heard. The other four are mixtures. Air contains ether. That is why air is not only felt, but also heard whistling. Fire contains ether and air. It is not only seen, but also heard crackling and felt hot. Water is heard, felt, seen, and tasted (any smell of it is due to earthy contaminations). And earth is heard, felt, seen, tasted, and scented. Therefore, in addition to the impure "coarse elements," the Sâmkhyas assumed as many "fine elements," imperceptible to common people. These *sûksma-bhûtas*, or *tan-mâtras*, alone are genuine elements in the true sense of the term

But when trying to make a choice between these things, to single out one of them for the role of the ultimate from which the others could be derived, he met with a difficulty. As a genuine Greek, as a naive, ametaphysical monist without our distinction between an independent external world and internal individual worlds dependent on it, Anaxagoras was not yet able to say: Those numerous simplest things have not *originated* from one thing, but are *dependent* upon one thing *for their existence;* and that thing is present in the external world and imperceptible to us.

But neither did it enter his head, in the interest of one or two kinds of these "things," to question the reality of all the others, as did Democritus after him.[1]

And so the problem of whether those various simplest things could be derived from any unique origin had to be answered by Anaxagoras in the negative, and he had to bear up with *an irreducible plurality of equally ultimate things.*

Essence of the Anaxagorean Elements

This seems to have been one (cf. p. 321, also p. 203, n. 1) of Anaxagoras' leading motives for abandoning the ideal of the oneness of a primary substance and for assuming *a plurality of ultimate elements of the world.*

These ultimate elements are exemplified by the *pairs of opposites* mentioned in the extant fragments. Each pair of these opposites corresponds to another field of sensation, or, to say it with an Aristotelian term, is *"specific as to the senses,"* ἴδιον πρὸς τὰς αἰσθήσεις (cf. Meteor. IV 8. 385a1).

Those pairs of opposites are usually called "the qualities." This is not quite correct as far as Anaxagoras is concerned. For his strict and consistent usage of "the warm," *e.g.*, instead of "warmth" – while, on the other hand, he speaks without ado of "quickness" (ταχυτής),[2] and not of "the quick" (τὸ ταχύ), – is not an awkward way of expression, but an intentional substitution for the common usage (cf.

since they are *only seen, only heard, only felt, only tasted,* and *only scented,* respectively, each corresponding to only one field of sensation. (Cf. R. Garbe, *Die Sâmkhya-Philosophie,* 2nd ed., 1917, p. 300 ff.)

[1] Democritus himself thought he did it "in favor of the intellect," but actually his *atomoi* are constructed of ingredients of the optic and haptic fields, – and he even knew it eventually (cf. fr. 125).

[2] fr. 9. (Simpl. phys. 35, 13).

p. 316), in accordance with the cardinal meaning of his doctrine of elements.

Anaxagoras apparently imagined those opposites not as "qualities," but as things (χρήματα) – as *things of spatial extensiveness.*

He thus realized all of the opposites indiscriminately, even those which have no space values in themselves, strictly speaking, but can only be given space values indirectly, by the association of ideas. That is to say, to Anaxagoras not only was a particle of "the bright" a part of space filled with color, to put it in modern terms, but to him also a particle of "the warm," e.g., was a part of space filled with warmth.

Therefore, whenever in the following the word "qualities" is used as a term to signify the Anaxagorean elements, the reader may keep in mind that this is done by falling back, so hard to avoid, to our habits of expression and from a view not properly Anaxagorean.

Nowhere, however, have I said that Anaxagoras regarded those spatialized, independent "qualities" as "subjective, secondary qualities."[1]

The Ostensibly Infinite Number of the Elements

Anaxagoras does not seem to have been entirely clear about the exact number of those elements. *He did not assign any definite number* and was content to call the elements

> numerous and of all kinds,
>
> πολλὰ καὶ παντοῖα.
>
> *fr. 4 (Simpl. phys. 34, 28, and 156, 1).*

The same point is proved by another passage in which in an extensive quotation from Anaxagoras it is likewise only stated:

> There are numerous particles of *numerous* (elements).
>
> μοῖραι δὲ πολλαὶ πολλῶν εἰσι.
>
> *fr. 12 (Simpl. phys. 157, 1).*

---

[1] Concerning the difference between my interpretation and P. Tannery's, cf. p. 313. – This philosophically relevant remark is one of those numerous sentences taken over without change from my Anaxagoras publication of 1917. That book has been listed among the literature on Anaxagoras in the subsequent editions of the *Ueberweg* (1919 and 1926). Therefore, one may safely assume that the sentence in F. M. Cornford's article on "Anaxagoras' Theory of Matter" (*Class. Quart.* [1930] p. 92), "Anaxagoras certainly did not regard any sensible qualities as 'subjective'," might have been meant as a confirmation and (tacit) acknowledgment of my contention.

Common opinion, accepted almost without opposition thus far, holds that Anaxagoras assumed an infinite number of elements. To my mind, such view is unfounded. At any rate, Anaxagoras cannot have assumed an infinite number of elements if the new interpretation of his doctrine of elements is correct.

The usual opinion is based on the words, "seeds infinite in quantity" (σπέρματα ἄπειρα πλῆθος), repeated several times within the preserved fragments, as, e.g., in fr. 4 (Simpl. phys. 34, 21, and 156, 1. Cf. also p. 213, n. 1.)

But this argument does not stand the test. Even if one has the older view of the Anaxagorean elements, one ought to leave open the question of whether the words, "seeds infinite in quantity," mean the number of the *kinds* of seeds or the quantity of the *particles* belonging to the various kinds.

This alternative disappears if we accept the new interpretation of the Anaxagorean elements. For then that conception according to which *the quantity of the moiras* of the different elements is meant by the cited words remains as the only plausible one.

Thus, the number of the elements themselves, the number of the kinds of seeds, was left undetermined by Anaxagoras.

The Distinctive Feature

Yet, for all the kinds of seeds, whatever their number, there is one indispensable characteristic, one condition, without which they cannot even pertain to that notion:

No likeness whatsoever, not even the slightest, must exist between them in anything, so that each kind must be as incomparable to any other kind as a color is to a temperature.

In the conclusion of an enumeration, Anaxagoras says:

> ... and, generally, of seeds infinite in quantity, *in no way like each other. For of the other ones, too,* (sc., of the other elements not explicitly mentioned here) *none resembles any other in any respect.*

> ... καὶ σπερμάτων ἀπείρων πλῆθος οὐδὲν ἐοικότων ἀλλήλοις. οὐδὲ γὰρ τῶν ἄλλων οὐδὲν ἔοικε τὸ ἕτερον τῷ ἑτέρῳ.

fr. 4 (Simpl. phys. 156, 1).

Incidentally, by this view any construction with particles differing only in shape, size, and velocity, like the *atomoi* of Leucippus and Democritus, is rejected from the outset.

The Primary Relation and Its Dual Working

It is a matter of fact that there is, e.g., no color, of which the "metaphysical carrier" (as we should call it today) would not be able to act equally upon the other senses as well.

This is a fundamental discovery, and Anaxagoras understands it as *the basic and primary interrelation of the elements.* He declares:

> *There is no isolated existence, but all (things) have a portion of every (element).* (Cf. p. 265 ff.)
>
> οὐδὲ χωρὶς ἔστιν εἶναι, ἀλλὰ πάντα παντὸς μοῖραν μετέχει.
>
> *fr. 6 (Simpl. phys. 164, 25).*

Likewise:

> *The (elements) in this one cosmos are not separated from one another.*
>
> οὐ κεχώρισται ἀλλήλων τὰ ἐν τῷ ἑνὶ κόσμῳ.
>
> *fr. 8 (Simpl. phys. 175, 11, and 176, 28).*

That is to say:

> There is no thing containing
>> particles of the bright and the dark
>>> (*color*)
>
> that would not contain as well
>> particles of the warm and the cold,
>>> (*temperature*)
>> particles of the rare and the dense,
>
> or what amounts to the same thing,
>> of the light and the heavy,
>>> (*pressure*)
>> particles of the moist and the dry,
>>> (*other haptic qualities*) etc.

I am intentionally saying that particles of the warm *and* the cold, etc., are in every thing, and not: particles of the warm *or* the cold, etc. For *that primary interrelation works in a dual operation.* It is valid not only between the qualities themselves, but also as to the two contrasting sorts of particles within each quality. There is, for instance, no warm that is not also combined with some cold, and viceversa. For Anaxagoras this is natural – "the most warm" is always also "the least cold," and viceversa:

The (elements) in this one cosmos are not separated from one another nor cut off with an axe (from one another), neither the warm from the cold nor the cold from the warm.

οὐ κεχώρισται ἀλλήλων τὰ ἐν τῷ ἑνὶ κόσμῳ οὐδὲ ἀποκέκοπται πελέκει οὔτε τὸ θερμὸν ἀπὸ τοῦ ψυχροῦ οὔτε τὸ ψυχρὸν ἀπὸ τοῦ θερμοῦ.

fr. 8 (Simpl. phys. 175, 11, and 176, 28).

And so it is with everything.

Equally Infinite Particles of Each Element

From this it follows that all the elements consist of *equally* infinite particles.

Therefore, if meant as numbers of the *moiras* of Anaxagorean *chremata* (elements), "∞ minus ∞" could no longer pass for a symbol for any finite number, but would have the value of zero. For otherwise the actual surplus would be "separated" (χωρίς):

... one must understand that none of all (the elements) is less or more numerous (literally: that all [of the elements] are by no means less or more numerous) (for it is not feasible to be more than all), but that *all* (*to each other*) *are equal* (in quantity) for ever. (Cf. p. 204)

... γινώσκειν χρή, ὅτι πάντα οὐδὲν ἐλάσσω ἐστὶν οὐδὲ πλείω (οὐ γὰρ ἀνυστὸν πάντων πλείω εἶναι), ἀλλὰ πάντα ἴσα ἀεί.

fr. 5 (Simpl. phys. 156, 9).

'The Great' And 'The Small'

The fundamental statement that there is no isolated existence is true also in that field in which the opposites are named, "the great" and "the small." This could be the field of *spatial extensiveness as such.*

Anaxagoras seems to have been aware of the fact that the optic sphere includes not the quality of color alone, since there is also color-less extensiveness.[1]

---

[1] In this connection must be mentioned Anaxagoras' experimental proofs that the air, though colorless and, therefore, invisible, is not a "nothing," not a vacuum:

Those trying to demonstrate that there is no vacuum ... like Anaxagoras ... prove *the air to be something* by bending leather bags and showing how strong the air is ....

οἱ μὲν οὖν δεικνύναι πειρώμενοι ὅτι οὐκ ἔστιν (τὸ κενόν) ... ὥσπερ Ἀναξαγόρας ... ἐπιδεικνύουσι ... ὅτι ἔστι τι ὁ ἀήρ, στρεβλοῦντες τοὺς ἀσκοὺς καὶ δεικνύντες ὡς ἰσχυρὸς ὁ ἀήρ ...

Arist. phys. IV 6. 213a22; A68.

An isolated existence of particles of "the small" or "the great" can never occur. For the number of the great-particles which exist in the universe and the number of the small-particles which exist in the universe – just as the numbers of the particles of all the other kinds of *moiras*, as explained above – are absolutely equal, namely, equally infinite. Thus an isolated surplus can never arise anywhere:

> And since also the portions of the great and of the small are equal in number, also in this respect all (elements) would be in everything, and isolated existence is impossible. . . .
>
> καὶ ὅτε δὲ ἴσαι μοῖραί εἰσι τοῦ τε μεγάλου καὶ τοῦ σμικροῦ πλῆθος, καὶ οὕτως ἂν εἴη ἐν παντὶ πάντα· οὐδὲ χωρὶς ἔστιν εἶναι . . .
>
> *fr. 6 (Simpl. phys. 164, 25).*

Consequently, *there is no smallest nor greatest:*

> For of the small there is no smallest, but always a smaller one . . . but also of the great there is always a greater one. And it (sc., the great) is equal to the small in number.
>
> οὔτε γὰρ τοῦ σμικροῦ ἐστι τό γε ἐλάχιστον, ἀλλ' ἔλασσον ἀεί . . . ἀλλὰ καὶ τοῦ μεγάλου ἀεί ἐστι μεῖζον. καὶ ἴσον ἐστὶ τῷ σμικρῷ πλῆθος.
>
> *fr. 3 (Simpl. phys. 164, 16).*

For an absolutely "smallest" would contain no great-particles at all, and an absolutely "greatest" would contain no small-particles at all. Such an "isolated existence," however, is out of the question: Even "the most great" is always "the least small" as well, and viceversa.
Hence:

> *With reference to itself,* each thing is both great and small,
>
> πρὸς ἑαυτὸ δὲ ἕκαστόν ἐστι καὶ μέγα καὶ σμικρόν,   *(ibid.)*

since it contains always both of these kinds of *moiras*, and only *with reference to something else* is it either great or small, being always great with reference to something smaller or small with reference to something greater.

Infinite Geometrical Divisibility

That there is no smallest, implies an *infinite geometrical divisibility of all things* because an absolutely smallest cannot be obtained by means of geometrical division. For otherwise the next step beyond the supposedly smallest would have to lead to nothing. This, however, is impossible. There is no literal *annihilation*, any more than there is a true *coming into existence* in its strict sense, that is, out of nothing. What is commonly so designated is *only a mixing and severing of elements which themselves are eternal:*

"To come into existence" and "to be annihilated" is wrongly used by the Hellenes; for no one thing comes into existence or is annihilated, but of things that (eternally [1]) exist [i.e., of the elements; "chremata" is here used ambiguously] (everything) is mixed together and (then) severed (again). And thus it might be correct (for the Hellenes) to say "to become mixed together" instead of "to come into existence," and "to become severed" instead of "to become annihilated."

τὸ δὲ γίνεσθαι καὶ ἀπόλλυσθαι οὐκ ὀρθῶς νομίζουσιν οἱ Ἕλληνες· οὐδὲν γὰρ χρῆμα γίνεται οὐδὲ ἀπόλλυται, ἀλλ' ἀπὸ ἐόντων χρημάτων συμμίσγεταί τε καὶ διακρίνεται. καὶ οὕτως ἂν ὀρθῶς καλοῖεν τό γε γίνεσθαι συμμίσγεσθαι καὶ τὸ ἀπόλλυσθαι διακρίνεσθαι.

fr. 17 (Simpl. phys. 163, 18).

Thus, since there is no true annihilation at all, that is to say, since whatever exists can never cease to exist, it cannot cease to exist by being divided, either:

Of the small there is no smallest, but always a smaller one. For it cannot be that what is should cease to be by being cut.

οὔτε γὰρ τοῦ σμικροῦ ἐστι τό γε ἐλάχιστον, ἀλλ' ἔλασσον ἀεί. τὸ γὰρ ἐὸν οὐκ ἔστι τομῇ [2] οὐκ εἶναι.

fr. 3 (Simpl. phys. 164, 16).

---

[1] That here "things that exist" has the meaning of "things that exist eternally," and not merely of "things that exist already before," is substantiated also by a passage in Aristotle. Commenting on this Anaxagorean idea, he says:

In another meaning, however (sc., than that of union and severance), they neither come into existence nor are annihilated, but *remain eternal throughout.*

ἄλλως δ' οὔτε γίγνεσθαι οὔτ' ἀπόλλυσθαι, ἀλλὰ διαμένειν ἀΐδια.

Arist. Metaphys. I 3. 984a15; A 43.

Concerning an alleged dependence of this tenet on the doctrine of Parmenides, see p. 323.

[2] I agree with Zeller who reads τομῇ instead of the τὸ μή handed down. And so does Burnet (*Early Greek Philosophy*, 4th ed., p. 258).

Infinity of Space Filled

The statement that there is no greatest implies the infinity of space filled, or, in other words, the *spatial infinity of the universe*.

A universe of finite magnitude would be a really "greatest." This means that here, also, a step beyond would have to lead to nothing.[1] Such "thought," however, is not feasible (οὐκ ἀνυστόν).

But according to that primary relation, small-particles are always mixed with that supposedly greatest. That means this "greatest" would not really be an absolutely greatest since it is always smaller than something still greater.

That all this has been taught by Anaxagoras can be learned from his own words, as we have seen. Besides, it can be proved also by a passage in Lucretius who, in his report on Anaxagoras, says pointblank:

> And yet, he does neither admit to be there a vacuum in things anywhere nor a limit of solids to be cut.
> Nec tamen esse ulla idem parte in rebus inane
> Concedit neque corporibus finem esse secandis.[2]

Lucret. I 843, 844; A44.

The great-small-element, then, to all appearances corresponds to the field of spatial extensiveness as such.

Yet, it is not certain beyond doubt that Anaxagoras was perfectly clear about this meaning of that element of his. The way he speaks about it in some fragments gives the impression he might have felt something like a difference in kind between this and the other pairs of opposites. In fact, as already mentioned, he obviously realized all of the opposites indiscriminately as having spatial extensiveness. This, however, would not have been necessary since the indispensable and unavoidable presence of great-particles and small-particles in every mixture of the elements would have sufficed to guarantee the spatial extensiveness of the mixture.

A Strange Juxtaposition And an Attempt at Solving the Riddle

The interdependence of the elements implies that no particle can exist alone, and that each belongs to a *molecular union*, as we should call it today, *in which all the elements are represented:*

---

[1] Many a modern reader may be enticed to say instead: "to a void space." But to Anaxagoras this would have been as nonsensical as a quadrangular circle. To him such a "void space" would have been nothing but an absolute nothing.

[2] This is also a proof that the version τομῇ (instead of τὸ μή) is correct.

Since matters stand thus, one has to realize that there are in all the grown-togethers [1] many and manifold (sc., seeds), and seeds of *all* elements ...

τούτων δὲ οὕτως ἐχόντων χρὴ δοκεῖν ἐνεῖναι πολλά τε καὶ παντοῖα (sc., σπέρματα) ἐν πᾶσι τοῖς συγκρινομένοις, καὶ σπέρματα πάντων χρημάτων ...

fr. 4 (Simpl. phys. 34, 28; 156, 1; 157, 9).

Before taking a further step in this attempt at philosophical reconstruction, we must continue for a while to deal with this sentence. For in the above it has not been quoted in its entirety. The words ending it, however, need a detailed interpretation because almost every one of them implies a problem.

For solving such problems one thing is indispensable: *to read microscopically.* Which is no more than due and proper when dealing with the words of a real philosopher.

The continuation of the sentence is:

καὶ ἰδέας παντοίας ἔχοντα καὶ χροιὰς καὶ ἡδονάς.

Commonly, this is translated as: "having all sorts of forms as well as of colors and tastes." Some scholars even translate "smells" instead of "tastes," as, for example, H. Diels (*Die Fragmente der Vorsokratiker*): "... die mannigfache Gestalten, Farben und Gerüche haben." But neither of these translations is quite correct, I regret to say.

Now, let us try in our way:

"Having" (ἔχοντα) refers to "seeds," not to "elements," for otherwise it would read ἐχόντων, the genitive. This is left ambiguous in the usual English and German translations.

From the connection "seeds of all elements" (σπέρματα πάντων χρημάτων) it follows that here "seeds" is not synonymous with "elements," but is used, in its other meaning, as a term for the particles of the elements, like *moiras* (cf. p. 189, n. 1).

Χροιή (*chroié*) is a word synonymous with χρώς, gen. χρωτός, and means, in the first place, "*surface of a body.*" [2] then also "the skin with the flesh under it," hence also "flesh," and "body," "solid," as well. Furthermore, it can also have the meaning of "color of the skin," "complexion," and thus, finally, can also be used in the sense of "color" in general, like χρῶμα (*chroma*).

---

[1] A term for "molecule." (Cf. p. 194)

[2] In Pythagorean usage, for instance, χροιή has almost regularly the meaning of "surface." (Cf. Arist. de sens. 3. 439a31; Plut. mor. p. 883C; al.)

I keep to the original and regular meaning "surface." Thus "manifold surfaces" means "manifold conditions of a surface," such as evenness, crookedness, convexity, corrugation, etc.

'Ιδέα (*idéa*) means "form," "shape," "figure," "configuration." Here I prefer "shape" since by this word the meaning "form of the outlines," "form of the contour," is best given. This is exactly what might be meant in that connection, in contradistinction to the "surfaces."

And what finally could be the meaning of ἡδονή (*hedoné*)?

It does not mean "smell," to begin with. Its regular and original meaning is "pleasant sensation," "pleasure," "enjoyment," "delight." Sometimes it means also "delicious taste," not emphasizing, however, taste, but delicious.

I keep to the ordinary meaning "pleasant sensation." The plural ἡδοναί (*hedonai*) could be understood either as comprising all the sensations of the various kinds insofar as they have assumed their form of pleasure: pleasant sight, melodious sound, pleasant odor, pleasant taste, delicious warmth, etc. (cf. p. 281). In this case, ἡδονάς, the last word of the sentence, would have to be tacitly completed by καὶ λύπας, "and pains." Or: ἡδοναί could be considered also a representative designation comprising the total nuances of the sensations of every kind, from their being indifferent through their becoming pleasant to their getting painful (cf. p. 277 ff). To decide whether the one or the other has to be assumed is a philological matter. Philosophically, each of the two possibilities amounts to the same thing: at any rate, whatever is said in that connection regarding pleasures is to be likewise applied to pains.

What, then, is the meaning of the entire closing part of that sentence?

One must not forget that the whole sentence is the summary of an explicit presentation of certain teachings. That is evident from the words, "Since these matters stand thus," in the beginning. That explicit presentation, however, is lost. Only the comprehensive ending has been handed down. Therefore, in this sentence every word is of outstanding weight.[1] Once again, then, what could have been the sense of that strange juxtaposition of shapes, surfaces, and pleasures (and pains)?

The answer is implied in the word ἔχοντα, "having":

[16] Strictly speaking, all of the Anaxagorean sentences handed down ought to be regarded in this way. When mentioning the work of Anaxagoras, Plato speaks of several "books" (apol. 26D; Phaedo 98B). Hence we must realize that these twenty-odd fragments kept from oblivion are merely certain particularly significant passages, such as introductions, *resumés*, and the like.

The Anaxagorean elements are the "qualities" of the various specific kinds. Seeds, or *moiras*, of these elements, of *all* the elements according to their primordial interrelation, are contained (ἐνεῖναι) in every molecule. These seeds, these *moiras*, the constituents of the molecule, are not carriers of those qualities; they *do not have* those qualities; they themselves *are* those qualities.

In addition, however, there are:

the various *shapes* of the *moiras* (and of the molecules, the shapes of which result from the commixture of the shapes of their *moiras*);

the various *surfaces* of the *moiras* (and of the molecules, the surfaces of which result from the commixture of the surfaces of their *moiras*); and finally,

the various *quantities* (absolute and relative) of the *moiras*, from the commixture of which within a molecule

the various *intensities* of every quality result which correspond to the intensities of the respective

sensation: *indifference, pleasure, pain,* and all the shades between. (Cf. pp. 279 f. and 282.)

All these are not Anaxagorean elements; there are no seeds, no *moiras* of them. But *the seeds of the elements have them.* The *moiras*, the seeds, *have* all those variable inherencies and potentialities: they *have* various shapes; they *have* various surfaces; and their commixtures *have* various intensities.

This being carried by carriers *having* them – that is what the *common feature* of the links of that strange juxtaposition consists in.

Incidentally, hypostatizing of bare shapes, establishing of an independent "realm of mere forms" – this step was reserved for a subsequent period. Anaxagoras himself might perhaps have answered such a proposition by disapprovingly shaking his head.

An Aggregation Terminology

For the actual present world state that relation of interdependence of the elements implies only that no particle exists alone, but that each belongs to a molecular union in which all the elements are represented.

However, it does not mean that in this actual world state equal numbers of particles of each element are present in every molecular union. Today – it was not always so (cf. p. 200) – there are all kinds of combining-ratios. For all substances known to us are different only by an inequality of the combining-ratios of the ultimate units, the *moiras*, within their penultimate units, that is, in modern terms, by the inequality of their molecular constitutions.

But is it not anachronistic to expect of Anaxagoras the modern molecular conception?

This consideration might disappear, should we succeed in removing, by this very "anachronism," one of the most painful obscurities in the tradition of the Anaxagorean doctrine.

In the reports on the system of Anaxagoras there are some terms, the meaning of which has not been plausibly stated thus far. It is not even certain whether they have been used by Anaxagoras himself or are inventions of later reporters. For they are not contained in the extant fragments of Anaxagoras' work. They are the terms ὁμοιομερές (*homoiomeres*) and ὁμοιομέρεια, plur. ὁμοιομέρειαι (*homoiomereia;* plur. *homoiomereiai*), in Latin, *homoeomeria*. The first of them is to be found mainly in the Aristotelian reports. The other terms are used only by some post-Aristotelian writers, as e.g. Lucretius, Plutarch, Sextus Empiricus, Diogenes Laertius, etc.

Schleiermacher, Breier, and Zeller, particularly, did not believe those terms to have come from Anaxagoras himself. In the extant fragments there are indeed enough other names for the ultimate elements and the ultimate particles of the elements. Hence the terms in question might easily have seemed superfluous, and it was plausible to suppose they were invented by Aristotle and others for reasons far removed from the Anaxagorean doctrine itself.

Now, one must not overlook that Aristotle might have attributed to Anaxagoras elements different from those he actually assumed. At any rate, Aristotle, as we have seen, has confounded with the term *homoiomeres* other terms which in Anaxagoras serve to signify the really ultimate elements (cf. p. 175). Accordingly, one may presume that those terms were possibly used by Anaxagoras himself, but signified other conceptions than did the terms with which they were confounded by Aristotle later on.[1]

If we assume something like a molecular conception in Anaxagoras, we can eliminate the confusion caused by Aristotle, without being

---

[1] Those terms were considered as probably going back to Anaxagoras himself by M. Heinze (*Ueber den Nous des Anaxagoras*. Berichte der königlich sächsischen Gesellschaft der Wissenschaften [1890]). But Heinze did not give any support to his conjecture, by a new interpretation, for example, of these terms.

compelled to consider the terms *homoiomeres* and *homoiomereiai* inventions by Aristotle or later authors, and the following *aggregation terminology* would result for the Anaxagorean system of elements:

μοῖραι (*moirai*)
>would be a designation for the ultimate particles, never existing actually isolated, of the

χρήματα (*chremata*),[1]
>the elements, likewise not isolable from one another.
>A term directly corresponding to our "molecule" would be lacking (cf., however, p. 194). But we may possibly imagine that

μέρεια (*mereia*) [2]
>could have been Anaxagoras' designation for a molecular aggregate of *moiras*.
>At any rate, however,

ὁμοιομέρειαι (*homoiomereiai*)
>might have been a name for molecules of equal constitution. That is why this term would correctly be used as a *plurale tantum*, being meaningless otherwise.

ὁμοιομερές (*homoiomerés*)
>would be a designation for any mass consisting of *homoiomereiai*, i.e., of *mereiai* of only one species.

ἀνομοιομερές (*anhomoiomerés*)
>could have been used for a mixture of unequal molecules. And finally,

---

[1] χρήματα (*chremata*) is used by Anaxagoras also in its common meaning, "things," as, for instance, in fr. 9 (Simpl. phys. 35, 13), or even only in the sense of "solid and liquid substances," as in fr. 1 (Simpl. phys. 155, 23; cf. p. 215). Such a shifting from the special use of a word as a *terminus philosophicus* back to its current, general meaning occurs in Anaxagoras time and again. *Moira, e.g.,* sometimes has also its usual meaning of "share" or "portion." (Cf. also p. 269, concerning ἐνεῖναι.)

Finally, the term σπέρμα (*sperma*), "seed," is in need of explanation. At times it is synonymous with *moira*, at times with *chrema*. If one asks, "with regard to what?," the dual use of this term is easily accounted for. The *moiras* are "seeds" with regard to the molecule because, compared with them, this is something new. For a molecule does not result from a summing up of *moiras*, but from a special kind of aggregation (cf. p. 193ff.) of *moiras* of all the elements. In the same sense, the elements themselves may be called "seeds" with regard to all the things existing really isolated. On the other hand, a molecule of a substance is no "seed" with regard to a mass of that substance.

[2] It is conceded that in other Greek sources the term *mereia* is only used in the sense of "part of a town," "part of a district."

ὅμοιον (*hómoion*)

would then be a term for a mass consisting, not of equal molecules, but only of equal *moiras*.

Such a *homoion* is an impossibility wherever the primary interrelation of the elements obtains. It would be possible only with an element not subjected to that relation of dependence, an element with full independence, "self upon itself."

Does Anaxagoras assume such an element?

As will be seen in the following chapter, he does.

Nous, the Ruler Element and Construction Engineer

Anaxagoras has imposed over the other elements *a ruler element*. And this reigning element alone is really "self upon itself." It is the only one beyond that relation of interdependence. *Nous* (Intellect, Mind) is the only element thoroughly pure, not mixed with any of the others:

Nous, however, is not mixed with any element, but is alone self upon itself.

νοῦς δὲ ... μέμεικται οὐδενὶ χρήματι, ἀλλὰ μόνος αὐτὸς ἐπ' ἑωυτοῦ ἐστιν.

fr. 12 (Simpl. phys. 156, 13).

For (Nous) is the thinnest of all the elements as well as the purest.

ἔστι γὰρ λεπτότατόν τε πάντων χρημάτων καὶ καθαρώτατον.

fr. 12 (Simpl. phys. 156, 19).

Homogeneity, Relative And Absolute, And Why Snow Is Also Black And Warm

Consequently, when speaking of Nous, one may speak of a *real homogeneity:*

Every (piece of) Nous is homogeneous, a larger as well as a smaller one. Nothing else, however, is homogeneous in itself,[1] but every single thing is and was (only) most distinctly that of which the most is contained in it.

νοῦς δὲ πᾶς ὅμοιός ἐστι καὶ ὁ μείζων καὶ ὁ ἐλάττων. ἕτερον δὲ οὐδέν

22

ἐστιν ὅμοιον οὐδενί,[1] ἀλλ' ὅτων πλεῖστα ἔνι, ταῦτα ἐνδηλότατα ἓν ἕκαστόν ἐστι καὶ ἦν.[2]

fr. 12 (Simpl. phys. 157, 2–4).

It is not evident at first glance that these words are to be understood in this way. As a matter of fact, common opinion is far from giving the passage this interpretation. However, relying on the context preceding and the wording of the sentence, one could understand its idea rather as follows:

Nous is the only thing really homogeneous. It would be meaningless, therefore, to apply to it those distinctions concerning aggregation as to other substances and speak of *nous-moiras, nous-mereias,* etc., since *its homogeneity does not depend on the unit of measurement.*

Those other substances which are commonly taken for homogeneous, the *homoiomereses* (ὁμοιομερῆ) – *i.e.,* substances consisting throughout of *homoiomereias,* or *mereias* of only one kind – may or may not be called homogeneous. If the *mereia* is taken as the ultimate unit, they are homogeneous: they consist of equal *mereias,* of molecules of only one kind. Their homogeneity is gone if the *moira* is taken as a measure because then a plurality is represented in every molecule, namely, the total number of all the kinds of *moiras.* The individual diversity of the various substances has been brought about only by diversity of the actual combining-ratios of the contrasting species of *moiras* within every one of the various qualities:

... every single thing is and was (only) most distinctly that of which the most is contained in it.[3]

That is why, for example, snow is only white "most distinctly," although it consists as well of particles of the black, and only cold

---

[1] οὐδενί is reflexive to οὐδέν. Therefore: "Nothing else is homogeneous *in itself.*" H. Diels translates: "Sonst aber ist nichts *dem anderen* gleichartig." Quite apart from the fact that, in this context, this is materially meaningless, it is incorrect philologically, too. For if Diels were right, it ought to read, instead: οὐδὲν δέ ἐστιν ὅμοιον ἕτερον τῷ ἑτέρῳ, as can be learned from the sentence immediately preceding in this fragment: παντάπασι δὲ οὐδὲν ἀποκρίνεται . . . ἕτερον ἀπὸ τοῦ ἑτέρου πλὴν νοῦ.

[2] ἓν ἕκαστον is the subject, ταῦτα is the predicate, and ἐνδηλότατα is the *adverb* of the superlative. With regard to certain hazy and misleading translations still commonly accepted, it does not seem superfluous to state explicitly such obvious things.

[3] It should be noted that it says: ἕτερον δὲ οὐδέν ἐστιν ὅμοιον οὐδενί, ἀλλ' ὅτων (plural!) πλεῖστα (plural!) ἔνι ταῦτα (plural!) ἐνδηλότατα ἓν ἕκαστόν (singular!) ἐστι καὶ ἦν. The plurals refer to the total number, represented in every molecule, of the kinds of *moiras.*

23

ALBRIGHT COLLEGE LIBRARY 147725

"most distinctly," although it consists as well of particles of the warm, etc. (Cf. Sext. Pyrrh. hypot. I 33, and Cic. Acad. II 31, 100.)

But as to Nous, those distinctions are devoid of meaning because *its homogeneity is really absolute.* For

every (piece of) Nous is a *homoion*, a larger as well as a smaller one,

even if one should have in view a piece as small as a molecule of a molecularized substance.

Spatial Extensiveness of Nous

Nous, then, is the reigning element.

However, Nous is an Anaxagorean element, and that means that *Nous* likewise, exactly as the other elements, *has spatial extensiveness.* Hence Nous can readily be called, in a quite literal sense, not only the purest, but even the "thinnest" of all the elements.

The fact that such "matter-like" attributes are given to Nous by Anaxagoras seems to imply a problem. That this is only a pseudo-problem will be shown in a subsequent chapter (cf. p. 321).

Nous' Immiscibility as a Prerequisite to Its Power

According to Anaxagoras' own words, the homogeneity of Nous, its being immixable with the other elements, is supposed to be *an absolutely indispensable prerequisite to its power* over the world:

> While the other (elements) have a share of every element, Nous is an infinite and autocratic being and is not mixed with any element, but is alone self upon itself. For if it were not upon itself, but mixed with any other (element), it would, (merely) by being mixed with any one (element), partake of all the elements altogether, since in every single (element) a share of every (other element) is contained, as I have demonstrated above. *And the elements mixed with it would check it so that it would not have power over any element in the same way as (it has) being alone upon itself.*
>
> τὰ μὲν ἄλλα παντὸς μοῖραν μετέχει, νοῦς δέ ἐστιν ἄπειρον καὶ αὐτο-κρατὲς καὶ μέμεικται οὐδενὶ χρήματι, ἀλλὰ μόνος αὐτὸς ἐπ' ἐωυτοῦ ἐστιν. εἰ μὴ γὰρ ἐφ' ἑαυτοῦ ἦν, ἀλλὰ τεῳ ἐμέμεικτο ἄλλῳ, μετεῖχεν ἂν ἁπάντων χρημάτων, εἰ ἐμέμεικτό τεῳ· ἐν παντὶ γὰρ παντὸς μοῖρα ἔνεστιν, ὥσπερ ἐν τοῖς πρόσθεν μοι λέλεκται· καὶ ἂν ἐκώλυεν αὐτὸν τὰ συμμεμειγμένα, ὥστε μηδενὸς χρήματος κρατεῖν ὁμοίως ὡς καὶ μόνον ἐόντα ἐφ' ἑαυτοῦ.
>
> *fr. 12 (Simpl. phys. 156, 13–19, and 164, 24).*

The meaning of the last sentence of this passage has remained *de facto* an enigma up to this very day. There are attempts enough at interpretation, though, but I do not know of a real explanation.

Rule by Nous evidently consists in its having power to move the molecules at will, but in a downright mechanical manner, by pressing or pushing or pulling. For Nous does not operate by means of commands like the God of the Bible. How should Nous be kept from moving the other elements or their molecular aggregates by being mixed with them?

Structure of the Anaxagorean Molecule

There is only one way to arrive at a solution: One must, first of all, become clear about the structure of the Anaxagorean molecule. That is to say, one must answer the question of how the union of *moiras* into a *mereia* might have been meant.

The first thought is to take the *moiras* of a *mereia* in the sense of "severed atoms held together within a 'motion district' (*Bewegungsbezirk*)."

Apart from the fact that Anaxagoras could not have imagined it in this way, merely because he did not operate with a vacuum – why should Nous become unable to move the other constituents of a molecule by being a member of a molecular union such as this? (For in this case that would be the meaning of "being mixed.") Let us take a case quite obvious and simple: Supposing the other constituents of a *mereia* were enclosed by a Nous-tegument. In that case one cannot understand how a molecular structure of this kind should prevent Nous from moving the whole *mereia* quite arbitrarily as long as Nous' ability to move itself is not taken away.

To avoid operation with a vacuum, one might suggest that the *moiras* of a *mereia* could have been meant as "volume-units stuffed with different qualities and amalgamated with each other."

Assume that one of these volume-units were filled with Nous. How could this Nous-particle be thus prevented from moving itself and, consequently, also the other parts of the *mereia*, directly or indirectly welded together with it? That would be just as incomprehensible. One might say, perhaps, motion would then be impossible because the whole infinite filling of space could form but one unmolecularized and therefore rigid mass. But that objection would not be legitimate. For even without void spaces in between would molecularization be possible: Whatever did not belong to the same molecule would likewise

25

be side by side, but not amalgamated. And also movements of the single molecules could take place within such a filling of space. For there could be not only motion systems closed in themselves, but even all kinds of movement of the single molecule, provided only that corresponding movements of all the other molecules are combined with them in every instance, according to Nous' physical knowledge present in every molecule.

Thus neither the "asunder" nor the "abreast" of the *moiras* of a *mereia* would clarify Anaxagoras' strange statement.

But what is more: *Neither an asunder nor an abreast makes any sense. For in both cases Anaxagoras would have been bound to imagine such a* mereia *to be black on the right, moist on the left, warm below, heavy above, fragrant before, and hard behind, or something like that – a monstrosity I would not dare to impute to our philosopher.*

If Anaxagoras really taught that the ultimate elements were those spatialized qualities, then the union of their *moiras* within a *mereia* could not have meant a relation of "asunder" nor a relation of "abreast." In consequence of his fundamental idea, as a real philosopher, he must have had in mind a relation of *into-one-another*, of a *true mutual penetration*.

Molecule: the 'Grown-Together'

As a matter of fact, only by this interpretation do some terms, otherwise colorless and unnoticed, acquire color and plasticity.

Take, for example, the term τὸ συγκρινόμενον (*to synkrinomenon*), "the grown-together," in the sentence:

> Since those matters stand thus, one has to realize that there are in all the grown-togethers many and manifold (seeds) ...
>
> τούτων δὲ οὕτως ἐχόντων χρὴ δοκεῖν ἐνεῖναι πολλά τε καὶ παντοῖα ἐν πᾶσι τοῖς συγκρινομένοις ...

Now it becomes quite obvious that this term *to synkrinomenon*, "the grown-together," "the fused," is an outright designation for the Anaxagorean molecule, and that ἐν πᾶσι τοῖς συγκρινομένοις exactly means "in all the molecules," "in every molecule."

Also the statement that the elements are "not cut off with an axe from one another" (cf. p. 181) is given an additional meaning since by that any relation of "asunder" or "abreast" is denied in a very plastic way.

Moreover, we understand now that the repeatedly used terms

μίγνυσθαι (*mignysthai*), or μίσγεσθαι (*misgesthai*), and μεμειγμένον εἶναι (*memeigménon einai*), that is: "to mix" and "to be mixed," in their original sense mean nothing but just this *true mutual penetration of qualities*. If you mix something fluid with something sweet, then quite evidently the mixture is not sweet in one part and fluid in another, but sweet and fluid throughout and in all its parts. The same space is then filled with both qualities.[1]

To think of "mixture" as of an "asunder" of the ultimate particles is characteristic of those assuming as ultimate particles solid corpuscles: Empedocles (see the remark by Galen on p. 345) and the Atomists (see the report on Democritus by Alexander of Aphrodisias on p. 419).

The Anaxagorean and the Modern Molecules

A philologist has raised the objection that "the molecular structure of the homogeneous substances is a hypothesis which conflicts with the principle of infinite divisibility." [2] This is a gross confusion of the modern molecule conception and the Anaxagorean molecule, or *mereia:*

The molecule of modern chemistry, realized as a *motion district of severed atoms*, can indeed mean a limit, though not of geometrical divisibility (as contrasted to actual physical division), but of divisibility into still smaller units homogeneous with the constitution of the molecule itself – if, namely, it is a molecule of a chemical compound and not of an "element" (in the modern, chemical sense of the term).

The Anaxagorean *mereia*, however, supposed to be a *penetration district of moiras*, implies not only no limitation of infinite geometrical divisibility – which alone is postulated by Anaxagoras –, but no

---

[1] All of the foregoing reconstruction of the structure of the Anaxagorean molecule has been taken over from my Anaxagoras publication of 1917. There, on pages 16 and 17, the doctrine of the genuine mutual penetration of the ultimate elements, this fundamental and truly pivotal idea of Anaxagoras', has been rediscovered for the very first time, as far as I know, since Anaxagoras' day. – A young English philologist by the name of J. E. Raven (in *The Classical Review* of December 1950) has more or less openly accused me of plagiarism for not having mentioned that also in *The Greek Atomists and Epicurus* by Dr. Cyril Bailey, "fusion" – in contradistinction to mere "juxtaposition" – is suggested as the solution of that riddle in Anaxagoras' elements doctrine. Well, it is too bad indeed that Mr. Raven has failed to ponder a minute or two over the fact that Dr. Bailey's book was published in 1928, whereas that first Anaxagoras publication of mine came out in 1917 ... Incidentally, Dr. Bailey himself was at least honest enough not to claim originality for that "at once ingenious and plausible point" (to quote Mr. Raven's words). On page 546 he has inserted, as a footnote, the vague, yet telling remark: "I believe that I owe the suggestion of this view originally to Professor J. A. Smith." (??!!)

[2] Cf. *Review of Religion*, May, 1950.

limitation of homogeneity, either. For all of the *moiras* (mutually penetrating each other) of a *mereia* are filling one and the same *entire* space of the *mereia* and, therefore, cannot be separated from one another, however small the particles may be into which the actual *mereia* could be imagined as being cut. The notion of the Anaxagorean *mereia* does not imply indivisibility, but merely actual physical undividedness.[1]

Impenetrability – Motion Resistance – Movability

Yet, the question as to the structure of the Anaxagorean molecule was only preliminary. It was indispensable to answer this question first because otherwise it would have been impossible to solve that other problem.

Here we have the solution of the riddle. It is now clear why Nous must be immixable with the other elements in order to be able to rule over them:

That the elements are penetrable to each other means that they do not resist each other. If Nous were mixable with the other elements, that is to say: if they were penetrable to Nous, it would not be able to rule over them, i.e., to move them. For if they do not resist Nous, it certainly can move itself as it likes; it can penetrate into their molecules and leave them again; but – its motion would not be able to cause their motion. It would not be able to pull or press or push them. It would no more be able to move them by its own motion than a moving shadow can move from the spot another shadow which it is going through.[2]

How it is to be understood that the power of Nous is conditional upon its absolute immiscibility, and that the contrary would be tantamount to an impediment of its rule, now appears to be clarified:

Molecules or elements penetrable to Nous would resemble Nous in power, in motive power, in so far as by their very penetrability they would be able to succeed in resisting Nous' motion impulses.

---

[1] Only the Democritean ἄτομοι (*atomoi*) were meant as "first quantities," πρῶτα μεγέθη (cf. Arist. de caelo III 4. 303a5), mostly tiny and sometimes of gigantic dimensions, the sizes and various shapes of which could not be changed either by division or growth through apposition (cf. p. 406).

[2] Even despite penetration, a determination and communication of motion could still be constructed, provided only that transmission of motion did not depend on penetration resistance, but on a primary law of pushing. This, however, is a possibility Anaxagoras did not become aware of. Regarding this possibility of construction, cf. Adolf Stöhr, *Philosophie der unbelebten Materie. Hypothetische Darstellung der Einheit des Stoffes und seines Bewegungsgesetzes* (Leipzig, 1907).

Anaxagoras, however, maintains that *there is nothing equal to Nous in power*. He says:

(*Nous*) has the greatest power.

ἰσχύει μέγιστον.

fr. 12 (Simpl. phys. 156, 20).

The Divine Mechanician

But whence does Nous get its motive power, its own motivity?

This power is an ingredient of Nous' sovereign nature. It belongs to Nous, never lost and from all eternity. For Nous is a being that rules out of an original plenitude of power of its own,

an autocratic being,

αὐτοκρατές.

fr. 12 (Simpl. phys. 156, 14).

Yet, *Nous is not omnipotent*. Nous has only the greatest power.

Nous' power is not boundless. Nous cannot deal with the elements by arbitrary will. For *they have the cause of their existence in themselves, exactly as Nous has the cause of its existence in itself*. If they were not from all eternity, Nous would not be able to create them (*creare*); since they exist already, Nous cannot annihilate them (*ad nihilum redigere*):

For no element comes into existence or is annihilated.

οὐδὲν γὰρ χρῆμα γίνεται οὐδὲ ἀπόλλυται.

fr. 17 (Simpl. phys. 163, 18).

Consequently, Nous cannot make out of the elements whatever it may please. For *not even the possibilities of their development are created by Nous*. (There is no genuine creationism, in the Biblical sense, in Greek thought.) *And whatever is discordant with those mechanical possibilities lying in the elements is unaccomplishable.*

But Nous is *cognizant* of all these possibilities of development. Nous knows all the different sequences of development to result from its interferences, *and thus can act accordingly*. For Nous has a knowledge not only of itself, but of all the other things as well:

(Nous) has all knowledge about all,

γνώμην γε περὶ παντὸς πᾶσαν ἴσχει,

fr. 12 (Simpl. phys. 156, 20).

and there is in the whole world no occurrence unbeknown to Nous, nothing that Nous has not known from all eternity:

29

Nous has known all (cf. p. 271).

πάντα ἔγνω νοῦς.

fr. 12 (Simpl. phys. 156, 25).

Hence *Nous' power is a function of its knowledge* of the given possibilities.

But all the same, Nous' will is not hindered by that. For – and this is the most characteristic feature of this divine mechanician – *he can do whatever he wills, because he does not will anything except exactly what can be done, exactly what he knows he can do.*

Without Renunciation or Ideal ...

It is usual to take the Nous of Anaxagoras for a deity "setting purposes" and Anaxagoreanism for a teleological doctrine.

True, Nous is a being that works consciously. And so is the omnipotent God of the Bible who creates the world out of nothingness to be subservient to His ends.

But there is a difference. Nous, not being a Creator, is only cognizant of what will result from his [1] interferences. Nous knows all the mechanical possibilities lying in the elements and, out of those various possible courses of a world, chooses the most beautiful and most variegated (not: "the best," which is much too hazy). But that is all, and those possibilities are not dependent on Nous, as explained above.

A deity, however, able to accomplish only that which "can be done," a deity that has to take into account those independent possibilities, a deity that would have to renounce the realization of any wishes not accommodated to those possibilities – such a deity cannot be said to "set purposes," without emptying this term of its proper sense. The world of Anaxagoras is certainly no blind mechanism; it is a seeing mechanism; but – a mechanism.

The Anaxagorean doctrine is usually labelled "teleological" in reference to these words: "Und alles ordnete der Geist an, wie es in Zukunft werden soll und wie es vordem war (was jetzt nicht mehr vorhanden ist) und wie es gegenwärtig ist." (H. Diels).

Anaxagoras himself, however, – provided we may give credence to the brilliant adjustment by Diels himself of the texts handed down – wrote:

---

[1] Sometimes, owing to Nous' being a god as well as an element, one cannot help saying "he" in reference to Nous.

καὶ ὁποῖα ἔμελλεν ἔσεσθαι καὶ ὁποῖα ἦν, ἄσσα νῦν μὴ ἔστι, καὶ ὁποῖα
ἔστι, πάντα διεκόσμησε νοῦς.

fr. 12 (Simpl. phys. 156, 25).

And, unfortunately, this sentence made up of Greek words and that
other sentence made up of German words are by no means to one
another as Greek text to German translation. For ὁποῖα ἔμελλεν ἔσεσθαι
no more means "wie es in Zukunft werden soll" ("how it shall come to
be in the future") than διεκόσμησε means "er ordnete an" ("he gave
orders, commands").

Διακοσμεῖν is a designation for the world-moulding, world-forming
activity of Nous. Διεκόσμησε means "er *ordnete*" ("he put in order, he
organized, arranged"), but not, "er *ordnete an*" ("he gave orders, he
gave commands"). And μέλλειν has never had the meaning of "shall"
as an imperative, to say nothing of the fact that ἔμελλεν is not the
present tense.

Therefore, ὁποῖα ἔμελλεν ἔσεσθαι *does not mean the purport of a
command*, but only denotes the totality of what had been impending,
what had been future, sc., at the moment immediately preceding
cosmopoeia. The preterit value in the word διεκόσμησε ("he has
arranged in order") is obviously meant from the view of the actual
reader at any given time. Thus the meaning of the whole sentence
might be:

> Whatever had been future (sc., taken from the last moment before
> the beginning of the formation of the world), that is, the totality
> of all actually past as well as the totality of all actually present,
> has been the work of Nous' organizing activity.

Here the totality of all actually future is not explicitly mentioned. It
could indeed not very well have been mentioned in the original
Anaxagorean text, first, because it is implicitly contained in the two
other determinations, and then for quite an obvious reason regarding
style: It could not have been said of it, διεκόσμησε ("he *has* organized").
These considerations might have been, also, among the reasons why
the mention of the future in all the three (slightly differing) quotations
in Simplikios (156, 25; 165, 33; 177, 5) has been deleted by Diels in his
reconstruction of the Anaxagorean text.[1]

[1] In the 5th and subsequent editions of *Die Fragmente der Vorsokratiker*, Dr.
Kranz, adopting a suggestion by Heinrich Gomperz, has somewhat mechanically
combined the three different versions in Simplikios of that Anaxagorean passage
into one all-embracing galimatias: "Und wie es werden sollte und wie es war, was

Thus, anyone who had not yet gathered it from the whole character of the system ought to have grasped from this single sentence alone that the doctrine of Anaxagoras is not teleological, strictly speaking, since ὁποῖα ἔμελλεν ἔσεσθαι means merely the world process as it would result if and when and as long as Nous works in the correct way.[1]

However, despite the aseity and autonomy of the moulded material, this universe is not a defective reproduction of a pattern enticing and elusive. Thoroughly unlike the cosmos of the Platonic Demiurge, this orderly running of the world of Anaxagoras was intended and is being operated by Nous just as it is, without renunciation or ideal.

COSMOGONY

How and from what kind of a primordial condition has Nous brought about the orderly variegation and motion that we see?

Anaxagoras may have realized this as follows.

The Primordial Condition

In the beginning, the universe, or *sympan* (τὸ σύμπαν [fr. 4; Simpl. phys. 34, 21]), – apart from Nous – was one, boundless, and immeasurable *homoiomeres* (cf. p. 189). For there was only one kind of *mereias:*
Every mereia *had the combining-ratio $1:1$ as to all the n elements.* Each *mereia* – and likewise the *sympan*, the total of the *mereias* – was a "*panta homou*" (πάντα ὁμοῦ), an "all together." [2]

jetzt nicht mehr ist, und alles was jetzt ist, und wie es sein wird, alles ordnete der Geist an." In a note he declares: "Es liegt Erweiterung der alten Formel ἦν καὶ ἔστι καὶ ἔσται vor," and in the Word Index (p. 144, line 22) he writes, literally: "stark erweiterte Seinsformel (ἔμελλεν ἔσεσθαι, ἦν, ἔστι, ἐστι, ἔσται) Anax. B 12." Yet, it does not seem to be exactly a characteristic habit of real, original philosophers to use "old formulas," "amplified" or otherwise, without regard to whether or not they make sense in a certain context.

[1] All of this criticism of Diels' translation was already contained in my first, rudimentary Anaxagoras reconstruction, *Die Philosophie des Anaxagoras. Versuch einer Rekonstruktion* (Vienna, 1917). It is gratifying that, after the death of Diels, Dr. Kranz has finally heeded that reprehension, at least partly, by substituting "wie es werden *sollte*" for Diels' "wie es in Zukunft werden *soll*." The other, much weightier part of the mistake, the rendering of διεκόσμησε as "*ordnete an*" instead of "*ordnete*," has still been left unchanged. Philosophically, however, there is a world-wide gulf between the two expressions. And so we see here one more instance of that trouble with so many philologists when they deal with philosophical texts: They have all the answers – but, alas, they do not know the questions.

[2] *Pantahomou* has not the same meaning everywhere in Anaxagoras. In the

'Pantahomou'

That is to say:

In every *mereia* there were

> as many moiras of the bright as of the dark,
> hence *no color at all* would have been visible
> to a spectator;

> as many moiras of the warm as of the cold,
> hence it had *no temperature at all;*

> as many moiras of the moist as of the dry,
> hence it was *neither moist nor dry;*

> as many moiras of the rare as of the dense,
> or, what amounts to the same thing,

> as many moiras of the light as of the heavy,
> hence it was *weightless throughout,*
> *it balanced, was unmoved,*
> *not through an incapacity*
> *of motion, but through*
> *its suppression;*

and so on.

These *pantahomou-mereias* contained also

> *as many moiras of the great as of the small.*

What is the meaning of that? Obviously, it does not mean that from the *pantahomou-mereias*, invisible at any rate, extensiveness as such is taken. But it might mean that throughout they are

> *all of absolutely the same "normal" magnitude.*

Therefore, as none of them is greater or smaller, consequently, than

fragment said to have been the beginning of Anaxagoras' work (Simpl. phys. 155, 23) it has, obviously and quite naturally (cf. p. 215), no particular sense at all but the usual one. Elsewhere, *pantahomou* is a short term for the primary interrelation of the elements. In this sense even every differentiated *mereia* is an "all together":

As in the beginning also now all is together.

ὅπωσπερ ἀρχὴν εἶναι καὶ νῦν πάντα ὁμοῦ.

fr. 6 (Simpl. phys. 164, 25).

Besides, however, *pantahomou* has also the special meaning of "combining-ratio 1:1." *In the following presentation the term "pantahomou" will be used in this particular meaning only.*

any other, it makes good sense to say that they are, by the combining-ratio 1:1,

> *neither great nor small* (cf. p. 182).

In other words:

These *mereias* seemed to be without any quality at all,

> *seemingly they did not exist at all,*[1]

only by compensation, as a result of their combining-ratio 1:1, or, in Anaxagoras' own words, "because the combination was the hindrance":

> But before these were severed when all still were together, *no surface quality whatsoever was perceptible: for the hindrance was the combination of all the elements,* of the moist and the dry, and of the warm and the cold, and of the bright and the dark (since also much earth [potentially] was therein [2]), and, generally, of seeds infinite in quantity, in no way like each other. For of the other

---

[1] Except that the finger of an imaginary observer would have felt resistance when trying to penetrate into them. For according to Anaxagoras, as reports Aristotle,

> the *apeiron* (= the undifferentiated *mereias*) is tight for the touch.

> τῇ ἁφῇ συνεχὲς τὸ ἄπειρον εἶναι.

Arist. Phys. III 4. 203a22; A 45.

[2] As already mentioned (p. 174), the words καὶ γῆς πολλῆς ἐνεούσης, "since also much earth was therein," are at any rate a remark of comment. The single genitive γῆς is not parallel with the preceding pairs of genitives. This passage is to explain why the primordial *migma* was imperceptible. If earth, and even "much earth," not mixed with anything contrasting that compensated its qualities, were *actually* contained, the *migma's* imperceptibility, conditional upon compensative mixture of all its components, would have been cancelled. Besides, the determination "in no way resembling each other" could not have been applied to the earth because of its resemblance to the dense, the cold, and the dark. But the words καὶ γῆς πολλῆς ἐνεούσης are not parallel syntactically with the preceding genitives. They are an intercalated *genetivus absolutus*, which is correctly expressed in Diels' translation, "zumal auch viel Erde sich darin befand." This *genetivus absolutus* is an illustration of the second, the fourth, and the sixth of the preceding genitives, and ἐνεῖναι obviously means in this passage "to be contained *potentially.*" Whether one attributes this remark of comment to Anaxagoras himself or to Simplikios is of no consequence whatsoever concerning this reconstruction of the Anaxagorean system. The Ionic form ἐνεούσης, however, cannot furnish a serviceable argument since here something like a *petitio principii* is involved. For any copyist when ascribing that remark to Anaxagoras himself was likely to change an original ἐνούσης (of Simplikios) into the Ionic ἐνεούσης. Incidentally, at the end of the enumeration (καὶ σπερμάτων ἀπείρων πλῆθος), I have translated the καί as a concluding "and generally." Whoever takes umbrage at such translation will be disabused by any school-dictionary of the Greek language.

ones, too (sc., which here are not mentioned explicitly), none resembles any other in any respect. Since these matters stand thus, one has to realize all the elements to be contained (already) in that *sympan*.

πρὶν δὲ ἀποκριϑῆναι ταῦτα πάντων ὁμοῦ ἐόντων οὐδὲ χροιὴ ἔνδηλος ἦν οὐδεμία· ἀπεκώλυε γὰρ ἡ σύμμιξις πάντων χρημάτων, τοῦ τε διεροῦ καὶ τοῦ ξηροῦ καὶ τοῦ θερμοῦ καὶ τοῦ ψυχροῦ καὶ τοῦ λαμπροῦ καὶ τοῦ ζοφεροῦ (καὶ γῆς πολλῆς ἐνεούσης [2]) καὶ σπερμάτων ἀπείρων πλῆθος οὐδὲν ἐοικότων ἀλλήλοις. Οὐδὲ γὰρ τῶν ἄλλων οὐδὲν ἔοικε τὸ ἕτερον τῷ ἑτέρῳ. τούτων δὲ οὕτως ἐχόντων ἐν τῷ σύμπαντι χρὴ δοκεῖν ἐνεῖναι πάντα χρήματα.

fr. 4 (Simpl. phys. 34, 21, and 156, 1).

The translators of this passage render χροιή (*chroié*) as "color." This is a mistake. There is no reason for assuming that here χροιή is not used in its original, regular meaning "surface" (cf. p. 186). But there are good reasons against such an assumption:

If χροιή meant "color," the explanation given by this passage as to why no "color" was perceptible would be nonsensical. For in this case only the "combination" of the bright and the dark would have been a plausible cause. This pair of opposites, however, is not even mentioned in the first, but only in the third place. On the other hand, what the moist and the dry, the warm and the cold should have to do with the visibility or invisibility of any color, one fails to understand.

But all the pairs of opposites mentioned here, as well as the other ones, are indeed perceptible *from the surface*. This also perfectly corresponds to the meaning of the whole idea. It is in fact *only on the outside* where those *pantahomou-mereias* are *not perceptible*, hence seemingly not existing at all, while *inside they actually contain all the "qualities," or elements.*

Thus, the total of these *mereias*, the *sympan*, is by no means a thing truly onefold that then would change into a multitude, like the *apeiron* of Anaximander. Anaxagoras did not accept the previous, naive conception of a changeable element. His elements are eternal and unchangeable.[1] Therefore, as follows from the whole argumentation, all the elements are *actually* contained in that seemingly onefold *sympan* already. As cited above:

> Since these matters stand thus, one has to realize *all the elements to be contained (already) in that sympan.*

[1] Their plurality is consecutive to their unchangeableness.

τούτων δὲ οὕτως ἐχόντων ἐν τῷ σύμπαντι χρὴ δοκεῖν ἐνεῖναι πάντα χρήματα.

fr. 4 (Simpl. phys. 34, 21).

Why the detailed delineation of the primordial condition is concluded by this sentence now appears to be evident.

With regard to such a starting-stage of cosmogony, a statement stressed by Anaxagoras again and again becomes much clearer.

Als already mentioned, Anaxagoras maintains that the numbers of the *moiras* of all the elements extant in the universe are equal. In that early chapter, we had to restrict ourselves to an incomplete quotation of the sentence containing that statement (cf. p. 181). Only now the whole sentence is comprehensible:

> Since they were differentiated in such a way (*i.e.*, out of a starting-stage like this), one must understand that none of all (the elements) is less or more numerous (for it is not feasible to be more than all), but that all (to each other) are equal (in quantity) *for ever*.

> τούτων δὲ οὕτω διακεκριμένων γινώσκειν χρή, ὅτι πάντα οὐδὲν ἐλάσσω ἐστὶν οὐδὲ πλείω (οὐ γὰρ ἀνυστὸν πάντων πλείω εἶναι), ἀλλὰ πάντα ἴσα ἀεί.

fr. 5 (Simpl. phys. 156, 9).

Those words in the beginning, "Since they were differentiated in such a way," *i.e.*, out of a starting-stage like this, with its combining-ratio 1:1, give the reason for the subsequent statement. That the numbers of the *moiras* of each element not only must be equal in the beginning but also must remain equal for ever, then becomes a matter of course.

An Endorsement by Aristotle

This condition of the primordial *migma*, the *pantahomou*, that seemingly it does not exist at all, since seemingly it lacks any quality, exactly corresponds to the following description by Aristotle of the implicit condition of the Anaxagorean mixture:

> As nothing was severed it is evident that it would not have been possible to predicate anything correct about that being (sc., the *migma*), that is to say, that it was neither white nor black nor grey nor of any other color, but *colorless*, of necessity. For (else) it ought to have been of any of these colors. But likewise it was *tasteless*, too, and, by that same reason, it was *lacking also of any other (quality) of the kind*. For it is not possible that that be of any

quality or any quantity or anything at all. For certainly some of the specialties specifically predicated ought to have been in it. This, however, is impossible *if all are mixed together,* for (else) they ought to have been severed already, whilst he (sc., Anaxagoras) maintains all to be mixed, except for Nous ...

ὅτε ... οὐδὲν ἦν ἀποκεκριμένον, δῆλον ὡς οὐδὲν ἦν ἀληθὲς εἰπεῖν κατὰ τῆς οὐσίας ἐκείνης, λέγω δ᾽ οἷον ὅτι οὔτε λευκὸν οὔτε μέλαν ἢ φαιὸν ἢ ἄλλο χρῶμα, ἀλλ᾽ ἀχρώματον ἦν ἐξ ἀνάγκης· εἶχε γὰρ ἄν τι τούτων τῶν χρωμάτων· ὁμοίως δὲ καὶ ἄχυμον, καὶ τῷ αὐτῷ λόγῳ τούτῳ οὐδὲ ἄλλο τι τῶν ὁμοίων οὐδέν· οὔτε γὰς ποιόν τι οἷόν τε αὐτὸ εἶναι οὔτε ποσὸν οὔτε τί. τῶν γὰρ ἐν μέρει τι λεγομένων εἰδῶν ὑπῆρχεν ἂν αὐτῷ, τοῦτο δὲ ἀδύνατον μεμιγμένων γε πάντων· ἤδη γὰρ ἂν ἀπεκέκριτο, φησὶ δ᾽ εἶναι μεμιγμένα πάντα πλὴν τοῦ νοῦ κτλ.

Arist. Metaphys. I 8. 989b6–15 (omitted by Diels and Kranz).

"Keeping Itself at a Standstill ..."

According to this interpretation, *the unmovedness of the pantahomoumereias comes from a mutual compensation of two opposite motion tendencies of these mereias themselves,* as we have seen (p. 201).

There is a statement by Anaxagoras that appears to be in good harmony with this fact, although designated as nonsense by Aristotle:

Anaxagoras, however, nonsensically speaks about the *apeiron's* standstill: for he says that the *apeiron "keeps itself at a standstill."*

Ἀναξαγόρας δ᾽ ἀτόπως λέγει περὶ τῆς τοῦ ἀπείρου μονῆς· στηρίζειν γὰρ αὐτὸ αὐτό φησι τὸ ἄπειρον.

Arist. Phys. III 5. 205b1; A50

That the *apeiron,* or sum total of the undifferentiated *mereias,* keeps *itself* at a standstill is by no means nonsensical, according to what has been explained above.

There is in Aristotle another passage explicitly attesting that before Nous' intervention the *migma* of the elements was at rest:

He (sc., Anaxagoras) ... says that, after all (things) having been (mixed) together and *resting the infinite time,* motion was brought in, and differentiation was caused, by Nous.

φησὶ ... ἐκεῖνος, ὁμοῦ πάντων ὄντων καὶ ἠρεμούντων τὸν ἄπειρον χρόνον, κίνησιν ἐμποιῆσαι τὸν νοῦν καὶ διακρῖναι.

Arist. Phys. VII 1. 250b24 (omitted by Diels and Kranz).

Incidentally, has Aristotle not asserted that to Anaxagoras the ultimate elements were flesh, bone, marrow, etc., in a word: solid substances? Then one cannot understand how it could escape his notice that those two conceptions were incompatible. For a *migma* composed of elements like these would hardly be able to remain at a standstill even for one moment, let alone for "the infinite time." It would have to start at once getting stratified according to the specific gravities of its different components. "The barley water becomes stratified if it is not stirred up" (ὁ κυκεὼν διίσταται μὴ κινούμενος, Theophr. de vert. 9). Anaxagoras knew that as well as did Heraclitus, I am sure. A *pantahomou* like this would not be able to rest, and having arrived at rest again after stratification, it would not be a *pantahomou* any longer.

Thus Aristotle did not even become aware that he imputed a prodigious physical absurdity to Anaxagoras.

As long as the Aristotelian interpretation of Anaxagoras was admissible, there was the great difficulty of interpreting acceptably the explicit statement of the initial standstill. This difficulty exists no longer.

The Whereabouts of Nous

Thus, in its primordial condition, the universe was a *homoiomeres* of infinite dimension.

But where was Nous at that time? The molecules are "unlimited in quantity" (ἄπειρα πλῆθος). Is there any space left for Nous?

Hippolytus in his report, going back to Theophrastus, on the Clazomenian's doctrine uses the following words:

> For first all (things) were (mixed) together, then *Nous came up* and arranged.
>
> ὄντων γὰρ πάντων ὁμοῦ, νοῦς ἐπελθὼν διεκόσμησεν.
>
> *Hippol. refut. I 8, 1 f.; A42.*

But where is Nous supposed to have come from? From another world beyond?

This might be quite out of the question. Anaxagoras no more reached beyond a naive, metaphysic-less monism than did the other early Greek philosophers (cf. p. 177). The idea of a plurality of worlds had not yet been conceived. Moreover, in spite of fervent efforts, this idea was found not even by those who, as for instance Democritus, would have been disentangled from their various constructing-troubles only through this idea.

Now, Archelaos, who was a disciple of Anaxagoras', is said to have taught that

> the *migma*, in a way, so to speak, is in Nous.
>
> τῷ νῷ ἐνυπάρχειν τι εὐθέως μῖγμα.
>
> *Hippol. refut. I 9, 1; 60A4.*

One could try to use this sentence for a solution of the problem. If in this way we succeed in arriving at a satisfactory result, then we should be allowed to take this sentence as one of those positions on which Archelaos agreed with his master Anaxagoras.

A proper "being in one another" in the sense of a true penetration is not meant here because of the exceptional position of Nous in this respect. Hence the restricting words "in a way, so to speak" (τι εὐθέως).

Consequently, there are only two more meanings of the *migma's* "being included" in Nous:

Nous, like an envelope, encloses the whole *migma* of the other elements. This is one possibility. In this case, however, the elements would not be "unlimited" (ἄπειρα). The Nous-envelope would be their limit, their πέρας. And moreover, this would contradict an explicit statement by Anaxagoras who says:

> Nous, however, being always (sc., everywhere), quite certainly is also now *wherever all the other (elements) are* ...
>
> ὁ δὲ νοῦς, ὅς ἀ‹εί› ἐστι, τὸ κάρτα καὶ νῦν ἐστιν ἵνα καὶ τὰ ἄλλα πάντα ...
>
> *fr. 14 (Simpl. phys. 157, 5).*

He says, "also now." That implies, "all the more so before."

Hence only the other possible meaning is left, and so Anaxagoras seems indeed to have realized it himself:

Every molecule is surrounded by Nous on all sides; Nous, as "the thinnest of all the elements" (cf. p. 190), fills up all the spaces between the molecules; *Nous is the non-molecularized medium in which the molecules are embedded.*

First Means of Cosmopoeia: Differentiation

The primordial condition of homogeneousness and isomerism was to be changed by Nous into the world's thousandfold variegation.

First of all, therefore, equality of the molecules had to be turned into a thorough inequality. *The combining-ratio 1:1 had to disappear.*

Disengagement of the Checked Qualities

Nous could obtain this effect, and by that disengage the checked capacities and qualities, by taking single moiras from their molecular unions and incorporating them into other molecules.[1]

This implies that that *primary relation*, according to which there is no isolation of *moiras* of the various elements, *is not valid "in statu nascendi,"* to use this modern term of chemistry.

On the other hand, it follows from that primary relation

that *the* pantahomou-mereias *must not have contained only one* moira *of every element* (nor even of any single element, which, however, is impossible anyway, according to pp. 181 and 204);

that, *later on,* mereias *left with only one* moira *of a single element could not be differentiated any more in the respective field, except by unequal additions;* and

that *any* mereias *reduced to only one* moira *of each element could not be taken, except by means of unequal additions, into any further process of differentiation.*

For *otherwise such* mereias, *in this way of differentiation, would have been liable to lose one or the other kind of* moiras *entirely.*

This, however, must not happen. The number of the *kinds* of *moiras,* that is, the number of the elements represented in a *mereia,* must always and for all *mereias* remain the same:

[1] Nous would have obtained the same result by unequally dividing the individual molecules:

Suppose $a_n\alpha_n b_n\beta_n \ldots$ to be the formula of the *pantahomou*-molecules. Then, *e.g.,* is

$$a_n\alpha_n b_n\beta_n \ldots = \underset{2\ \ 3\ \ 4\ \ 5}{a_n\alpha_n b_n\beta_n} \ldots + \underset{2\ \ 3\ \ 4\ \ 5}{a_n\alpha_{2n} b_{3n}\beta_{4n}} \ldots ;$$

or:

$$= \underset{5\ \ 4\ \ 3\ \ 2}{a_n\alpha_n b_n\beta_n} \ldots = \underset{5\ \ 4\ \ 3\ \ 2}{a_{4n}\alpha_{3n} b_{2n}\beta_n} \ldots ;$$

etc.

But Anaxagoras apparently did not think of this possibility.

For this disengagement is not a thorough rent,

οὐ γὰρ παντελὴς διασπασμός ἐστιν ἡ διάκρισις,

> Simpl. phys. 461, 20; A53 (fragment 10 Schaubach).

but *none* becomes severed or disengaged from any other *entirely*.

παντάπασι δὲ οὐδὲν ἀποκρίνεται οὐδὲ διακρίνεται ἕτερον ἀπὸ τοῦ ἑτέρου.

> fr. 12 (Simpl. phys. 157, 1).

One need but bear in mind that a *mereia* with only one *moira* of each kind would also contain only one *moira* of the great and only one *moira* of the small. If this sole great-*moira* were taken away, the *mereia* *would become a really, absolutely smallest* (cf. p. 182). However, Anaxagoras explicitly says:

> As "*the smallest*" *cannot be there at all, it might also not be capable of being separated and getting on itself*, but, on the contrary, as in the beginning (i.e., before differentiation) also now (i.e., after differentiation) (only) *all* (the elements) might be capable of being together: also among the differentiated (*mereias*) (the) many (elements) are contained *equal* in number in *all* of them, in the greater ones and in the smaller ones as well.
>
> ὅτε τοὐλάχιστον μὴ ἔστιν εἶναι, οὐκ ἂν δύναιτο χωρισθῆναι οὐδ' ἂν ἐφ' ἑαυτοῦ γενέσθαι, ἀλλ' ὅπωσπερ ἀρχὴν εἶναι καὶ νῦν πάντα ὁμοῦ· ἐν πᾶσι δὲ πολλὰ ἔνεστι καὶ τῶν ἀποκρινομένων ἴσα πλῆθος, ἐν τοῖς μείζοσί τε καὶ ἐλάσσοσι.
>
> fr. 6 (Simpl. phys. 164, 25).

The changing of the combining-ratio 1:1 into many unequal combining-ratios is done with regard to the two contrasting sorts of *moiras* which in each of the specific qualities correspond to the opposites:

> From the rare the dense is severed, and from the cold the warm, and from the dark the bright, and from the moist the dry. (But there are many *moiras* of many [elements].) None, however, is severed or disengaged from any other entirely ...
>
> ἀποκρίνεται ἀπό τε τοῦ ἀραιοῦ τὸ πυκνὸν καὶ ἀπὸ τοῦ ψυχροῦ τὸ θερμὸν καὶ ἀπὸ τοῦ ζοφεροῦ τὸ λαμπρὸν καὶ ἀπὸ τοῦ διεροῦ τὸ ξηρόν. μοῖραι δὲ πολλαὶ πολλῶν εἰσι. παντάπασι δὲ οὐδὲν ἀποκρίνεται οὐδὲ διακρίνεται ἕτερον ἀπὸ τοῦ ἑτέρου ...
>
> fr. 12 (Simpl. phys. 156, 29–157, 2).

Hence *differentiation* need not take place in all the fields in the same way, but *can be performed quite unequally* within the various pairs of opposites.

Consequently, it can easily happen that *mereias* are produced which, while unequal in everything else, are *equal* in their contents of the rare and the dense, that is to say, *in their specific gravities.*

Differentiation can even be omitted in one or the other field, as may be exemplified by the air-*mereias,* the *colorlessness* of which obviously is to be explained in this way, or by the *mereias* of *scentless* or *tasteless* substances, etc.

In short: *Coordination of the combining-ratios* within the individual *mereias* is apparently *left to the will of Nous.*

True, the coordination of some kinds of *mereias* is somehow stated in the extant fragments:

> The dense [overbalancing the rare also present, hence compensating it and effective itself through the surplus only] and moist [this and the rest by analogy] and cold and dark moved inward to that place where now there is the *earth*, but the rare and warm and dry (and bright [cf. p. 175, note n. 3) moved outward to the remoteness of the *ether.*
>
> τὸ μὲν πυκνὸν καὶ διερὸν καὶ ψυχρὸν καὶ τὸ [1] ζοφερὸν ἐνθάδε συνεχώρησεν, ἔνθα νῦν <ἡ γῆ>, τὸ δὲ ἀραιὸν καὶ τὸ [1] θερμὸν καὶ τὸ [1] ξηρὸν (καὶ τὸ [1] λαμπρὸν) ἐξεχώρησεν εἰς τὸ πρόσω τοῦ αἰθέρος.
>
> *fr. 15 (Simpl. phys. 179, 3).*

Yet, no rule of coordination – according to which, say, with a decline of the rare-contents and increase of the dense-contents proportionate analogies in all the other fields would have to correspond – can be gathered from these statements.

Among all the differentiations, those effecting an unequal percentage of the rare and the dense (*specific density*) and of the great and the small (*specific magnitude*) in the individual *mereias* were of the greatest consequence for *the mechanism of cosmogony.*

The Beginning of Cosmopoeia

The world-building activity of Nous

started, first, from some small (district) . . . ,

---

[1] The articles might have come from the pen of a copyist who did not quite comprehend the meaning.

πρῶτον ἀπό του σμιχροῦ ἤρξατο . . .,

fr. 12 (Simpl. phys. 156, 23).

chosen quite to Nous' liking.

Proceeding from this district, Nous' activity gained more and more ground. Not that Nous wandered. Being the medium between the *mereias*, Nous is ever present everywhere. It took place in such a way that Nous *successively began operating* in the various spheres around this centre-kernel. For if intending a true cosmogony, Nous had to avoid a differentiation simultaneous in all points of the infinite universal space and had to be intent on obtaining *a differentiation gradually progressing in globular waves.*

The reason why Nous had to do so, in order to attain that purpose, will become clear presently.

Let us suppose that that tiny initial district consisted of

100 *pantahomou-mereias.*

Then the differentiation with regard to the rare and the dense and to the great and the small might have been accomplished in such a manner that Nous, by regrouping their *moiras*, transformed

50 *pantahomou-mereias*

into

2 very heavy and very small *mereias* of *earth*,

and

48 very light   and very great *mereias* of *ether;*

and

50 *pantahomou-mereias*

into

10   heavy and   small *mereias* of *water*

and

40   light   and   great *mereias* of *air.*

Illustrated mathematically:

a_1 shall be the notation of a dense-*moira;* α_1, of a rare-*moira;*
b_1 the notation of a small-*moira;* β_1, of a great-*moira.*
c and γ shall denote the two sorts of *moiras* of any other specific quality. And

$a_3\alpha_3b_3\beta_3c_3\gamma_3$... is supposed to be the formula of *pantahomou.*

Thus,

$$100\ a_3\alpha_3b_3\beta_3c_3\gamma_3\ldots = \quad 2\ a_{51}\alpha_3b_{51}\beta_3c_3\gamma_3\ldots +$$
$$+\ 48\ a_1\alpha_3b_1\beta_3c_3\gamma_3\ldots +$$
$$+\ 10\ a_7\alpha_3b_7\beta_3c_3\gamma_3\ldots +$$
$$+\ 40\ a_2\alpha_3b_2\beta_3c_3\gamma_3\ldots$$

(I do not pretend to assert that Anaxagoras himself calculated in this way. But there is no reason why we should not thus illustrate his idea mathematically today.)

The two earth-*mereias* were made to rush towards each other by Nous. Then, by mutual compensation, they lost their motion and became the resting centre of the originating cosmos. (Needless to say, "resting" is meant as to locomotion only.) This earth-kernel was covered by the 10 water-*mereias;* these were enveloped by the 40 air-*mereias;* and these, in turn, by the 48 ether-*mereias.*

This differentiation was repeated all around, and the new products had to be *stratified* in every instance according to their specific gravities – so that

all of the same kind came together,

... συνελθεῖν τε τὰ ὅμοια ...

(Hippol. refut. I 8, 2; A42).

–, *oriented to the resting kernel* of the first differentiation. And in every instance there resulted *more ether than air, more air than water, and more water than earth:*

For these (sc., air and ether) are contained in the totals as the largest (substances) by quantity and by magnitude as well.

ταῦτα γὰρ (sc., ἀήρ τε καὶ αἰθὴρ) μέγιστα ἔνεστιν ἐν τοῖς σύμπασι καὶ πλήθει καὶ μεγέθει.

fr. I (Simpl. phys. 155, 23).

The words, "by magnitude as well," indicate that Anaxagoras thought the ether and the air occupy such a large space not only because there are more *mereias* of them than of the other substances, but also because their *mereias* themselves are very voluminous. For according to the above calculations,

an ether-*mereia* would be
         not only twice as light,
         but also twice as great
                  as an air-*mereia;*

44

an air-*mereia*,

> not only four times as light,
> but also four times as great
>> as a water-*mereia;*

and a water-*mereia*

> twelve times as light and also
> twelve times as great
>> as an earth-*mereia.*

But on the other hand, within the embedding Nous the distances between ether-*mereias* and the distances between air-*mereias* need not be larger than the distances between earth-*mereias* or water-*mereias.*

Nous produces from the *pantahomou* not only these four substances, but the full number of the kinds of *mereias* possible.[1] Therefore, in this presentation the terms *earth, water, air,* and *ether* are to be taken as representative designations for four sections of the line of the different densities, or specific gravities. This line is continually graded, though. But those four sections are meant to correspond to *the four physical conditions.* For according to the almost common ancient Greek conception, there is also a special etheric condition that precedes the gaseous condition in the same sense as the gaseous condition precedes the liquid condition.

Why Cosmogony Had To Start from One Point

Now it is evident why cosmogony had to start from one point.

If Nous had differentiated in all points of space simultaneously, an infinite multitude of stratified globules staying unmoved side by side would have been obtained or, at best, a chaos of motions, in the sense of the kinetic theory of gas, without any result for a world structure.

Therefore, differentiation had to be done *successively in the various spheres* around the centre-kernel, while, on the other hand, it had to be performed *simultaneously in the entire sphere included* at a time:

> And after Nous had begun to move (sc., by doing away with compensation of the two opposite motion tendencies), on the part

---

[1] This full number of the kinds of *mereias* possible produced by Nous from the *pantahomou*, the full number of possible combining-ratios, is not infinite in the strict sense of the word, but certainly very great and, at any rate, practically undefinable. It may be that this, too, induced later reporters to ascribe to Anaxagoras the assumption of an "infinite" number of such "elements" as could be paralleled with the four Empedoclean *stoicheia.*

45

(ἀπό) of the *whole* moved (district) severance took place, and (always) as much as Nous made to move, this was stratified *in its entirety*.

καὶ ἐπεὶ ἤρξατο ὁ νοῦς κινεῖν, ἀπὸ τοῦ κινουμένου παντὸς ἀπεκρίνετο, καὶ ὅσον ἐκίνησεν ὁ νοῦς, πᾶν τοῦτο διεκρίθη.

fr. 13 (Simpl. phys. 300, 27).

Which means that differentiation was progressing in globular waves. *Otherwise, compensation of motion of the world-kernel would have been lost again.*

Needless to say, in all those movements of stratification Nous gives way accordingly.

'Peri-échon – Proskrithénta – Apokekriména'

The *pantahomou*-masses surrounding the growing cosmos at a given time are:

τὸ περιέχον (*to peri-échon*), "the enclosing"; also: "the mass of the enclosing" (τὸ πολὺ τοῦ περιέχοντος) or "the enclosing mass" (τὸ πολὺ περιέχον).

The *mereias* in the process of being differentiated and stratified at a given time are:

τὰ προσκριθέντα (*ta proskrithénta*), literally: "the just being added ones thereto by severance."

The *mereias* already differentiated and stratified at a given time are:

τὰ ἀποκεκριμένα (*ta apokekriména*), "the severed ones."

The passages containing these important terms are:

... For also air and ether are severed from *the mass of the enclosing*, and just *the enclosing* is infinite in quantity.

... καὶ γὰρ ἀήρ τε καὶ αἰθὴρ ἀποκρίνονται ἀπὸ τοῦ πολλοῦ τοῦ περιέχοντος καὶ τό γε περιέχον ἄπειρόν ἐστι τὸ πλῆθος.

fr. 2 (Simpl. phys. 155, 30).

Nous, however, ... also now is wherever all the other (elements) are: in *the enclosing mass* and in *the just being added ones by severance* and in *the severed ones*.

ὁ δὲ νοῦς ... καὶ νῦν ἐστιν ἵνα καὶ τὰ ἄλλα πάντα, ἐν τῷ πολλῷ πε- ριέχοντι καὶ ἐν τοῖς προσκριθεῖσι [1] καὶ ἐν τοῖς ἀποκεκριμένοις.[2]

fr. 14 (Simpl. phys. 157, 5).

---

[1] *Aoristus ingressivus!*
[2] *Perfectum praesentiale!*

Exegetic Paraphrase of Fragment Number One

This stage of starting differentiation and gradual stratification must be distinguished from that very first world-stage, the stage of the undifferentiated *mereias*.

It is only this second world-stage that the following sentences, said to have been the beginning of the first book of the Anaxagorean work, can refer to. For here air and ether are mentioned: differentiation, consequently, has already begun. These sentences, commonly known as fragment number one in the usual collections, are:

All things were together, infinite both in quantity and smallness; for even the small was infinite. And though all were together, nothing was perceptible in consequence of smallness: for air and ether enveloped all (things), both together being infinite. For these (sc., air and ether) are contained in the totals as the largest (substances) by quantity and by magnitude as well.

ὁμοῦ πάντα χρήματα ἦν, ἄπειρα καὶ πλῆθος καὶ σμικρότητα· καὶ γὰρ τὸ σμικρὸν ἄπειρον ἦν. καὶ πάντων ὁμοῦ ἐόντων οὐδὲν ἔνδηλον ἦν ὑπὸ σμικρότητος· πάντα γὰρ ἀήρ τε καὶ αἰθὴρ κατεῖχεν, ἀμφότερα ἄπειρα ἐόντα· ταῦτα γὰρ μέγιστα ἔνεστιν ἐν τοῖς σύμπασι καὶ πλήθει καὶ μεγέθει.

fr. 1 (Simpl. phys. 155, 23).

Among the Anaxagorean fragments, this is one of the most difficult to interpret. Mere translation does not suffice. Here a detailed exegetic paraphrase is needed.

In these introductory statements air and ether are mentioned in contradistinction to the "things." Hence, *here "things" means only the solid and liquid substances* and does not comprise also gaseous things like air and ether, in full accordance with common ancient daily life phraseology. And as a matter of course, words are likely to be used in their common meaning at the outset of a book, as one cannot very well begin with special *termini technici*. That is also why in this fragment *chremata* ("things") does not have the meaning of "elements."

Now, in the very first moments after the beginning, from a tiny district, of differentiation by Nous, this "together" of the "things" –

All things were together,

ὁμοῦ πάντα χρήματα ἦν

– this small starting-district, was not simply "small." Those differentiated things gathering in and around the kernel still were even *infinitely small*, since consisting only of a few *mereias* initially; and nevertheless, they were *infinite in quantity as well:*

infinite in quantity as well as in smallness;

ἄπειρα καὶ πλῆθος καὶ σμικρότητα·

For that "small something" (σμικρόν τι, cf. p. 210) itself, that infinitely small starting-district, was, on the other hand, infinite in quantity, too, –

for the small, too, was infinite.

καὶ γὰρ τὸ σμικρὸν ἄπειρον ἦν.

– since there was in the whole universe an infinite number of such small districts chosen by Nous as starting-points of cosmogonies (as will be shown later, cf. p. 297 ff.).

Yet, though all solid and liquid things so far differentiated were together in such a tiny starting-district, still *nothing could be perceived initially, but only because of the initial smallness of their aggregation.* Apart from that initial smallness, however, there would have been *no other hindrance to visibility* for an imaginary human spectator. For all those differentiated solid and liquid things, already colored by differentiation, within that tiny starting-district were enveloped by *transparent* air and ether only. These, consequently, would not have been any hindrance to visibility. Thus, only the initial smallness of aggregation, nothing else, constituted the hindrance:

And though all were together, nothing was perceptible *in consequence of smallness:* for air and ether enveloped all (things).

καὶ πάντων ὁμοῦ ἐόντων οὐδὲν ἔνδηλον ἦν ὑπὸ σμικρότητος· πάντα γὰρ ἀήρ τε καὶ αἰθὴρ κατεῖχεν,

To "air and ether" Anaxagoras adds the words:

both together being infinite;

ἀμφότερα ἄπειρα ἐόντα·

This is not exactly correct. For within a world district growing by differentiation the number of the air- and ether-*mereias* is no more infinite, though constantly growing larger, than that of the other *mereias*. But if one considers that the still undifferentiated *mereias* of the *peri-echon* likewise are in a gaseous state, then air, ether, and the non-differentiated, together, really are infinitely large. And indeed, Anaxagoras corrected his statement himself by explaining:

48

Air and ether, namely, are also severed from the mass of the *peri-echon*, and just this *peri-echon* is infinite in quantity.

καὶ γὰρ ἀήρ τε καὶ αἰθὴρ ἀποκρίνονται ἀπὸ τοῦ πολλοῦ τοῦ περιέχοντος καὶ τό γε περιέχον ἄπειρόν ἐστι τὸ πλῆθος.

fr. 2 (Simpl. phys. 155, 30).

However, not only air and ether are strictly speaking not infinite in quantity: even *the whole resultant cosmos*, being formed from the differentiation products and comprising the "things" and air and ether, *is but finitely large at any given time.*

And yet, *it is quite impossible to determine how many mereias this finite quantity consists of.* For this quantity is not constant but variable, since it grows larger from instant to instant,

> so that the quantity of the *(mereias)* being severed cannot be figured out, neither by calculating (λόγῳ) nor by counting off (ἔργῳ).
>
> ὥστε τῶν ἀποκρινομένων μὴ εἰδέναι τὸ πλῆθος μήτε λόγῳ μήτε ἔργῳ.
>
> *fr. 7 (Simpl. de caelo 608, 24).*

But this, at least, can be stated: Every increase in small, heavy *mereias* is accompanied by an increase of correspondingly still more ether- and air-*mereias*. That is to say that, at any rate, there is *always more ether and air than water and earth* (cf. p. 212),

> for (among all the products of differentiation) these (sc., air and ether) are contained in the "totals" (*i.e.*, in each total complex of growing cosmos plus *proskrithenta* plus *peri-echon* = in the single world-systems, cf. p. 297 ff.) as the largest (substances) by quantity (of their molecules) and by (molecular) dimension as well (cf. p. 212).
>
> ταῦτα γὰρ μέγιστα ἔνεστιν ἐν τοῖς σύμπασι καὶ πλήθει καὶ μεγέθει.

Between the *pantahomou*-stage proper, as described in fr. 4 (Simpl. phys. 156, 1; cf. p. 202), and this stage of beginning differentiation, this difference is the most significant: Here nothing was perceptible "because of *smallness*" (ὑπὸ σμικρότητος), whilst in the stage of non-differentiation nothing had been perceptible because "(compensating) *combination* of all elements was the hindrance" (ἀπεκώλυε γὰρ ἡ σύμμιξις πάντων χρημάτων).

Second Means of Cosmopoeia: Rotation

Had rendering the *mereias* unequal been the only activity of Nous, a stratified globe with strata continually increasing would have been the primitive result.

That was not what the Nous intended. If this had been the only evolution of the *pantahomou* possible, Nous would perhaps not have interfered at all. A lifeless, dreary ball in which no sunny day, no night moonlit and glittering with stars would have been achievable might scarcely have presented an objective to entice Nous to building.

There were, however, other possibilities, finer ones and more artistic, and Nous, the omniscient physicist and engineer and architect, knew them and willed them and was cognizant of the methods to be used for realizing them.

This is *the chief means* Nous employed for moulding the cosmos such as it is shown to our eyes today:

Going round about,

περιχώρησις (*perichoresis*)   *fr. 12 (Simpl. phys. 156, 22).*

with its "*force*" (βίη):

It is namely the quickness (of going round about) that produces force.

βίην δὲ ταχυτὴς (sc., τῆς περιχωρήσιος) ποιεῖ.
fr. 9 (Simpl. phys. 35, 13).

That is to say: *Rotation with its centrifugal force.*

The results achieved through the co-operation of this component shall be examined in the following.

The Two Sorts of Motion and Their Allotment to Two Principles

The mereias *would never have been able to take a crooked path by themselves.* Spontaneously, they are capable of rectilinear motion only, or even, if the world centre is already taken into account, of motion rectilinear up and down only. *Nous alone is capable of any non-rectilinear spontaneous motion.*

Hence Nous effected a rotation of the mereias *by rotating itself* – first in the primordial globule and then in each sphere further included, around an axis chosen quite to Nous' liking but put through the centre of the world kernel – *and thus dragging along the embedded* mereias:

Nous effected by its might [1] the whole rotation, too, so that *(Nous) went around* from the very outset. And first *(Nous) began going around* from some small (district), but *is going around farther* . . .[2]

καὶ τῆς περιχωρήσιος τῆς συμπάσης νοῦς ἐκράτησεν,[1] ὥστε περιχωρῆσαι τὴν ἀρχήν. καὶ πρῶτον ἀπό του σμικροῦ ἤρξατο περιχωρεῖν, ἐπὶ δὲ πλέον περιχωρεῖ . . . .[2]

fr. 12 (Simpl. phys. 156, 21–24).

Anaxagoras apparently allotted the sorts of motion to two principles. He was induced to do so by the obvious fact that by themselves *"lifeless" bodies only go up and fall*, while *any other kind of motion* is to be met *only with living beings or, with lifeless bodies, only when the will of a living being interferes.*

A Mental Experiment

Actually, then, this highly important means of rotation and centrifugal force had been combined with the disengagement of the automotion of the *mereias* from the very beginning, from the very first differentiation, or, at the latest, immediately after the first differentiation.

For a better didactic arrangement of presentation, however, in order to make the single components more distinct in their individual modes

---

[1] Literally: "It ruled over . . ." But here κρατεῖν obviously has the same meaning as in the preceding sentences of that fragment, *i.e.*, "to rule by moving," "to move" (cf. p. 193).

[2] One should not close one's eyes any longer to the clear wording of these sentences. περιχωρεῖν means exactly "to go around," and ὥστε περιχωρῆσαι τὴν ἀρχήν means plainly and literally: "so that it went around from the very outset." And just as in the sentence ending with these words (and the two preceding sentences), also in the sentence immediately following (just as in the two subsequent sentences), νοῦς *is the grammatical subject:* νοῦς is the subject of ἤρξατο περιχωρεῖν ("it began going around") as well as of ἐπὶ πλέον περιχωρεῖ ("it goes around farther") and of περιχωρήσει ἐπὶ πλέον ("it will go around still farther"). This seems to me rather incontestable. Diels translates: "So hat er auch die Herrschaft über die gesamte Wirbelbewegung, so dass er dieser Bewegung den Anstoss gibt. Und zuerst fing dieser Wirbel (!) von einem gewissen kleinen Punkt an, er (sc., dieser Wirbel) greift aber weiter und wird noch weiter greifen." (In the Kranz-editions merely "Wirbelbewegung" has been changed into "Umdrehung.") Aside from other, minor grammatical errors, this, to say the least, is a gross obscuring in the first sentence and a common blunder in the second. And if other philologists translate ὥστε περιχωρῆσαι τὴν ἀρχήν as "dergestalt, dass sie (sc., die Wirbelbewegung) anfing, herumzuwirbeln," it is not only nonsensical, but likewise simply wrong grammatically.

of acting, I am going to draw out their simultaneity into a succession – by way of a mental experiment, so to speak.

The function of the one component has been described in the foregoing.

Now differentiation shall have produced already a stratified globe of some size. Only in this moment shall the other component start acting, and henceforth the magnitude of the cosmos shall remain constant, influx of further material from the *peri-echon* shall be interrupted, until centrifugal force will have made up for what I am supposing it to have missed.

The Effects of Rotation upon the Earth and the Waters, and upon the Original Line of Fall

Centrifugal force caused *the earth* in the middle of this cosmos *gradually to lose its spherical form and become increasingly oblate, until it assumed the shape of a flat disk,*

> the·earth, however, to be flat in shape,
>
> τὴν δὲ γῆν τῷ σχήματι πλατεῖαν εἶναι,
>
> *(Hippol. refut. I 8, 3; A42; and elsewhere).*

and, finally, was even transformed into a hollow, surrounded by big rolls of mountains ascending toward its circumference.[1]

In the middle of this hollow the waters flowed together, forming an enormous ocean. For the effect, in the sense of tossing outwards, of centrifugal force on the heavy, bulky stones is much stronger than on the less heavy water:

> These (sc., the stones) get outwards (sc., in consequence of rotation) more than the water.
>
> οὗτοι δὲ (sc., οἱ λίθοι) ἐκχωρέουσι μᾶλλον τοῦ ὕδατος.
>
> *fr. 16 (Simpl. phys. 155, 21).*

True, this strict separation is not in conformity with *the present distribution of water and land.* But Anaxagoras seems to have assumed

---

[1] This reconstruction of the final shape of the earth as a hollow surrounded by mountains is based upon a doctrine of Archelaos', a follower of Anaxagoras'. Archelaos taught that

> first it (sc., the earth) was a basin, being high on its circumference but concave in the middle.
>
> λίμνην . . . εἶναι (sc., τὴν γῆν) τὸ πρῶτον, ἄτε κύκλῳ μὲν οὖσαν ὑψηλήν, μέσον δὲ κοίλην.
>
> *Hippol. refut. I 9, 4; 60 A 4.*

that from this first condition of the earth surface its actual state *might have resulted later*, as a consequence of two causes:

In his opinion, one part of

the waters *evaporated* under the influence of the sun.

. . . διατμισθέντων ὑπὸ τοῦ ἡλίου τῶν ὑγρῶν . . .

Diog. Laert. II 8; A1; and elsewhere.

(One cannot do entirely without naivetés, after all, even with "the greatest natural philosopher" of the Greeks [ὁ μὲν φυσικώτατος 'Αναξαγόρας . . .] Sext. Emp. VII 90.)

Another part of the waters *sank down into the many caves of the earth,*

for it (sc., the earth) is cavernous and contains water in the hollow spaces.

εἶναι γὰρ αὐτὴν (sc., τὴν γῆν) κοίλην καὶ ἔχειν ὕδωρ ἐν τοῖς κοιλώμασιν.

Hippol. refut. I 8, 5; A42.

Anaxagoras may have imagined these subterranean hollow spaces to result from laxations of the solid structure of the earth, as an effect of centrifugal force.

The most conspicuous manifestation of centrifugal force is the fact that everywhere on earth *the bodies fall in the direction rectangular to the horizontal plane*, instead of falling toward the geometrical centre of the earth.

This original falling direction toward the centre implies a tendency to obliqueness, to deviation from the perpendicular, and this trend increases in proportion to the distances from the axis. But centrifugal force, while being zero in the middle of the disk, likewise grows with the increasing radius and, consequently, is always strong enough at any point to surmount the trend to obliqueness of the fall's original direction.

It is presupposed, here, that the angular velocity of the rotating earth is the same everywhere. This may safely be assumed with regard to the solid physical condition.

Why the Rotation of the Earth Has Been Passed Over in Silence

As in the first stages of cosmogony, *the earth is still rotating around the world axis with a velocity far surpassing all known velocities.* Today, also, the earth is not excluded from

the rotation rotated now by the stars and the sun and the moon
and the air and the ether that are produced through severance.

. . . τὴν περιχώρησιν ταύτην, ἣν νῦν περιχωρέει τά τε ἄστρα καὶ ὁ ἥλιος
καὶ ἡ σελήνη καὶ ὁ ἀὴρ καὶ ὁ αἰθὴρ οἱ ἀποκρινόμενοι.

fr. 12 (Simpl. phys. 156, 27).

Their (sc., of the rotating things) quickness, however, does not
resemble the quickness of any thing (literally: "any thing in
quickness") among the things existing with men now, but at any
rate is many times as quick.

ἡ δὲ ταχυτὴς αὐτῶν (sc., τῶν περιχωρούντων) οὐδενὶ ἔοικε χρήματι τὴν
ταχυτῆτα τῶν νῦν ἐόντων χρημάτων ἐν ἀνθρώποις, ἀλλὰ πάντως
πολλαπλασίως ταχύ ἐστι.

fr. 9 (Simpl. phys. 35, 13).

However, to all appearances *this sharing of the earth in the rotation
was not taught expressly by Anaxagoras.* For otherwise he would
probably have mentioned the earth, too, in the sentence quoted above
in which those celestial bodies taking part in the *perichoresis* are
enumerated. This is somewhat striking.

*It may be that Anaxagoras even avoided uttering it explicitly, in order
not to give too much offense.* One must not forget: Dealing with natural
history of heaven and earth was quite a perilous amusement in those
times, outside of Ionia. In proof of this, one need but point to the fact
that Anaxagoras himself came very near being killed in Athens when it
had got abroad that he regarded Helios and Selene as glowing clods of
stone.

There is no knowing, after all, whether Anaxagoras did not intentionally abstain from saying many another thing as well. He might
have understood that a martyrdom for the sake of enlightenment was
neither due nor of use to mankind, since their narrowmindedness was
too spiteful and too inherent.

An Endorsement by Plutarch

There is a confirmation by Plutarch of this view, an endorsement
really thrilling:

Anaxagoras was the first to put down in writing the clearest as
well as boldest of all explanations of the irradiations and shadow
of the moon. But neither was Anaxagoras himself considered
venerable on that account, nor was that explanation praised by

all people. *On the contrary, it was still kept dark and spread step by step in a few words only and with precaution or in strict confidence. For in those days, natural philosophers and "star-gazing babblers" were not tolerated, they were persecuted (even)* [literally: "mal-treated"], *as if levigating the Godhead into irrational causes, blind forces, and fated, necessary occurrences. That is why Protagoras fled, and the life of Anaxagoras whom they had thrown into dungeon, could narrowly be saved by Pericles, for his own sake.*

ὁ γὰρ πρῶτος σαφέστατόν τε πάντων καὶ θαρραλεώτατον περὶ σελήνης καταυγασμῶν καὶ σκιᾶς λόγον εἰς γραφὴν καταθέμενος Ἀναξαγόρας οὔτ’ αὐτὸς ἦν παλαιὸς οὔτε ὁ λόγος ἔνδοξος, ἀλλ’ ἀπόρρητος ἔτι καὶ δι’ ὀλίγων καὶ μετ’ εὐλαβείας τινὸς ἢ πίστεως βαδίζων. οὐ γὰρ ἠνείχοντο τοὺς φυσικοὺς καὶ μετεωρολέσχας τότε κακουμένους, ὡς εἰς αἰτίας ἀλόγους καὶ δυνάμεις ἀπρονοήτους καὶ κατηναγκασμένα πάθη διατρίβοντας τὸ θεῖον, ἀλλὰ καὶ Πρωταγόρας ἔφυγε καὶ Ἀναξαγόραν εἰρχθέντα μόλις περιεποιήσατο Περικλῆς.

Plutarch. Nic. 23; A18.

Intrinsic Reasons for the Rotation of the Earth

Therefore, if one intends to reconstruct, not in a philological sense, but philosophically, then also reasons of inner consistency based on the technique of composition may, no, must co-operate, and the question must be not only: "What has been written in the text?" but also: "What might the philosopher have thought to himself?". And when dealing with a thinker of Anaxagoras' rank, we may assume, perhaps, naive presuppositions and starting-points, but never any inconsistency or nonsense in the construction itself.

Thus, the fact that in the texts it is passed over in silence cannot prevent me from believing that Anaxagoras imagined *the earth to share in the "perichoresis,"* or rotation, not only at the beginning of cosmogony, but *for ever.* He had to construct in this way, since otherwise he could not have worked out the flatness of the earth. For *if the rotation of the earth had stopped, its oblateness, also, would have had to get lost again, and the spherical shape, to come back.*

Is the earth, then, supposed to rotate with that incomparable speed, although we do not feel it?

This conception would hardly have presented any difficulty to Anaxagoras. He needed merely to remember this fact: When sailing in the open sea, one likewise would not be aware of the ship's movement, except by inferring it from the oarsmen's manipulations or the whizzing of the sails and the roaring of the waves. And yet the ship moves faster than the strongest fellow can run. Only the movements aboard ship are felt, not those of the ship itself. Certainly, it could be quite so with the earth.

On the other hand, however, *Anaxagoras explicitly says that the air partakes in the* perichoresis. *Consequently, for this reason alone, he was forced to keep the earth rotating as well.* Otherwise he would not have been in a position to explain the fact that there was no feeling this continual, furious rotation of the air.

The Effects of Rotation upon Air and Ether

What effects resulted from centrifugal force for the air stratum and the ether stratum?

To answer this question is extremely difficult, considering that in the air-*mereias* and the ether-*mereias* the rare-percentage surmounts the dense-percentage. Their lightness, consequently, should not mean a very low degree of heaviness, but a quality working against heaviness, strictly speaking. Thus the *mereias* in which the rare prevails would have no trend toward the centre of the cosmos, but a trend away from it. To the *mereias* in which the dense prevails a tendency of "moving inward" (συγχωρεῖν) would belong; to those with the rare prevailing, a tendency of "moving outward" (ἐκχωρεῖν) (cf. fr. 15 [Simpl. phys. 179, 3].) But as to this problem, one cannot venture to say whether Anaxagoras did carry out this idea to its extreme consequences. And it is obviously impossible merely by way of reconstruction to determine how centrifugal force might act upon such "light" molecules.

However, in the reports on the doctrine of Anaxagoras, there are some passages in which the effect of that action is simply stated, without any deduction, as, for instance, in Plutarch. Lys. 12 (A12), where a "(living) force (literally: tension) of rotation" (τόνος τῆς περιφορᾶς) is mentioned quite generally. From this one may gather that it did not occur to Anaxagoras to think of any other difference but a gradual one in the respective effects upon heavy and light bodies of centrifugal force.

It may be that the effects of this "force produced by quickness" were merely plagiarized, so to speak, from the world of obviousness by Anaxagoras, but *not further analysed*. There is a significant indication, even, that he took indeed all of it *from mere observation*, without having been able to resolve it into more elementary components: *his opinion that Nous alone is capable of that kind of spontaneous motion by which centrifugal force is produced.*

On the other hand, to become familiar with the fact as such of centrifugal force and its behaviour – which prompted his statement that also during cosmogony

mere rotation as such effected severance

ἡ δὲ περιχώρησις αὐτὴ ἐποίησεν ἀποκρίνεσθαι

fr. 12 (Simpl. phys. 156, 28).

–, he only needed go for a stroll through the Kerameikos of Athens.

Rotation and Stratification

Separation of the substances in the sense of stratification to their specific gravities was not only not arrested, but even strengthened by centrifugal force.

Anaxagoras expressly says:

And after Nous had begun to move (sc., by doing away with compensation of the two opposite motion tendencies), on the part of the whole moved (district) severance took place, and (always) as much as Nous made to move, this was stratified in its entirety. However, while thus there was motion and stratification (anyway), *rotation but greatly intensified stratification.*

καὶ ἐπεὶ ἤρξατο ὁ νοῦς κινεῖν, ἀπὸ τοῦ κινουμένου παντὸς ἀπεκρίνετο, καὶ ὅσον ἐκίνησεν ὁ νοῦς, πᾶν τοῦτο διεκρίθη· κινουμένων δὲ καὶ διακρινομένων ἡ περιχώρησις πολλῷ μᾶλλον ἐποίει διακρίνεσθαι.

fr. 13 (Simpl. phys. 300, 27).

How the Earth Remains Suspended

We could now halt our stopping the influx of material from the *peri-echon* and demonstrate how the *proskrithenta* (cf. p. 214) are acted upon by gravity and centrifugal force together.

But first let us consider one little remaining problem, contained in a rather obscure passage in Hippolytus (taken from Theophrastus [1]) concerning the mechanical relationship between the earth and the air.

Anaxagoras is said to have held

the earth ... to remain suspended in consequence of its magnitude and in consequence of there not being any vacuum and because

---

[1] Cf. Arist. de caelo II 13. 294b13 (13A20), and 295a16.

the air, being strong enough, carries the earth sitting on it.

τὴν γῆν ... μένειν μετέωρον διὰ τὸ μέγεθος καὶ διὰ τὸ μηδὲν εἶναι κενὸν καὶ διὰ τὸ τὸν ἀέρα ἰσχυρότατον ὄντα φέρειν ἐποχουμένην τὴν γῆν.

Hippol. refut. I 8, 3; A 42.

If it were admissible to impute to Anaxagoras a belief in an absolute "above" and "below," this sentence should mean to explain how the earth does not fall "down" but persists in its state of suspension.

There is, however, one very awkward thing about it: The factors mentioned in that sentence would not be able to protect the earth from falling down. Largeness of the mass could but enhance a fall within the aerial region, and the air, becoming displaced, would not be strong enough to check the fall.

Yet, Anaxagoras was indeed not so naive as to believe in an absolute "above" and "below." [1] In the same report, some lines before the passage quoted, it says that Anaxagoras taught

all the heavy things to move to the middle.

πάντα τὰ βαρέα συνελθεῖν ἐπὶ τὸ μέσον.

Thus, in Anaxagoras' opinion, the heavy does not gravitate "downwards," but toward the centre of the axis of rotation.

Suppose the meaning of that sentence is that, while the earth is rotating on the spot in a certain manner, any change of this definite kind of rotation is prevented by atmospheric resistance which in consequence of the great size of the earth is sufficiently strong.

Three possibilities of a rotation of the earth disk are conceivable: (1) the axis of rotation can be rectangular to the disk in its centre; (2) the axis of rotation can be oblique to the disk; and (3) the axis of rotation can coincide with a diameter of the disk.

If the air did not rotate itself, a trifling frictional resistance would result in the first case. In the second and third instances, however, an air displacement resistance would arise, increasing in accordance with the largeness of the disk even unto insuperability.

But the air does rotate, in Anaxagoras' opinion. It rotates around an axis obviously coinciding with the axis of the earth rotation. (The other case, rotation around a different axis, though imaginable theoretically, can be disregarded. One would not understand where such irregularity should come from.)

[1] Cf., in contradistinction, Arist. Phys. IV 1. 208b14, and de caelo IV 1. 308a18.

In the first of those cases possible, *i.e.*, rotation around a central axis rectangular to the plane of the earth, the air's rotation equal in direction and velocity would imply even a cessation of the weak frictional resistance of the air. The third case, rotation around a diameter, would likewise mean a cessation of the air displacement resistance that would have arisen with the air at rest. (The second of those possibilities, rotation around an axis oblique to the plane of the disk, is too unnatural for consideration.) Now, as has been pointed out, the earth disk has resulted from a previous earth ball that has become oblate by its rotation. For this reason alone, no form of rotation other than one around an axis rectangular to the disk in its centre is possible. And how this manner of rotation could be changed into any of those other manners of rotation, one fails to understand.

Thus, that obscure passage in Hippolytus is still in need of clarification. It may be, however, that the meaning is this:

While rotating around the world axis, could the earth not in addition oscillate to and fro along this axis, every point of the earth describing a spiral line instead of a circle? This would indeed be a possible idea. Yet, *when the air from above the earth rushes about the earth disk into the air below the earth, this storm under the earth does not make the earth shift along the axis, but causes merely a shaking in the sense of an earth-quake:*

> Earth-quakes arise when the air from above rushes into the air under the earth: For when this (air below the earth) is moved, also the earth sitting on it is shaken by it.
>
> σεισμοὺς δὲ γίνεσθαι τοῦ ἄνωθεν ἀέρος εἰς τὸν ὑπὸ γῆν ἐμπίπτοντος· τούτου γὰρ κινουμένου καὶ τὴν ὀχουμένην γῆν ὑπ' αὐτοῦ σαλεύεσθαι.
>
> *Hippol. refut. I 8, 12; A42.*[1]

In this the earth is *like a stretched drumskin:*

> ... the earth being flat and drumskin-like ...
>
> ... πλατεῖα οὖσα καὶ τυμπανοειδὴς ἡ γῆ ...
>
> *Simpl. phys. de caelo 520, 28; A88.*

If you press a drumskin down with your finger at one spot, immediately a corresponding convexity rises at another spot, but the drumskin as a whole does not give way. The drumskin, however, is fastened at its circumference, while the earth disk is not. Where does the similar behaviour of the earth come from?

[1] Cf. Arist. Meteor. II 7. 365a32; A 89.

This "remaining suspended" of the earth in the middle of the world is vouched for "by its (enormous) size." *Since, owing to the earth disk's enormous size, resistance of the air from both directions is insuperable, neither a gust of air down to the earth* (not perceptible to us) *nor a gust of air from the opposite side can make the earth leave the middle of the world axis.* Both of the air masses, the one which

"carries the earth sitting upon,"

"ἐποχουμένην φέρει τὴν γῆν,"

and the other which

sitting upon is carried by the earth,

ἐποχούμενος φέρεται ὑπὸ τῆς γῆς,

are equal contributors to that mechanical effect.

Differentiation And Rotation Acting Together

The fictitious constancy of size of the cosmos shall now be revoked, and differentiation in the *peri-echon* – interrupted for the sake of a better presentation of the effects of centrifugal force – shall continue.

Now, what happens to the *proskrithenta* (cf. p. 214)?

The 'Proskrithenta' and Their Conglomerations

The proskrithenta *are under the joint influence of gravity and centrifugal force* everywhere, the line of the axis itself excepted.

In this very line, any *mereia* coming in from the *peri-echon* must reach (and remain in) that stratum which corresponds to its specific gravity in a rectilinear fall toward the earth centre. For in this line the fall's rectilinearity cannot be disturbed since here the intensity of centrifugal force equals zero.

That is also why in that line no conglomerations are possible.

Everywhere else there is opportunity for conglomerations of the proskrithenta.

The new *ether-mereias* find their place immediately in the outermost strata of the cosmos.

The *air*-particles, *water*-particles, and *earth*-particles *trickle inwards* across the ether-strata, and when finally reaching the air-stratum, they can be *conglobated to complete clouds*. And these, in turn, dissociate so that the air content remains in the aerial sphere, the water- and earth-contents stream down to the earth in form of *rain* that contains earth-particles:

> For out of the clouds water is severed, but out of the water, earth.
>
> ἐκ μὲν γὰρ τῶν νεφελῶν ὕδωρ ἀποκρίνεται, ἐκ δὲ τοῦ ὕδατος γῆ.
>
> *fr. 16 (Simpl. phys. 155, 21, and 179, 6).*

From the *pantahomou-mereias* of the *peri-echon* also *stone-particles* are produced. These are nothing but *earth-particles congealed*, owing to a greater content of the cold-element.

On their way into the cosmos, *the stone-particles are worked upon by centrifugal force with particular intensity*, much more than water:

> Stones congeal out of earth, owing to the cold. These, however, get more outwards than the water.
>
> ἐκ δὲ τῆς γῆς λίθοι συμπήγνυνται ὑπὸ τοῦ ψυχροῦ, οὗτοι δὲ ἐκχωρέουσι μᾶλλον τοῦ ὕδατος.
>
> *fr. 16 (Simpl. phys. 155, 21).*

As a consequence, stone-particles conglomerate to full stone clods very quickly and already in strata far distant from the centre.

Then, under the joint action of gravity and centrifugal force, *such a stone clod will sink across the ether* from stratum to stratum – not in a radial path, of course – *until it reaches a stratum, the "force" (βίη) of which will be strong enough to prevent it from sinking farther, at least* pro tempore.

Why Angular Velocity and Centrifugal Force Must Increase from Without Inwards

The intensity of centrifugal force is not equal everywhere.

Within every sphere, the intensity of centrifugal force is continually graded from a maximum at the equator to zero at the poles.

There is another gradation, besides: *the gradation of the total values of the individual spheres themselves.* And here, according to Anaxagoras' construction, the arrangement is that *angular velocity and, consequently, centrifugal force as well increase from without inwards.*

If, instead, angular velocity were equal in all the spheres, the intensity of centrifugal force would have to increase from within outwards. It would reach its actual maximum at the equator of the actually outermost sphere at any given time. Consequently, from a certain size of the growing cosmos, centrifugal force in the outermost stratum – apart from the poles and their nearest surroundings – would for a long time be strong enough to keep the *proskrithenta* from penetrating into the cosmos. The *proskrithenta*-masses would be jammed until they would have grown to such immensity that they would finally be able to force their entrance and passage and then would burst in upon the whole cosmos stratified by then, catastrophically destroying it forthwith.

Yet, this would only occur if rotation did not set in simultaneously with differentiation, whereas in this case something quite different would happen. From a certain moment, centrifugal force would preponderate over gravity, and another system of strata produced by the centrifugal force's stratifying activity would be forming around the kernel stratified by then. And this additional system, the strata of which would be arranged in an order strictly reverse to the order of the kernel, would remain isolated from that kernel for ever, forming a shell that would incessantly be growing thicker and thicker.

Hence an increase of centrifugal force from without inwards was the only possibility serviceable to Anaxagoras.

If looking for a plausible starting-point, he certainly could suppose that Nous, at first, spinned with the same *absolute* velocity in each sphere joining rotation. Then whatever was different today Anaxagoras was free to interpret as secondary results. The equality of angular velocity within the whole earth, *e.g.*, could have resulted from intensive cohesion as an average angular velocity. Generally, whenever it turned out necessary in the course of evolution, Nous could change the original relation between the velocities of the various spheres. In this way, Nous caused, *e.g.*, the innermost air strata to rotate with the same angular velocity as the earth and conferred on the future moon-heaven and the future sun-heaven velocities of rotation many times as great as the velocity conferred on the earth and the innermost air strata. Only the principle had to be heeded that angular velocity and centrifugal force had to increase inwards at least as far as to the future moon-sphere.

This arrangement of the velocities corresponds also to the fact that in the extant reports the whole rotation is sometimes called "whirlpool" and "whirl," δίνη and δίνησις (Arist. de caelo II 13. 295a9 [A88]; and elsewhere). It is characteristic of a whirl to be most torrential toward the middle.

Origin of the Stars

Let us assume the clod of stone (or of metal) mentioned above has reached an ether stratum the centrifugal force of which is strong enough to prevent it from sinking farther for the present. It remains in that sphere and takes part in its *perichoresis*.

But the velocity of such a clod is smaller than the velocity of the surrounding medium: the clod is *swimming* in the ether-sea.

Through this swimming in the warm ether *an enormous friction* takes place, as a result of which *the clod begins to glow and shine*. That is to say: *The stone, heavy and cold originally, has changed into a fiery, radiant, revolving star.*

> Though stone-like and heavy, they (sc., the stars) are shining in consequence of the (frictional) resistance and breaking [in the sense of "surf"] of the ether and, being clasped by (centrifugal) force, are dragged along by the whirl and strain of rotation. Presumably in this way, they had been prevented from falling hither (to us) also in the beginning when the cold and heavy (substances) were severed out of the whole.
>
> λιθώδη . . . ὄντα (sc., τὰ ἄστρα) καὶ βαρέα λάμπειν μὲν ἀντερείσει καὶ περικλάσει τοῦ αἰθέρος, ἕλκεσθαι δὲ ὑπὸ βίας σφιγγόμενα δίνῃ καὶ τόνῳ τῆς περιφορᾶς, ὥς που καὶ τὸ πρῶτον ἐκρατήθη μὴ πεσεῖν δεῦρο τῶν ψυχρῶν καὶ βαρέων ἀποκρινομένων τοῦ παντός.
>
> *Plutarch. Lys. 12; A12.*

> The sun and the moon and all the stars to be burning stones dragged along round about by the ether's rotation.
>
> ἥλιον δὲ καὶ σελήνην καὶ πάντα τὰ ἄστρα λίθους εἶναι ἐμπύρους συμπεριληφθέντας ὑπὸ τῆς αἰθέρος περιφορᾶς.
>
> *Hippol. refut. I 8, 6; A42.*

This, then, is Anaxagoras' theory that the stars are glowing clods of stone or metal.[1]

---

[1] The epitomist Aetios, oddly enough, summarizes the Anaxagorean teaching about the origin of the stars in this way (literally!):

> Anaxagoras (says) that the encircling ether is fiery by nature, but that through the strain of the whirl it has pulled up(!) rocks from the earth (!!) and, by burning them up (!), has transformed them into stars.
>
> Ἀναξαγόρας τὸν περικείμενον αἰθέρα πύρινον μὲν εἶναι κατὰ τὴν οὐσίαν, τῇ δὲ εὐτονίᾳ τῆς περιδινήσεως ἀναρπάσαντα πέτρους ἀπὸ τῆς γῆς καὶ καταφλέξαντα τούτους ἠστερωκέναι.
>
> *Aetios II 13, 3; A 71.*

Among all the ancient authors, Aetios alone has managed to turn Anaxagoras' ingenious hypothesis into such egregious nonsense.

How Anaxagoras Came to His Hypothesis

The way Anaxagoras came to arrive at this famous doctrine is extremely interesting.

It is stated he taught that the sun (sc., as well as the stars generally) was a glowing clod, a *mydros*,[1]

because of the burning's immensity.

διὰ τὸ ἄμετρον τῆς πυρώσεως.

Olympiod. in Meteor. p. 17, 19; A19.

That is to say, he seems to have reasoned as follows:

True, also things not made of fireproof material can burn and gleam, but after a short time they come to an end of their burning, they burn away. Consequently, if there is to be not only a comparatively short flaring up in the sky each time, but stars *continually* gleaming, the material employed must be fireproof.

Yet, this is still not enough to guarantee an "immensity of burning." For even if a thing consists of fireproof material but is set ablaze by any accidental, transitory cause, the burning must come to an end, finally, because of the continual subsequent loss of heat.

But Anaxagoras did not fail to consider this point, too. For actually, his stars get their glow from the motion of the medium in which they are swimming and the friction arising in this way. Thus *continual loss is being compensated by continual restitution.*

Motion of the medium itself, however, cannot stop unless Nous itself stops "going around."

One may imagine that an achievement such as the present-day "caloric death" theory would have been sneered at by Anaxagoras as a particularly "silly fancy" (ἄτοπόν τι). Or he would even have with indignation rejected such a theory. To take the World-Nous for clumsy is an unprecedented impertinence (ὕβρις), he might have muttered.

The Stone of Aigospotamoi

The stone clod, then, changed into a star, shares in the *perichoresis* of that sphere of which the centrifugal force is able to compensate its heaviness. Thus the star discontinues to sink.

---

[1] The Greek terms used in the reports are: μύδρος (mydros), Olympiod. in Meteor. p. 17, 19 Stüve; μύδρος διάπυρος, Diog. Laert. II 8 and 12, and Harpocr.; μύδρος πυρόεις, Diog. Laert. II 15; μύλος διάπυρος, Joseph. c. Ap. II 265; βῶλος Eurip. "Phaeton" FTG fr. 783; λίθος διάπυρος, Xenoph. Memor. IV 7, 7; λίθος ἔμπυρος, Hippol. refut. I 8, 6; πέτρος διάπυρος, Aet. II 20, 6.

Yet, only for a time. For a long time, perhaps. But not for ever. For *the magnitude of a star is not constant.*

A star is not alone in the sphere in which it is swimming at a given time. In that sphere there are other *mydroi* that previously reached it. And besides, differentiation goes on incessantly outside in the outermost remoteness (πρόσω) of the cosmos. That is to say, continually new *proskrithenta* arise and consequently new *mydroi* as well. And all these *mydroi* would penetrate into the cosmos along ways similar to the ones pursued by the *mydros* in question. Inevitably, therefore, *mydroi* of both groups, some of those having been in that sphere before and some of those having reached it later, will come into *collisions* with our clod, or, rather, star.

It is plausible that such occurrences do not pass off particularly smoothly. On the contrary, such a *mydros* rushing headlong can hit our star so vehemently that a piece will break off and crash down to the earth as an *aerolith*, like the famous stone of Aigospotamoi:

> It is said Anaxagoras foretold that, when a slipping or shaking occurs among the bodies held fast in the sky, a flinging and a falling down of one (piece) broken off will take place.
>
> λέγεται δὲ 'Αναξαγόραν προειπεῖν, ὡς τῶν κατὰ τὸν οὐρανὸν ἐνδεδεμέ-νων σωμάτων γενομένου τινὸς ὀλισθήματος ἢ σάλου ῥίψις ἔσται καὶ πτῶσις ἑνὸς ἀπορραγέντος.
>
> *Plutarch. Lys. 12; A12.*

As to these proceedings, the (known) stone-fall, also, became a proof, it is said. For a huge stone had darted down – from Heaven, in the opinion of the people at large – to Aigospotamoi. And even today it is still pointed out, as it is a subject of (superstitious) awe to the inhabitants of the Chersonese.

> οἱ δὲ καὶ τὴν τοῦ λίθου πτῶσιν ἐπὶ τῷ πάθει τούτῳ σημεῖόν φασι γενέσθαι· κατηνέχθη γάρ, ὡς ἡ δόξα τῶν πολλῶν ἐξ οὐρανοῦ,[1] παμμε-γέθης λίθος εἰς Αἰγὸς ποταμούς. καὶ δείκνυται μὲν ἔτι νῦν σεβομένων αὐτὸν τῶν Χερσονησιτῶν.
>
> *Plutarch. Lys. 12; A12.*

One can imagine that the fall of this meteorite (in 468/7 B.C.) was a welcome support of his hypothesis to Anaxagoras. And so did Plutarch

---

[1] I put the comma after οὐρανοῦ. The version with the comma after πολλῶν instead, accepted by Diels (and Kranz), does not make much sense nor would it be an explanation as to why that stone was "a subject of awe to the inhabitants of the Chersonese."

understand it. The reports,[1] however, that the fall was predicted by Anaxagoras can only have this meaning, if any, that he "predicted," not the fall of this particular meteoric stone, but such stone-falls generally and theoretically, just as it is stated in the first of the two passages in Plutarch cited above.

Will the Stars Crash Down to the Earth in Time to Come?

Despite the pieces flung off, however, because of its union with the other *mydroi* the star in question is growing larger and larger, heavier and heavier, and finally too heavy. It will be released, so to speak, by its sphere and sink again until it can remain in another sphere with a sufficiently stronger centrifugal force:

> Anaxagoras has declared that the whole sky (sc., meaning "total of all the stars," of course,) consists of stones; that they have united as a consequence of the vehement rotation; and that *they will be released in the future and sink down.*
>
> τὸν δὲ ᾽Αναξαγόραν εἰπεῖν ὡς ὅλος ὁ οὐρανὸς ἐκ λίθων συγκέοιτο· τῇ σφοδρᾷ δὲ περιδινήσει συνεστάναι [2] καὶ ἀνεθέντα‹ς› [3] κατενεχθήσεσθαι.
>
> Diog. Laert. II 12; A1.

Naturally, this is true not only as to the future. Also the present places of the various stars are different from what were their places in the beginning. This follows from the very manner of their origin:

> None of the stars is in the place of its origin (today).
>
> εἶναι δὲ καὶ τῶν ἄστρων ἕκαστον οὐκ ἐν ᾗ πέφυκε χώρᾳ.
>
> Plutarch. Lys. 12; A12.

In days gone by, they sank into the spheres in which they are now revolving, and they will sink still deeper in days to come.

Is this supposed to continue irresistibly in this way? Did Anaxagoras indeed believe that these proceedings would end for every star by its crashing down to the earth some day when its time will have come?

Such result would not have been quite satisfactory, to be sure.

Nous could have avoided this effect by spinning itself, and thereby

---

[1] Diog. Laert. II, 10 (A1); Pliny Nat. Hist. II, 149 f. (A11), and elsewhere.
[2] συνίσταμαι "unite," "join."
[3] ἀνίημι = "let go something held fast." Instead of ἀνεθέντα which is meaningless in this context, I read the word as ἀνεθέντας.

everything else in the respective sphere, with a velocity correspondingly greater whenever a star was about to become too heavy.

Yet, this conception of velocities endlessly increasing would not have been quite the thing, either. And Anaxagoras did certainly not make such an assumption. For if he did, he would not have let the stars sink at all.

However, there was another way of avoiding such a result and, to all appearances, Anaxagoras did make use of it, although not only for solving this problem alone. This point will be dealt with in a subsequent chapter.

Apparent and Real Magnitude of the Stars

Wherever in addition to gravity centrifugal force is at work, there are conglomerations of the *proskrithenta* and, consequently, also *mydroi*.

The hugest conglomerations arise where centrifugal force is strongest: *in the equatorial zone.* For by this very cause more material capable of uniting is forming there than elsewhere. On the other hand, it is these places where, to become too heavy and sink deeper, a star must grow to a much bigger mass than anywhere else. And as a matter of fact, the greatest stars – the planets, the moon, and the sun – are precisely in this zone (that has to be realized as still lying in the equatorial plane of the earth).

Anaxagoras drew a strict distinction between apparent and real magnitude of the stars. As is well known, he maintained that *in reality the sun might be larger than the Peloponnesus*, and that *the moon contained complete mountains and valleys:*

> It (sc., the sun) ... to be larger than the Peloponnesus, but the moon to contain ...[1] summits and gorges.
>
> μείζω (sc., τὸν ἥλιον) τῆς Πελοποννήσου ... τὴν δὲ σελήνην ... ἔχειν ... καὶ λόφους καὶ φάραγγας.
>
> *Diog. Laert. II 8 (A1); also in Hippol., and elsewhere.*

Which is not particularly surprising, considering that, according to Theophrastus, Anaxagoras has made the greatest number of original contributions, as far as the various senses are concerned, in the analysis of the sensations of sight. This was to him the "great" sense (cf. p. 284,

---

[1] The complete passage in Diog. Laert. reads: ".. but the moon to contain *homes*, but also summits and gorges," as if Anaxagoras had asserted the moon to be inhabited. This is a misunderstanding easily refuted (cf. p. 297).

n. 1), obviously because of its supreme degree of variegation and differentiation:

> ... he says original things of his own about all the senses and *particularly about sight* because it is the *great* sense ...

> ... ἴδιον ἐπὶ πάσαις λέγει ταῖς αἰσθήσεσι καὶ μάλιστα ἐπὶ τῇ ὄψει, διότι τὸ μέγα αἰσθανόμενόν ἐστιν ...

> *Theophr. de sensu 37; A92.*

And he even dealt with optics to solve problems of scenography and perspective, if the report in Vitruvius is reliable.[1]

Anaxagoras did not doubt that the moon was nearer to the earth than the sun:

> The moon ... to be still deeper than the sun, nearer to us.

> εἶναι δὲ τὴν σελήνην κατωτέρω τοῦ ἡλίου πλησιώτερον ἡμῶν.

> *Hippol. refut. I 8, 7; A42.*

Consequently, he may have assumed that in reality the moon was surpassed by the sun in magnitude much more even than it seemed to be, and that the other stars, being more distant from the earth than the sun, certainly are larger than a naive observer would believe. But all the same, Anaxagoras may not have had any doubt that of all the stars the sun was still the largest.

That Difficult Moon ...

The sun, just like any star, is a glowing stone clod, a *mydros*, though of enormous magnitude. And so should be the moon, Anaxagoras had to deduce from his astrophysical views.

But here he met with a difficulty. There was apparently no reason why the moon should be anything but a *mydros*. On the other hand, it was since Thales an established fact that *moonlight was nothing but reflected sunlight*. And Anaxagoras approved of this fact, of course:

> Thales was the first to say that it (sc., the moon) was lighted up by the sun. And so said Anaxagoras.

[1] Vitruvius VII, pr. 11: "Primum Agatharchus Athenis Aeschylo docente tragoediam scaenam fecit et de ea commentarium reliquit. ex eo moniti Democritus et Anaxagoras de eadem re scripserunt, quemadmodum oporteat ad aciem oculorum radiorumque extentionem certo loco centro constituto lineas ratione naturali respondere, uti de incerta re certae imagines aedificiorum in scaenarum picturis redderent speciem et quae in directis planisque frontibus sint figurata alia abscedentia alia prominentia esse videantur."

Θαλῆς πρῶτος ἔφη ὑπὸ ἡλίου φωτίζεσθαι . . . ᾿Αναξαγόρας ὁμοίως.

Aet. II 28, 5; A77.

The moon . . . to have its light not from itself, but from the sun.

τὸ δὲ φῶς τὴν σελήνην μὴ ἴδιον ἔχειν, ἀλλὰ ἀπὸ τοῦ ἡλίου.

Hippol. refut. I 8, 8; A42.

Or, in Anaxagoras' own words:

The sun confers upon the moon the bright.

ἥλιος ἐντίθησι τῇ σελήνῃ τὸ λαμπρόν.

> fr. 18 (Plutarch. de fac. in orb. lun. 16 p. 929B). (Cf. also Plato Cratyl. p. 409A; A76.)

Besides, however, Anaxagoras could not have overlooked the obvious fact that *the moon did not give any heat.*

Neither do we feel the glow of the stars, it is true. Yet, this is no analogon, for they are much too distant:

The heat of the stars, however, is not felt because of their great distance from the earth.

τῆς δὲ θερμότητος μὴ αἰσθάνεσθαι τῶν ἄστρων διὰ τὸ μακρὰν εἶναι τὴν ἀπόστασιν τῆς γῆς.

Hippol. refut. I 8, 7; A42.

But the moon is not even as distant from the earth as is the sun.

Anaxagoras tried to harmonize his theory with the facts in this way: Essentially, he said, the moon, too, is a *mydros.* But there is *some irregularity as to the mixture of its mass: Also much of the cold and much of the dark is mixed with it. And as a consequence, the heat produced by friction and the corresponding light are compensated:*

Anaxagoras (declared) the moon to be an annealed solid, containing flat grounds and mountains and gorges.

᾿Αναξαγόρας . . . στερέωμα διάπυρον ἔχον ἐν ἑαυτῷ πεδία καὶ ὄρη καὶ φάραγγας (sc., τὴν σελήνην).

Aet. II 25, 9; A77.

(But,) according to Anaxagoras, there is an irregularity in the mixture of the solid, as it is not only earth-like (having high and flat and hollow parts), but is, besides, mixed with the cold. And with the shining fiery the dark is mixed. And these (sc., the cold and the dark) bring about the shadiness (sc., of the moon). That is why this star is called falsely-luminous.

'Αναξαγόρας ἀνωμαλότητα συγκρίματος διὰ τὸ ψυχρομιγὲς ἅμα καὶ γεῶδες, τὰ μὲν ἐχούσης ὑψηλὰ τὰ δὲ ταπεινὰ τὰ δὲ κοῖλα. καὶ παραμεμῖχθαι τῷ πυροειδεῖ τὸ ζοφῶδες, ὧν τὸ πάθος ὑποφαίνει τὸ σκιερόν· ὅθεν ψευδοφανῆ λέγεσθαι τὸν ἀστέρα.

Aet. II 30, 2; A77.

Anaxagoras' Invisible Celestial Bodies

The most distant spheres are spangled with stars all over. But *in the inferior strata there is only one star in every sphere:* the moon in the moon-sphere, the sun in the sun-sphere, and only one planet in each of the various planet-spheres.

To all appearances, this was felt as something like a flaw by Anaxagoras. For he assumed that, just as in the heaven of the stars, *also in the strata below*, i.e., in the heavens of the planets and in the sun-heaven and the moon-heaven, *mydroi* were spread *all over, but not visible to us*, presumably because they were too small and became outshined:

The sun, the moon, and all the stars are fiery stones dragged around by the ether's rotation. But (also) *below the stars* there are certain bodies, dragged around along with the sun and the moon (that is to say: in the same spheres), though invisible to us.[1]

ἥλιον δὲ καὶ σελήνην καὶ πάντα τὰ ἄστρα λίθους εἶναι ἐμπύρους συμπεριληφθέντας ὑπὸ τῆς αἰθέρος περιφορᾶς. εἶναι δ' ὑποκάτω τῶν ἄστρων ἡλίῳ καὶ σελήνῃ σώματά τινα συμπεριφερόμενα ἡμῖν ἀόρατα.[1]

Hippol. refut. I 8, 6; A42.

Anaxagoras seems to have made this assumption for no other reason but because he did not want to accept such inartistic asymmetry. True, he is said [2] to have employed those invisible celestial bodies also for an explanation of solar and lunar eclipses, in addition to the other, well-known causes of these phenomena, causes even said to have been thoroughly analysed for the first time by Anaxagoras, according to

---

[1] These Anaxagorean invisible celestial bodies *beneath the heaven of the stars*, revolving in the sun-sphere and the moon-sphere, are something completely different from those "earth-like formations *in the region of the stars*, moving around together with them" (εἶναι δὲ καὶ γεώδεις φύσεις ἐν τῷ τόπῳ τῶν ἀστέρων συμπεριφερομένας ἐκείνοις), fathered by Hippolytus (I 7, 5; 13 A 7) upon Anaximenes.

[2] Aet. II 29, 6 and 7; A77.

Hippolytus.[1] Yet, for that purpose there was no need for him to contrive those bodies.

Third Means of Cosmopoeia: Dismemberment of the Axis

Yet, this condition of the cosmic system was still different from the world as it is today, since all of this *diakosmesis* was still unfit to bring about an alternation of day and night. For still *the entire* perichoresis *was everywhere taking place around the one axis* chosen in the beginning when Nous started cosmogony from that tiny district. Consequently, the circles described around that axis by the sun and the moon could only lie in the plane of the earth disk itself, and the orbits of the other stars were either in this very plane or parallel with it.

In other words, *there was neither rising nor setting for any star. All the stars were continually and simultaneously visible.* The moon, the sun, and the planets were revolving around the earth in the heaven-equator which coincided with the earth-equator. And the starred sky was set upon the horizon like a well-fitting cupola.

If Nous intended to avoid such uniformity, if a condition resembling that of today was to be brought about, *the identity of the axes of rotation for all the spheres had to be abolished.*

Individual Rotation for Every Sphere

Nous had to divide the one common *perichoresis* into a very system of *perichoreses*. The one unique axis had to be cut into pieces, so to speak. Only in this way could each sphere, fully independent of the others, be enabled to execute its own *perichoresis*.

And as a matter of fact, Anaxagoras did realize it in the way described. According to the report in Diogenes Laertius, Anaxagoras taught:

> Originally, the stars were moving *like a cupola*, so that on the top of the earth (*i.e.*, from the surface of the earth) the celestial vault (*i.e.*, the starry sky) was *continually* visible. Later on, however, they got their slanting position.

> τὰ ἄστρα κατ' ἀρχὰς μὲν θολοειδῶς ἐνεχθῆναι, ὥστε κατὰ κορυφὴν τῆς γῆς τὸν ἀεὶ φαινόμενον εἶναι πόλον, ὕστερον δὲ τὴν ἔγκλισιν λαβεῖν.

> *Diog. Laert. II 9; A1.*

---

[1] Refut. I 8, 10; A42.

Only by this assumption of Nous breaking the axis of rotation was Anaxagoras enabled to harmonize his theory with the obvious physical world. Now it was easy for him to bring about the actual condition from the one preceding it in his construction: Nous was free not only to change the velocities of the various spheres according to need (cf. p. 230), but also to *turn each axis* of rotation correspondingly, while retaining their mutual intersecting point in the earth-centre, needless to say.

Anaxagoras even gained a further advantage in this way. As everybody knows, the direction of the rotation of the heaven of stars is opposite to the direction of the rotations of the other spheres. How is this to be explained? Should Nous have reversed the original direction of its own rotating? There was no need for Anaxagoras to resort to such a supposition. He was allowed to let Nous keep the original direction and merely turn the axis by 180 degrees.

Explanation of the Milky Way

During that cosmic condition characterized by the oneness for all the spheres of the axis of rotation, the whole sky had been bespangled with stars uniformly. By transformation into the present condition, the symmetrical distribution of the stars was not abolished, though, but as a consequence such alternation in the conditions of light came about as can be observed today.

As it is now, during the sun's way *above* the earth all the other stars are outshined, giving an impression as if the sun were alone in the sky. During the sun's way *below* the earth, the other stars become visible, but it looks as if their distribution were *unequally dense*. Those stars which come into the direct shadow of the earth can display their illuminating power most intensively, while the light of the others is being weakened by reflected sunlight. Which is the Anaxagorean explanation of the Milky Way:

> The Anaxagoreans ... assert that the Milky Way is the light of certain stars; (that) the sun, namely, when moving below the earth, does not irradiate (literally: "see") some of the stars; (that) the light of all those stars enveloped in its rays does not become visible (because it is being checked by the rays of the sun); (that) on the other hand, the own light of all those stars adumbrated by the earth, so that they cannot be irradiated by the sun, is exactly what the Milky Way is.

οἱ δὲ περὶ ᾿Αναξαγόραν . . . φῶς εἶναι τὸ γάλα λέγουσιν ἄστρων τινῶν.
τὸν γὰρ ἥλιον ὑπὸ τὴν γῆν φερόμενον οὐχ ὁρᾶν ἔνια τῶν ἄστρων. ὅσα
μὲν οὖν περιορᾶται ὑπ' αὐτοῦ, τούτων μὲν οὐ φαίνεσθαι τὸ φῶς (κω-
λύεσθαι γὰρ ὑπὸ τῶν τοῦ ἡλίου ἀκτίνων). ὅσοις δ' ἀντιφράττει ἡ γῆ,
ὥστε μὴ ὁρᾶσθαι ὑπὸ τοῦ ἡλίου, τὸ τούτων οἰκεῖον φῶς φασιν εἶναι τὸ
γάλα.

Arist. Meteor. I 8. 345a25; A80.

Hence, also this phenomenon has been made possible only by the
dismemberment of the axis of rotation.

The Orbits and the Turnings of the Sun and of the Moon

Thus, as to the orbit of the sun, between today's actual condition
and the previous state the difference is that now the solar heaven's
equator does not belong any more to the same plane as does the equator
of the earth, in other words: that now the sun is alternately above and
below the earth.

Besides, there is another difference. The daily circles described by
the sun now are not in one and the same plane. Or, strictly speaking,
now the sun is describing no circles at all, but a helical line: during six
months a helical line ascending and during the other six months a
helical line descending.

This, however, implies a problem. *How is it that the sun is not
executing its orbit perpetually in the equinoctial?*

Even this is easily accounted for by that division of the original axis:

Let us visualize the sun to have been in a certain sphere, and in the
equator of the sphere. Presently that operation of "breaking" the axis
is performed. As a result, the axis of rotation of one of the nearest lower
spheres will form an angle with the axis of what had been the sun-
heaven until then. In this moment or later, the sun shall become too
heavy for its sphere and rush into that lower sphere the centrifugal
force of which is supposed to be sufficiently stronger. Henceforth, the
sun will perform its revolution in the direction of the rotation of its
new sphere and stop sinking toward the world's centre.

But the fall tendency will last. And from then on, since not parallel
with any parallel of that sphere, this fall tendency will manifest itself as
a component of the movement of the sun in that *the sun will never again
return to the starting-points of its daily orbits.* That means: The sun will
not describe daily circles any longer, but something like a spiral line, a
helical line.

The sun cannot have reached that sphere in the sphere's equator, i.e., in the plane of equinox. *Hence, upon arriving at this plane in the course of the helical line, the sun will not remain in it, but will continue its winding orbit.*

True, if the sun were as large as the earth or still larger, and the surrounding medium as dense as the air surrounding the earth, then all this would not be possible. In spite of that component, the sun would be forced to remain in the parallel it had arrived at when rushing into the sphere. The medium's resistance would be too strong to allow the sun to leave that plane. The same mechanism would set in by which the earth is prevented from leaving its place in the middle of the world (cf. p. 228).

But the sun is much smaller than the earth. It is merely somewhat larger than the Peloponnesus, after all. Besides, the medium – although mingled with the *proskrithenta*-molecules streaming through from the *peri-echon* – is at any rate rarer than the air surrounding the earth. Therefore, the sun is able to overcome the medium's resistance and execute a screw-shaped orbit.

Yet, this cannot go on *in infinitum*. Resistance is growing because *the medium is being condensed more and more by the sun's compressing it perpetually.* And so the medium is given *power* by the sun itself *to push it back, finally.*

Then, driven by this repulsion, the sun will describe a helical line in the opposite direction, pass the sun-heaven's equator once more, and reiterate the play on the other side.

This goes on to and fro, again and again. Twice a year there is an equinox, and twice a year the sun is forced to a turning back, to the *winter solstice* and the *summer solstice:*

> Anaxagoras (sc., realized solstice to take place) through repulsion by the air in the north [by the air in the south likewise, of course]. The sun itself, by compressing the air, renders it powerful through that very condensation.
>
> Ἀναξαγόρας (sc., τροπὴν ἡλίου γίγνεσθαι) ἀνταπώσει τοῦ πρὸς ταῖς ἄρκτοις ἀέρος, ὃν αὐτὸς (sc., ὁ ἥλιος) συνωθῶν ἐκ τῆς πυκνώσεως ἰσχυροποιεῖ.
>
> *Aet. II 23, 2; A72.*

The same applies to the orbit of the moon.

There is only some difference concerning its *turnings*, in Anaxagoras' opinion. The sun is pushed back by a dry and warm medium. But in the repulsion of the moon's orbits frequently co-operates *the cold-element* contained in the watery vapor that sometimes is already conglobated to clouds in the moon-heaven:

> The sun and the moon as well are turned when repelled by the air. The moon, however, often is turned because it cannot overcome the cold.
>
> τροπὰς δὲ ποιεῖσθαι καὶ ἥλιον καὶ σελήνην ἀπωθουμένους ὑπο τοῦ ἀέρος. σελήνην δὲ πολλάκις τρέπεσθαι διὰ τὸ μὴ δύνασθαι κρατεῖν τοῦ ψυχροῦ.
>
> *Hippol. refut. I 8, 9; A42.*

Thus Anaxagoras has succeeded in clarifying these phenomena, too, by that division of the original axis.

In this way, Anaxagoras has even avoided what afterwards Plato did not know how to steer clear of, and what appears somewhat forced in his interpretation of those phenomena. According to Plato, the stars are fixed in their centres at definite points of their respective spheres. Consequently, for explanation of the orbits of the sun and the moon Plato had no other way out than to assume the very axes of their spheres to pendulate.

The "(generative) power of rotation" (ἡ δύναμις ἐν τῇ περιχωρήσει), to use a Pythagorean-like term, was herewith exhausted. Nothing more could be accomplished in this way.

When Will Cosmogony Come to Its End?

The world-forming activity of Nous, as far as hitherto delineated, began in a tiny district, expanded from there more and more in spherical undulation, and *has not yet finished expanding* up to this day, in Anaxagoras' opinion:

> First (Nous) started going around from some small (district), but (Nous) is going around farther (even now) and will expand its going around still farther (i.e., over spaces still wider) also in the future.
>
> πρῶτον ἀπό του σμικροῦ ἤρξατο περιχωρεῖν (sc., ὁ νοῦς), ἐπὶ δὲ πλέον περιχωρεῖ, καὶ περιχωρήσει ἐπὶ πλέον.
>
> *fr. 12 (Simpl. phys. 156, 23).*

Was that supposed by Anaxagoras to continue in infinitum?
This question shall remain without an answer for a while.

"THERE ARE SOME IN WHICH NOUS, TOO, IS CONTAINED" *

The Bodies

Not yet was materialized the total of possibilities in the *pantahomou*.

A great many other formations, fine and artistic, could be moulded from those substances produced by means of differentiation. A great many other forms, indeed, and among them particularly those things with *psyche:* all kinds or organisms breathing and living, the whole vast variety of plants, animals, human beings.

Construction against Stratification

Nous was fully cognizant of that. For when producing molecular constitutions different from the combining-ratio 1:1, Nous had made also blood-molecules and flesh-molecules and bone-molecules and the like.

But by the means applied up to this point, a formation of organisms was not accomplishable. In this way, *at best, single lumps could have resulted, with the various constituents of organisms deposited in layers according to their specific gravities.*

Therefore, if Nous wanted to succeed in constructing the organisms of the various styles despite the general trend to stratification, *Nous had to interfere in a special way.*

If Nous Were Like the God of the Bible ...

Yet, mere moulding, mere building up but once, would not have been enough for Nous to accomplish this intention.

True, if the Nous of Anaxagoras were like the God of the Bible, then perhaps even this would have sufficed. For then moulding would have implied an order given to matter, previously created and then moulded, to persevere in its forms until counter-order. Where a "Let there be!" is enough for creation, a "Let it keep on!" may be enough to preserve the formedness of things.

August Gladisch [1] has tried to make it plausible that Anaxagoras in his conception of Nous' cosmopoeia may have been influenced by the Bible.

* Anaxagoras.
[1] "Anaxagoras und die alten Israeliten," in: Niedner's *Zeitschrift für historische Theologie* (1849), 4th issue, no. 14, and *Anaxagoras und die Israeliten* (Leipzig, 1864).

It is one of the most serious counter-arguments that in Anaxagoras' doctrine there is no *creatio ex nihilo*. But Gladisch endeavored to refute this argument by contesting that a true *creatio ex nihilo* was not taught by the Bible.

In one of his writings [1] he says:

> In dem ersten Verse: "Im Anfange schuf Gott den Himmel und die Erde," soll der Ausdruck "schuf" bedeuten: schuf aus dem Nichts; und der Ausdruck "den Himmel und die Erde" soll bedeuten: eine chaotische Masse! Hier wird uns erstens zugemutet, wir sollen diese Bedeutung des Wortes בּרא sofort zugeben, ohne dass sie durch eine einzige Stelle der hebräischen Schriften erwiesen wird, in denen das Wort vielmehr nur in der Bedeutung "machen" überhaupt, ja auch geradezu in der Bedeutung "aus vorhandenem Stoffe bereiten" vorkommt.[2] ... Wir könnten uns vielleicht entschliessen, das Unglaubliche zu glauben, dass gleichwohl der Verfasser der Schöpfungsurkunde, er allein unter den Hebräern, das Wort in der bestimmten Bedeutung "aus dem Nichts erschaffen" gedacht und gebraucht habe. Allein, sogar dieser Entschluss, wenn wir ihn fassen wollten, wird uns durch die Urkunde selbst unmöglich gemacht: denn ... hier findet man dasselbe Wort nicht bloss von der ersten angeblichen Hervorrufung des Ganzen aus dem Nichts, sondern auch von der Bildung des Einzelnen aus dem vorhandenen Stoff, V. 21, und am deutlichsten V. 27 von dem aus einem Erdenkloss geformten Menschen. Trotzdem sollen wir im ersten Verse zu dem Worte nur dreist ergänzen: aus dem Nichts! Doch das ist noch nicht die ganze Zumutung, sondern zweitens auch dies, dass der Ausdruck "den Himmel und die Erde" im ersten Verse eine chaotische Masse bezeichne, sollen wir nur so geradhin glauben, ungeachtet selbst Diejenigen, welche uns den Glauben zumuten, noch niemals gewagt haben und wohl auch niemals wagen werden, diese Bedeutung des Ausdruckes in ein hebräisches Wörterbuch aufzunehmen. Der Verfasser der heiligen Urkunde soll bei dem ersten Verse die Anschauung eines finstern Chaos, welches Gott aus dem zu ergänzenden Nichts hervorrufe, um hernach, vom dritten Verse ab, daraus das gegenwärtig sichtbare Weltganze zu bilden, vor seiner Seele haben, und soll diese Anschauung eines finstern Chaos

---

[1] *Anaxagoras und die alten Israeliten* (Niedner's Zeitschrift, 1849), p. 535.

[2] Gladisch seems to have overlooked the fact that in no other passages this word could have the meaning of *creare e nihilo*.

mit den Worten aussprechen, welche jedem Hebräer das bereits
gebildete gegenwärtig sichtbare Weltganze, den Himmel und die
Erde, vor die Seele stellten! Welch einer seltsamen Art zu schrei-
ben muss er fähig erachtet werden! Einer, der für seine Vorstel-
lung keinen nur verwandten Ausdruck fand, der Jenes dachte,
aber Dieses hinschrieb, ein solcher soll der Verfasser der heiligen
Urkunde sein! Wenn eine Worterklärung wie die, welche wir hier
vor uns haben, bei andern Schriftwerken, z.B. griechischen oder
lateinischen, vorgebracht werden sollte, so würde sie ohne Zweifel
das höchste Erstaunen erregen; bei den heiligen Schriften der
Israeliten aber ist diese Auslegung, die in Wahrheit eine Hinein-
legung und augenfällige Unterschiebung genannt werden muss,
aus den ältesten Zeiten her eingeführt und so geheiligt, dass auch
jetzt noch selbst die gründlichsten Forscher sich von ihr nicht
durchaus loszusagen vermögen.

It might be quite interesting to become acquainted with the altogether antagonistic view of a man who, one may safely assume, had at
least as good a command of the Hebrew language as had Gladisch.
Samson Raphael Hirsch, the famous rabbi of Frankfurt, in his
Pentateuch edition, published 1893 in Frankfurt-on-the-Main, com-
ments upon the first word of the first chapter of Genesis as follows:

Die Lautverwandtschaft mit רעש und רחש, wovon das Eine eine
Ortsbewegung und das Andere eine innere Bewegung bedeutet,
lehrt, dass wir ראש als den Sitz der Bewegung, als dasjenige Organ
zu begreifen haben, von welchem alle äussere und innere Bewegung
den Ausgang nimmt. Daher heisst ראשית der Anfang einer Bewegung, der zeitliche Anfang, nie der räumliche. Der räumliche
Anfang heisst wie das Ende קצה; es sind eben die beiden End-
punkte einer Ausdehnung, die, je nachdem man seinen Stand-
punkt nimmt, Anfang oder Ende sein können. בראשית וגו' heisst
somit: im Anfang alles Werdens war es Gott, der schuf; oder mit
den beiden nachfolgenden Objekten zusammengefasst: uranfäng-
lich schuf Gott den Himmel und die Erde. Jedenfalls spricht
בראשית das Faktum aus, dass dem Schaffen Gottes Nichts voran-
gegangen, dass der Himmel und die Erde nur aus dem Schaffen
Gottes hervorgegangen. Es ist damit die Schöpfung aus Nichts,
יש מאין, konstatiert, eine Wahrheit, die den Grundstein des Be-
wusstseins bildet, welches die Lehre Gottes uns aufbauen will, etc.

78

And *ad vocem* ברא:

> Die verwandten Wurzeln: פרע, פרא, פרח, ברה, ברח, die sämtlich ein Hinausstreben und Hinaustreten aus einer Innerlichkeit oder einer Gebundenheit bedeuten, ergeben für ברא ebenfalls den Begriff des Hinaussetzens in die Aeusserlichkeit; heisst ja auch chaldäisch ברא ohne weiteres das Draussenseiende, draussen. ברא ist somit das Aeusserlichmachen eines bis dahin nur im Innern, im Geiste Vorhandengewesenen. Es ist jenes Schaffen, dem nichts anderes als der Gedanke und der Wille vorausgegangen. Es ist das eigentliche יש מאין (*creatio ex nihilo*) und wird daher nur von dem Schaffen Gottes gebraucht. Ehe die Welt ward, war sie nur als Gedanke in dem Geiste des Schöpfers – menschlich zu sprechen – vorhanden. Der Schöpfungsakt machte diesen Gedanken äusserlich, gab diesem Gedanken ein äusseres, konkretes Dasein. Die ganze Welt im ganzen und einzelnen ist somit nichts als verwirklichte Gottesgedanken.

'Creatio ex Nihilo' – Viewed Psychologically

Yet – I am ready, nevertheless, to admit that, on the basis of the Biblical context, one has perhaps no right to assume that the author of that Genesis text already had the strict notion of a *creatio ex nihilo*. As early as the days of the *Mishnah* and the *Talmud*, the rabbis were quite alive to the fact that not seldom Scripture amazingly corresponded to popular view and phraseology. That is why, for logical justification, they laid down the principle: *"The Doctrine has spoken* (sc., intentionally) *like the tongue of the sons of Adam* (sc., in order to be understood by them),"* (דברה תורה כלשן בני אדם).[1]

In such cases, however, the question of whether or not an idea is precisely formulated is of no great importance. Here the mere fact that a logically precise *formulation* is lacking is far from being proof that *the idea itself* is lacking. Such ideas as *creation, emanation, effulguration,* etc., are rooted in a person's character or even in the psychic fundamentals of a whole race. A man can be a true creationist, psychologically speaking, without arriving at a formulation of the idea of *creatio ex nihilo* in this logical precision ever in a lifetime.

---

[1] *Talmud Babli's* tracts: *Babah Meziah* 31, 2; 94, 2; *Kiddushin* 17, 2; *Berachoth* 31, 1; *Arachin* 3; *Kerithoth* 11; *Yebamoth* 71; *Kethuboth* 67; *Gittin* 41; *Nedarim* 3; *Sanhedrin* 56; 64; 85; 90; *Makkoth* 12; *Abodah zarah* 27; *Sebachim* 28; *Niddoh* 32; 44. – For this list of passages I am indebted to the kindness of the late Rev. Dr. S. Rubin of the former Jewish Theological Seminary of Vienna.

The same may have occurred here. The idea of creation is a genuinely Jewish idea. It got its explicit formulation rather late, it is true. But this means only that the characteristic and distinctive traits of the Jews' own nature were not thrown into particular relief and clearness by them until they became acquainted with the natures of other peoples. Psychologically viewed, however, there is a complete identity of two things: the idea of *creatio ex nihilo*, on the one hand, and the conception, on the other hand, that the mere command "Let there be!" is sufficient to conjure up the universe, although this command is not oriented to any mechanical possibilities or impossibilities of matter. This is a relationship of exactly the same identity as that between the tree and the seed-grain from which it has sprung up.

One might perhaps suspect that the idea of a *creatio ex nihilo* was taken over into Judaism from the foreign, Greek philosophy. But this would be a mistake. *Of the numerous instances in ancient Greek philosophy of a "not being"* (μὴ ὄν), *from which or in which the cosmos is formed (not created!), none is a true "nihil."* It may be that the Greek positions were misinterpreted by the Jews in the sense of their own Jewish, creationistic constitution. But this would only lend support to my opinion.

The Anaxagorean Nous, however, is not the Jewish God, not a Creator absolutely omnipotent, who out of nothingness conjures up the world to be subservient to His ends, the ends of the Lord. The Nous of Anaxagoras is a Hellenic artist, the architect of the world, a mathematical and physical intelligence of the highest rank, but of a might only relatively highest. A skilful mechanician, knowing all that can be made of the world, but performing as well all the conditions indispensable for accomplishing the chosen possibilities.

For Nous, therefore, it would not have sufficed to mould the various organisms but once and then abandon them to themselves. *The artistic structures would have been destroyed by that general stratification in no time.*

A command of Nous to persevere would not have overcome destruction, either. Not even the will of Nous is a wizard. Otherwise there would have been no need for Nous to do the differentiation of the *pantahomou-mereias* with Its own hand, so to speak, or to effect that general rotation by rotating Itself. For these ends, too, a mere command would have sufficed.

Therefore, unless the formed organisms were to decompose immediately, Nous had to make use of all those means making possible the prevention, in a mechanical way, of the components of organisms from stratification to their specific gravities. And since Nous knows everything, it knows of course all these means, too, and also how to handle them. The godship of Nous consists, above all, in its omniscience, not in an omnipotence of its liking.

'Primordial Generation' and 'Generation from One Another'

Hence, Nous itself must operate as the moulding and preserving principle, not only in the case of the first specimens, but whenever an organism is to come into existence.

According to Anaxagoras, there is the very first production of organisms by Nous immediately from their constituents, the so-called *primordial generation*, and there is, subsequently, the so-called *generation from one another* of organisms by Nous:

> The living beings ... to originate (first) from moist and warm and earth-like (substances), but later on from one another.
>
> ζῷα γίνεσθαι ἐξ ὑγροῦ καὶ θερμοῦ καὶ γεώδους, ὕστερον δὲ ἐξ ἀλλήλων.
>
> *Diog. Laert. II 9; A1.*

In comparison with primordial generation, the subsequent generation from one another means merely a *simplification*, not a becoming autonomous and independent.

That the intervention of Nous was indispensable in each individual case could be learned by Anaxagoras from the fact that copulation often occurred without result for propagation. Whenever Nous has not decided on a living being to take birth, copulation is for pleasure alone.

Once more one may point to a characteristic difference between the Biblical God and the Nous of Anaxagoras. With the God of the Bible, mere blessing is sufficient for propagation of the first specimens of organisms.

First Measure against Decay: Breathing

Now, what are the measures by the taking of which Nous is keeping the organisms alive, preserving them from their constituents being stratified to their "dense"- and "rare"-contents? What are the *working-functions* (the *Betriebsfunktionen*, to apply the term of Wilhelm Roux), the somatic activities of Nous, *to counterbalance those losses continually inflicted on the organisms* by the stratification tendencies of inorganic nature?

Nous sees the losses compensated – that means: *preservation* – and supercompensated – that means: *growth* – by making them good from the organisms' environment in various ways.

The first and basic and simplest activity against decomposition is *breathing*.

The Meaning of 'Psyche'

Aristotle, already, is at a loss to know what is the meaning proper, in Anaxagoras, of "psyche." He complains of Anaxagoras having expressed himself not clearly enough about it nor about the difference between *"psyche"* and *"nous"*:

Anaxagoras speaks about them less plainly.

Ἀναξαγόρας ἧττον διασαφεῖ περὶ αὐτῶν.

Arist. de anima I 2. 404b1; A100.

For now, says Aristotle, he seems to distinguish strictly between *nous* and *psyche*, now he applies the two terms in a way as if they referred to the same being:

Anaxagoras seems to distinguish *psyche* and *nous* ... but he employs *both together like one reality*.

Ἀναξαγόρας δ' ἔοικε μὲν ἕτερον λέγειν ψυχήν τε καὶ νοῦν ... χρῆται δ' ἀμφοῖν ὡς μιᾷ φύσει.

Arist. de anima I 2. 405a13; A100.

It is usual to take *psyche* for the name of a *thing* and translate it as "soul." But the question is whether the word was used in this sense by Anaxagoras. And this question must rather be answered in the negative.

Originally, as already pointed out (cf. p. 59), *psyche* is a designation for breath; not for the air exhaled and inhaled, but for the respiratory movement, for *breathing*. And also from the linguistical view is *psyche* originally no designation for a thing, but *a substantival designation for an occurrence*:

Ψυχή is to ψύχειν exactly as βολή is to βάλλειν, τροπή to τρέπειν, στροφή to στρέφειν, μονή to μένειν, etc., or as *passio* is to *pati, lectio* to *legere, (com)pressio* to *premere*, etc., or as motion is to move, action to act, failure to fail, enjoyment to enjoy, seizure to seize, comprehension to comprehend, etc., or as *Fall* is to *fallen, Gang* to *gehen, Wurf* to *werfen, Traum* to *träumen, Genuss* to *geniessen, Griff* to *greifen, Begriff* to *begreifen*, etc.

Therefore, it could very well be that to Anaxagoras *psyche* was not the name of a thing, *not a name for something that performs certain functions, but a name for those functions themselves, while that something performing the functions is Nous.*

In this way, the terms *psyche* and *nous* would indeed designate different ideas and yet refer to one reality, and only "both together" (it reads: ἀμφοῖν!) would mean "one nature" (μία φύσις), since function can never subsist independently, apart from the functioning thing.

'Larger Psyche' and 'Smaller Psyche' and the Weakness of Human Perception

On the basis of this interpretation of *psyche*, an otherwise incomprehensible statement would make good sense. One of the Anaxagorean fragments contains the following sentence:

> All those having *psyche*, a larger one as well as a smaller one, are ruled over by Nous.
>
> καὶ ὅσα γε ψυχὴν ἔχει καὶ μείζω καὶ ἐλάσσω, πάντων νοῦς κρατεῖ.
>
> *fr. 12 (Simpl. phys. 156, 21).*

If one translates *psyche* as "soul," what shall be the meaning of "differences in size" of the souls? [1] But if ὅσα ψυχὴν ἔχει means "whatever has breath," "whatever is breathing," in other words: all the organisms, then it makes sense to distinguish "larger *psyche*" and "smaller *psyche*":

In Anaxagoras' opinion, whatever does not breathe is no organism. Yet, there are some kinds of organisms which in fact do not seem to breathe, as for instance the worms, the mussels, and, above all, the plants. With regard to such cases, Anaxagoras points out that *the sharpness of the human organs of sense just happens to have its limits* [2]:

> In consequence of their weakness we cannot discern the real fact.
>
> ὑπ' ἀφαυρότητος αὐτῶν (sc., τῶν αἰσθήσεων) οὐ δυνατοί ἐσμεν κρίνειν τἀληθές.
>
> *fr. 21 (Sext. Emp. adv. math. VII 90).*

---

[1] The most easy-going is it, of course, not to connect καὶ μείζω καὶ ἐλάσσω with ψυχήν and, as did Diels, to translate: "Und über alles, was nur eine Seele hat, *Grosses wie Kleines*, hat der Geist die Herrschaft." (Dr. Kranz has modified this into "die grösseren wie die kleineren Wesen," which is quite the same easy-going evasion.)

[2] This is the meaning of that Anaxagorean "weakness" of human perception, and *not a scepticism in principle* as it has been interpreted by Sextus Empiricus in accordance with his own scepticism (cf. p. 276 f.).

That is why we are not aware, say, of tiny changes of color:

> For if we take two colors, black and white, and then pour, drop by drop, from the one into the other, the eye will not be able to distinguish the little by little changes, although they are actually taking place.
>
> εἰ γὰρ δύο λάβοιμεν χρώματα, μέλαν καὶ λευκόν, εἶτα ἐκ θατέρου εἰς θάτερον κατὰ σταγόνα παρεκχέοιμεν, οὐ δυνήσεται ἡ ὄψις διακρίνειν τὰς παρὰ μικρὸν μεταβολάς, καίπερ πρὸς τὴν φύσιν ὑποκειμένας.
>
> *(ibid.)*

And quite the same occurs with the breath of those species of organisms: Their breathing happens to be too slight, *their "psyche" is much too small*, to be perceptible to a human observer.

Therefore, Anaxagoras explicitly taught that even the plants are breathing:

> Anaxagoras maintained that they (sc., the plants) have breath as well.
>
> Ἀναξαγόρας γὰρ εἶπε ταῦτα (sc., τὰ φυτά) ἔχειν καὶ πνοήν.
>
> *Nic. Damasc. [Arist.] de plantis I 2. 816b26; A117.*

But on the other hand, he also endeavored to demonstrate, as a proof of his assertion, the mechanism of breathing in such organisms:

> Anaxagoras, however, (and Diogenes) say that all (the organisms) breathe, and (therefore) explain (also) about the fishes and the mussels in which manner they breathe.
>
> Ἀναξαγόρας δὲ (καὶ Διογένης) πάντα φάσκοντες ἀναπνεῖν περὶ τῶν ἰχθύων καὶ τῶν ὀστρείων λέγουσι τίνα τρόπον ἀναπνέουσιν ...
>
> *Arist. de respirat. 2. 470b30; A115.*

At any rate, then, *psyche* was not the name of a thing to Anaxagoras, but a designation for a *function*, at least for the function of breathing.

But it is not unlikely, even, that *psyche* was used by Anaxagoras not only in this narrower sense, but *also as a representative name for the total of the "somatic activity"* (σωματικὴ ἐνέργεια[1]) *of Nous, for the total of the "working-functions" preserving the organism from decay.*

This would not be without analogy. The same thing was usual in Indian philosophy (cf. above p. 138f.). In the Sâṃkhya system every

---

[1] Cf. Aet. V 25, 2; A 103.

working-function in the organism is imagined as a kind of breath. And already as far back as the earlier Upanishads, *prâna* ("breath") is likewise used in the broadest sense.[1]

Second Measure against Decay: Nutrition and Digestion

Another function, meant to compensate and if need be super-compensate those continual losses, is *nutrition* from, and *digestion* of, the eatable and drinkable substances in the organism's neighborhood.

The nourishment of most kinds of organisms cannot be obtained from their immediate surroundings. Therefore, in these cases *the embedding Nous has to make use of its own free motivity.* For wherever Nous does not do so, motion happens but in the mounting and falling directions. And even this occurs only when bodies are taken from those positions which correspond to their specific gravities, while otherwise they remain in the relative rest of *perichoresis.*

Now, part of an organism's *food* consists of substances *similar* to the substances to be supplied, such as flesh, but another part, of substances *dissimilar* to them, as bread and others. This implies a problem. *Something lost is replaceable only with something similar. How is it, then, that bread does nourish, nevertheless?*

An Ancient Interpretation

Anaxagoras is said to have answered this question in quite a strange way: Bread becomes flesh and blood and bones, etc.; a true becoming, however, is not thinkable; consequently, *bread just consists of flesh-particles and blood-particles and bone-particles, etc.*!

That is indeed how the respective tenets of Anaxagoras were interpreted. A few examples may suffice:

> He (sc., Aristotle) shows us the reason why Anaxagoras came to such a conjecture ... Anaxagoras, however, came to this idea (sc., that every individual *homoiomereia* contains all in itself in the same way as does the whole [of the world]) because of his con-viction that *nothing originates from the not-being*, and that *every* (sc., *organism*) *can nourish itself by similar things only*. Now, he saw everything originating from everything, though not immedi-ately, but successively. (For from fire air originates, from air, water, from water, earth, from earth, stone, and from stone, fire

[1] Cf. Richard Garbe, *Die Sâmkhya-Philosophie*, 2nd ed., 1917, pp. 318 and 319, and Paul Deussen, *System des Vedanta*, pp. 353–356 and 359–363.

again,[1] and *from one and the same food supplied, as e.g. bread, many dissimilar things originate, such as muscles, bones, veins, sinews, hair, nails, and also, occasionally, wings and horns. But on the other hand, like can grow by like only.) That is why he assumed all those things to be contained already in the food, as well as wood and bast and fruit to be contained in the water, inasmuch as the trees live on it.* For this reason, he declared that all things are mixed in everything, and that origination comes about by means of disseverance. ... He saw that from every one of the things now differentiated all (kinds of things) were being severed, *such as from bread muscles and bones and the other [constituents of organisms], since all of them were jointly contained in it and mixed together.* From that he concluded that all the existing [substances] had been mixed also before severance [all the more].

τὴν αἰτίαν ἡμᾶς διδάσκει (sc., ὁ ᾿Αριστοτέλης), δι᾿ ἣν εἰς τοιαύτην ἔννοιαν (sc., ἑκάστην ὁμοιομέρειαν ὁμοίως τῷ ὅλῳ πάντα ἔχουσαν ἐνυπάρχοντα) ὁ ᾿Αναξαγόρας ἦλθεν ἡγούμενος μηδὲν ἐκ τοῦ μὴ ὄντος γίνεσθαι καὶ πᾶν ὑπὸ ὁμοίου τρέφεσθαι. ὁρῶν οὖν πᾶν ἐκ παντὸς γινόμενον, εἰ καὶ μὴ ἀμέσως, ἀλλὰ κατὰ τάξιν (καὶ γὰρ ἐκ πυρὸς ἀὴρ καὶ ἐξ ἀέρος ὕδωρ καὶ ἐξ ὕδατος γῆ καὶ ἐκ γῆς λίθος καὶ ἐκ λίθου πάλιν πῦρ [1] καὶ τροφῆς δὲ τῆς αὐτῆς προσφερομένης οἷον ἄρτου πολλὰ καὶ ἀνόμοια γίνεται, σάρκες ὀστᾶ φλέβες νεῦρα τρίχες ὄνυχες καὶ πτερὰ δὲ εἰ οὕτω τύχοι καὶ κέρατα, αὔξεται δὲ τὸ ὅμοιον τῷ ὁμοίῳ)· διὸ ταῦτα ἐν τῇ τροφῇ ὑπέλαβεν εἶναι καὶ ἐν τῷ ὕδατι, εἰ τούτῳ τρέφοιτο τὰ δένδρα, ξύλον καὶ φλοιὸν καὶ καρπόν. διὸ πάντα ἐν πᾶσιν ἔλεγε μεμῖχθαι καὶ τὴν γένεσιν κατὰ ἔκκρισιν γίνεσθαι ... ὁρῶν οὖν ἀφ᾿ ἑκάστου τῶν νῦν διακεκριμένων πάντα ἐκκρινόμενα οἷον ἀπὸ ἄρτου σάρκα καὶ ὀστοῦν καὶ τὰ ἄλλα, ὡς πάντων ἅμα ἐνυπαρχόντων αὐτῷ καὶ μεμιγμένων ὁμοῦ ἐκ τούτων ὑπενόει καὶ πάντα ὁμοῦ τὰ ὄντα μεμῖχθαι πρότερον πρὶν διακριθῆναι.

Simpl. phys. 460, 4; A45.

It seemed to him (sc., to Anaxagoras) to be a main difficulty (to understand) how anything should be able to originate from the

---

[1] The use of πῦρ in the sense of "fire" ("from stone fire again") is proof that this exemplification by Simplikios is not to be traced to Anaxagoras himself. In Anaxagoras' phraseology, πῦρ is synonymous with αἰθήρ, in accordance with older, previous usage (cf. Heraclitus). As Aristotle explicitly remarks, "He (sc., Anaxagoras) calls 'fire' and 'ether' the same." (τὸ πῦρ καὶ τὸν αἰθέρα προσαγορεύει ταὐτό. De caelo III 3. 302b4; cf. p. 175). In the passage commented upon by Simplikios, Aristotle merely says: "As he saw everything becoming from everything . . ." (διὰ τὸ ὁρᾶν ὁτιοῦν ἐξ ὁτουοῦν γιγνόμενον . . .)

not-being or perish into the not-being. *Now, the food we take is simple and "one-like," bread and water, and from it hair, vein, artery, muscle, sinews, bones, and the other parts [of an organism] are nourished. Because of these facts, one must admit that in the food taken all the existing (substances) are contained.*

ἐδόκει γὰρ αὐτῷ (sc., τῷ Ἀναξαγόρᾳ) ἀπορώτατον εἶναι, πῶς ἐκ τοῦ μὴ ὄντος δύναταί τι γίνεσθαι ἢ φθείρεσθαι εἰς τὸ μὴ ὄν. τροφὴν γοῦν προσφερόμεθα ἁπλῆν καὶ μονοειδῆ, ἄρτον καὶ ὕδωρ, καὶ ἐκ ταύτης τρέφεται θρὶξ φλὲψ ἀρτηρία σὰρξ νεῦρα ὀστᾶ καὶ τὰ λοιπὰ μόρια. τούτων οὖν γιγνομένων ὁμολογητέον ὅτι ἐν τῇ τροφῇ τῇ προσφερομένῃ πάντα ἐστὶ τὰ ὄντα.

Aetios I 3, 5; A46.

In later antiquity, then, this was the common interpretation of Anaxagoras' views concerning the problem of food.

Evidently, the blame has to be laid at Aristotle's door. He had been the first to father upon Anaxagoras the queer teaching that such things as flesh, bone, marrow, in short, constituents of organisms, were the ultimate elements of the world, and that, therefore, certain substances commonly considered homogeneous, such as air and ether, were mixtures of particles of flesh and bone and "all the other seeds" (cf. p. 175). Those later authors were influenced in this respect by the Stagirite, needless to say.

The Genuine Anaxagorean Teaching

How could this obvious mistake have arisen? After all, that assertion of Aristotle's cannot have been a mere fabrication.

Anybody who did not, or not thoroughly, comprehend the cardinal idea of Anaxagoras' elements doctrine could easily have misunderstood the original formulation of his genuine teaching as to this problem.

From his presuppositions, Anaxagoras must have concluded that in bread and the other victuals seemingly dissimilar the same had to be contained as was contained in flesh, in blood, in bone, etc. This, however, did not mean that the ones consisted of the others, but that both consisted of the same thirds – i.e., of those ultimate elements: rare- and dense-moiras, bright- and dark-moiras, warm- and cold-moiras, moist- and dry-moiras, etc., etc.

The differences between those substances consist but in an inequality of the combining-ratios of the *moiras* within the *mereias*, in an inequality of the *"homoiomereian* formulas." For *"flesh" and "bread,"* etc.,

87

are nothing but dissimilar names for the same elements in dissimilar molecular constitutions.[1]

Thus, of course, everything can become from everything, even from any single molecule every other molecule (cf. p. 208, n. 1), but at any rate, from an adequate number of *mereias* of one constitution, *mereias* of any other constitution, provided only that the *moiras* of the elements are *regrouped* in the right way each time.

This, too, can only be done by Nous. For Nous alone with numerical exactness knows the combining-ratios of the elements for the *mereias* of every stuff.

Hence, for preservation of the organism, Nous has to perform also *the physiological function of digestion:* Nous has to regroup the seemingly dissimilar foodstuffs into the elementary combining-ratios of the various organic parts to be replaced or enlarged at a given time. This is done in the same way in which Nous had transformed, and is still transforming, the seemingly quality-less *mereias* of the *pantahomou* to render them different and distinguishable.

And What about Fragment Number Ten?

Before leaving this topic, we have still to deal with a sentence apt to render questionable all of this hypothesis on the Anaxagorean elements doctrine – provided, of course, that that sentence proved authentic.

As one can learn from Migne's *Patrologia Graeca* (XXXVI, 911), the

---

[1] This solution of the more than two thousand years old riddle has been adopted by Prof. G. Vlastos in an article on "The Physical Theory of Anaxagoras" (in: *The Philosophical Review*, January 1950, pp. 31–57), displaying the results of his own labors to penetrate into Anaxagorean thought. He praises "the logical elegance of this proposal" which he confesses to "have not seen ... explicitly made in the literature, except in F. M. Cleve's recent *Philosophy of Anaxagoras* (New York, 1949)," and he declares himself to be "directly indebted to Mr. Cleve at this important point." This is all the more gratifying as in Mr. Vlastos' opinion this is the *only* "idea in this book which is original, sound, and of capital importance." Yet, even that solitary praise cannot be accepted without some qualification, I am sorry. That "proposal," namely, is not so "recent" as Mr. Vlastos would make us believe. It is contained already in my Anaxagoras publication of 1917 on page 73. This publication, since quoted in the subsequent editions of the *Ueberweg*, has all the time after 1917 been available to anybody interested in Anaxagoras. And as a matter of fact, whatever is tenable in the 26 pages of Mr. Vlastos' article can be found in that monograph. Thus, Mr. Vlastos appears to be not only "directly indebted" to me for that one idea, but also indirectly indebted to me for the durable ideas he has adopted from Cornford, Peck, Bailey (cf. p. 195, n. 1) *e tutti quanti*. – Incidentally, of all those who after 1917 wrote about Anaxagoras, Jean Zafiropulo alone – as far as I know – has mentioned his indebtedness to that old monograph of mine (in his book *Anaxagore de Clazomene*, Paris, 1948).

codex Monacensis no. 216 contains a scholion by an Anonymus to one
of the speeches of St. Gregory Nazianzene, the Christian bishop (329–
389/90 A.D.). This scholion begins with a warning not to believe in
those teaching all to be in all, and then gives a short and rather
superficial statement of one of the principles of Empedocles and
Anaxagoras, respectively. And the concluding sentences of the scholion
are:

> But all that is false. For how should contrasts be together?
>
> ἅτινα πάντα ψευδῆ ἐστι. πῶς γὰρ τὰ ἐναντία τοῖς ἐναντίοις συνέσονται;

This presentation by the Anonymus is very likely to be conditional
upon that passage in Simplikios (first half of the sixth century A.D.),
quoted above, about the Anaxagorean problem of food, as also H.
Diels appears to have found out. For the pertinent sentences in
Simplikios have obviously been used in one part of that scholion. But
there is a difference: The Anonymus speaks of γονή (goné), "evolution
of the embryo," not of τροφή (trophé), "food." Which seems to indicate
some carelessness of that anonymous reporter who, at any rate, was not
interested in giving a particularly correct presentation of the pagan
philosopher's doctrine, but rather in advancing what he took for its
repudiation.

This scholion contains a sentence cited in a way as if it were an
authentic quotation from Anaxagoras' writings:

> For how should, he (sc., Anaxagoras) says, from not-hair hair
> originate and flesh from not-flesh?
>
> πῶς γὰρ ἄν, φησίν, ἐκ μὴ τριχὸς γένοιτο θρὶξ καὶ σὰρξ ἐκ μὴ σαρκός;

And indeed, without taking heed at the somewhat suspicious
surroundings of this sentence, H. Diels has bestowed upon it the rank
of an ostensibly genuine Anaxagorean fragment by inserting it in his
collection as number ten.

However, one need not agree:

Considering the very source of the sentence, its alleged authenticity
stands on a weak foundation.

Moreover, the whole style of this rhetoric question, with the cunning
chiasmus in the arrangement of its words, looks by no means very
Anaxagoras-like.

At any rate, however, to take this sentence for an authentic dictum
by Anaxagoras would imply a *petitio principii*, since *only if Aristotle's
interpretation of Anaxagoras' elements doctrine is correct, those words*

could pass for Anaxagorean. (Consequently, it is not permitted, either, to use those words as proof of the Aristotelian interpretation being correct.)

But quite apart from all that – if that sentence were to be accepted as a genuinely Anaxagorean argumentation, then, by the same reason and in the same way, Anaxagoras ought to have rejected his own ingenious hypothesis on the origin of the stars by asking: "How should star originate from not-star?"

Third Measure against Decay: Perception

There seems to be still another somatic activity of Nous designed to protect the body from decay and to compensate the losses sustained.

The system of Anaxagoras contained also something like a "theory of perception," the main reports on which are to be found in a writing of Theophrastus' fragmentarily handed down under the title, Περὶ αἰσθήσεως καὶ αἰσθητῶν (*"De sensu"*).

It is extremely difficult, and requires great cautiousness, to worm out a true Anaxagorean meaning from these reports, and at times it is hard to decide whether the difficulty stems from the "obvious and vast corruption" of the text [1] or from the way Theophrastus deals with the subject.

What could have been to Anaxagoras the purport of a "theory of perception"?

Certainly not the question of how by action of a lifeless, unconscious "matter" upon an organism the various specific perceptions of that organism's "consciousness" come about. This problem, being consecutive to the assumption of a "matter" (– be it in its modern or even only its Aristotelian sense –), would have been meaningless to Anaxagoras who did not have such notion as "matter without consciousness" (cf. p. 321).

Neither was there to Anaxagoras a fundamental difference between organisms and "lifeless" things, since both after all consisted of *mereias*, of "grown-togethers" (cf. p. 194) from *moiras* of the "things in no way resembling each other," the various specific "qualities," *i.e.*, from *moiras* of those various pairs of opposites.

These themselves, being eternal elements of the world, have no origin at all, and since everywhere and at any time every *mereia* is

---

[1] Cf. Gustav Kafka, emphasizing "die offenbare und weitgehende Verderbnis des theophrasteischen Fragmentes De sensu..." (*Philologus*, LXXII [1913], 65.)

surrounded and touched and thereby known (cf. p. 271) by the infinite, embedding Nous, the *moiras* and their *mereias* are always an actual *Bewusstseinsinhalt* in the infinite divine "consciousness" of Nous.

This divine consciousness, however, is the sole consciousness-unit we have obtained so far in this hypothetical reconstruction of the Anaxagorean system (cf. p. 264f.). Therefore, as this reconstruction has not yet yielded separate, individual consciousness-units for the organisms, we are, strictly speaking, not yet in a position to reconstruct the meaning of an Anaxagorean theory of perception, but have still to postpone such an attempt.

But in the midst of Theophrastus' presentation of what he claims is the Anaxagorean doctrine on perception, there is a striking statement that seems to be significant and essential in an unexpected sense:

> For (Anaxagoras says) that whatever is equally warm and cold (sc., as the organism) [This obviously means: "whatever contains 'warm' and 'cold' in the same combining-ratio as does the organism." It reads "warm *and* cold," not, warm *or* cold!], when approaching (sc., the organism), neither warms nor cools; and that also the sweet and the sharp [the sour] are not cognized through themselves, but through the warm the cold, through the briny the potable, through the sharp the sweet, *corresponding to the deficiency of each. For "all (the elements)," he says, "are contained in us."*

> τὸ γὰρ ὁμοίως θερμὸν καὶ ψυχρὸν οὔτε θερμαίνειν οὔτε ψύχειν πλησιάζον οὐδὲ δὴ τὸ γλυκὺ καὶ τὸ ὀξὺ δι᾽ αὐτῶν γνωρίζειν,[1] ἀλλὰ τῷ μὲν θερμῷ τὸ ψυχρόν, τῷ δ᾽ ἁλμυρῷ τὸ πότιμον, τῷ δ᾽ ὀξεῖ τὸ γλυκὺ κατὰ τὴν ἔλλειψιν τὴν ἑκάστου. πάντα γὰρ ἐνυπάρχειν φησὶν ἐν ἡμῖν.

> *Theophr. de sensu 28; A92.*

---

[1] γνωρίζειν is the infinitive of the active voice. The seemingly lacking grammatical subject of this *accusativus cum infinitivo* is obviously the same as in the preceding *acc. c. inf.* opening the paragraph, namely: τὸν αὐτὸν δὲ τρόπον καὶ τὴν ἁφὴν καὶ τὴν γεῦσιν κρίνειν, just as also γνωρίζειν is parallel to κρίνειν. And so, in the respective parts of the sentence in question, τὴν ἁφήν and τὴν γεῦσιν, respectively, have to be tacitly added as the grammatical subjects of γνωρίζειν. However, to make things simpler and to avoid for the time being a discussion on whether, from an Anaxagorean view, really "touch" and "taste" are the ones which "discern and cognize" their percepts, I have converted the phrase into the passive voice.

What Is the Meaning of 'Corresponding to the Deficiency ...'?

The *mereias* of an organism consist of the same ultimate elements as do all the other things.[1] And since even in every *mereia* all the elements are represented, they are, consequently, represented also in the whole organism composed of those *mereias: "All (the elements) are contained in us."* That is clear.

But Theophrastus speaks also of a *"deficiency of each."* What does this stand for?

The meaning cannot be that in the organism any element become lost or be altogether lacking. For this is impossible even with any individual *mereia* (cf. p. 208, also p. 184).

However, "deficiency" need not mean that a thing is not present at all. It can also mean that a thing is not present in its appropriate quantity. There can be a deficiency *of* a thing and *in* a thing:

Anaxagoras could have assumed that *an organism*, or its molecules, *must contain the elements in strictly definite combining-ratios.* To give the simplest example, let us suppose that in the various living beings warm-*moiras* and cold-*moiras* have to be combined in definite ratios *as a standard.* In modern terms, one would say: This organism has a definite specific heat or caloricity.

Now, if an organism were a thoroughly stable and stiff and unchangeable building, those combining-ratios would never be capable of being deranged. Hence, also a deficiency in anything, an ἔλλειψις, could not occur with it.

But an organism is a very unstable building. It is in continual danger of destruction through the stratification tendencies, preserved from it

---

[1] That the organisms consist of the same elements as everything else could be the real meaning of this passage in Irenaeus (II 14, 2 A113.):

> Anaxagoras, however, who also was called "the atheist," taught the living beings to have grown from seeds fallen from heaven unto the earth.
> Anaxagoras autem, qui et atheus cognominatus est, dogmatizavit facta animalia decidentibus e caelo in terram seminibus.

Decidere e caelo, "to fall from heaven," could refer to the coming from the *periechon*, and, above all, *semina*, "seeds," is obviously the translation of the Anaxagorean σπέρματα (cf. p. 189). In this way, the sentence would get a truly Anaxagorean meaning, although it might not have been so understood by Irenaeus. Otherwise, one would have either to refuse any credence to that report or to father upon Anaxagoras something like a "Migration Theory." But to impute a modern whim of that kind to Anaxagoras would mean a lack of reverence for a man whom his friends justly called "Nous" (Plutarch. Pericl. 4), paralleling him with the god he propagated.

only by the continual restitutive activity of Nous, and is exposed also to many other perturbations.

Therefore, as the "normal" combining-ratios in an organism are always being deranged, Nous must see all the perturbations undone at any given time by replacing from the neighborhood the deficit –

filling up again the deficient,

ἐπαναπληροῦν τὸ ἐνδεές,

(cf. Theophr. de sensu 8; 31A86).

– and giving to the neighborhood the surplus, respectively, that is to say, in any case restoring the *status quo ante,*

rendering it the same as before, ἐπανισοῦν.

(cf. ibid.)

In other words: *Nous has to correct deranged combining-ratios* in the fields of the various specific pairs of opposites *through opposite combining-ratios,* or, for short:

through the opposites (sc., of the 'opposites'),

τοῖς ἐναντίοις (sc., τῶν ἐναντίων).[1]

Theophr. de sensu 27; A92.

Thus it seems to have been an Anaxagorean idea that not only breathing, and nutrition through eating and drinking, but somehow also perception is a compensation-function, a "working-function," one of the restitutive somatic activities of Nous.[2]

Decay

An organism keeps on living only as long as Nous applies to it those means against decay.

The moment Nous ceases to operate in those special ways, the organism, unprotected, lies open again to stratification and will decompose, will die.

---

[1] Incidentally, Theophrastus' distinction between those constructing – or, as he would say, "making" – perception "through the like" and those constructing it "through the opposite" fails as far as Anaxagoras is concerned. According to him, it is true, perception comes from opposite combining-ratios of two contrasting "qualities." But these themselves must always belong to *one and the same pair of opposites.* And so it is both: a "cognition by the opposite" and a "cognition of like by like" as well.

[2] It might be not improper to recognize in this Anaxagorean idea the ancient form of the modern view that appropriate nervous stimulation, as a passing through between overexcitement and underexcitement, is indispensable for life.

An Epitomist's Report and Its Anaxagorean Sense

In Aetios there is a passage that could serve as a proof that the two statements above correspond exactly to Anaxagoras' own opinion.

According to Anaxagoras, says Aetios,

there is also a death of *psyche* [1]: the *diachorismos*.

εἶναι δὲ καὶ ψυχῆς θάνατον· [1] τὸν διαχωρισμόν.

Aet. V 25, 2; A103.

What is the meaning of *psyche* and what of *diachorismos* in this sentence?

Diachorismos means "severance." But of what? And from what? This is not stated. In the next neighborhood of the quoted sentence, however, we read that, according to the teachings of Empedocles,

death takes place by severance of the ethereal, the aerial, the liquid, and the solid [literally: the earth-like], of which the human body's mass is composed.

τὸν θάνατον γίγνεσθαι διαχωρισμῷ τοῦ πυρώδους ‹καὶ ἀερώδους καὶ ὑδατώδους καὶ γεώδους›, ἐξ ὧν ἡ σύγκρισις τῷ ἀνθρώπῳ συνεστάθη.

Aet. V, 25, 4; 31A85.

Hence one may safely assume that in the passage on Anaxagoras likewise *diachorismos* means *severance from one another of the constituents of the organism.*

As to *psyche*, Aetios no doubt understood this word as a thing's name in the sense of "soul." But the problem is to find out the original meaning of that sentence, no matter how it might have been understood or misunderstood by Aetios. Therefore, it should be proper to take here *psyche* in its older meaning (cf. p. 252) as the name of a function, designating either *breathing* or, in its broader sense, *the total of the preserving working-functions.*

The sentence in question is contained in a chapter superscribed, "To Which of the Two Belong Sleep and Death, Respectively: to Soul or to Body?" (Ποτέρου ἐστὶν ὕπνος καὶ θάνατος, ψυχῆς ἢ σώματος.) That chapter in Aetios consists of none too correct summaries of the teachings on this topic of Aristotle, Anaxagoras, Leucippus, and Empedocles. Each of these successive paragraphs contains also a conclusive remark concerning that topic, a topic, however, set by Aetios, the epitomist, not by those men, the philosophers.

[1] I adopt Richard Meister's suggestion to put a stop before τὸν διαχωρισμόν. (*Zeitschrift für die deutschösterreichischen Gymnasien* [1919], issues 1 and 2, p. 76.)

Sleep and Death – Physiologically

And now let us quote the whole passage about Anaxagoras:

> Anaxagoras (says) that corresponding to a relaxation of the somatic activity [of whom?] sleep arises; (for this is a corporeal state, not a psychical one;) but that there is also a death of *psyche:* (the body's) decay.

> Ἀναξαγόρας κατὰ κόπον τῆς σωματικῆς ἐνεργείας γίνεσθαι τὸν ὕπνον· (σωματικὸν γὰρ εἶναι τὸ πάθος, οὐ ψυχικόν·) εἶναι δὲ καὶ ψυχῆς θάνατον· τὸν διαχωρισμόν.

> *Aet. V 25, 2; A103.*

Anaxagoras was certainly not in a position to foreknow what the views would be from which, some centuries later, an epitomist would arrange a presentation of those ancient philosophers' teachings. For Anaxagoras the problem was to understand the mysterious fact of the body's decomposition: *How is it that, after having remained intact despite the general stratification tendency for such a long time, the organism decomposes nevertheless in the end?* This was Anaxagoras' problem, but not how to answer such questions as whether sleep and death belong to "body" or to "soul."

That is why I have put in parenthesis, as evidently a conclusion by the epitomist, the second sentence in the paragraph (the infinitive εἶναι notwithstanding). But the other two sentences may perhaps be traced to some genuine Anaxagorean text, read though not thoroughly understood by Aetios, the epitomist.

In this case, however, the *somatic activity* here would mean the somatic activity *of Nous,* of course, and *psyche* would be *another designation for exactly the same:* the total of the somatic working-functions. Then the two pairs of contrasts are, on the one hand, *sleep* and *decay,* and on the other hand, *relaxation* and *"death,"* i.e., full cessation. And those sentences would have to be read, consequently, with this accentuation: "By *relaxation* of the somatic activity (of Nous) *sleep* is caused. But there is also a *death* (*i.e.,* a full cessation) of psyche·: (and that is what the body's) *decay* (is)."

If, instead, one accentuates as is usual: "There is also a death of *psyche,*" then the effect would be pure nonsense. For *then the contrasting statement would have to be that sleep is the death of the body*! Which is neither true, of course, nor the purport of that sentence.

Thus, the meaning would be:

Decay takes place by "psyche" definitively stopping, that is, by Nous ceasing to exercise "psyche," that is to say, to exercise the working-functions by which the organism had been protected from decay during its lifetime.

This interpretation is debatable, perhaps, but – possible.[1]

The Souls

The activities of Nous as described so far could have accounted, in the main, for the formation and physiological working of the organisms. Yet, *in a psychological sense, the organisms were still lifeless.*

True, the *mereias* forming an organism, just as all the other *mereias* in the world, are complexes of grains of those ultimate "things," the qualities, or "unfinished percepts," to use an Aristotelian term.[2] It is likewise true that the activity of Nous is forcing those *mereias* into the "morphological unity" of the organism, as a modern biologist would call it. But this union does not do away with the pulverization of the "unfinished percepts," it cannot give them an ability of coalescing into a large consciousness-unit, because that "morphological" union does not produce a real, genuine unity, the individual *mereias* of an organism still remaining ultimately asunder.

In their disjointedness, however, they are but an object of cognition to the only knower-individual then in existence, to Nous.

Nous Still the Only Person in the Universe

But even supposing those complexes of grains of "unfinished percepts" kept together to the morphological unity of an organism were able to coalesce into a larger consciousness-unit. Then thinking and volition, mirth and grief, in short: personality, would still be lacking in such consciousness. The personality-element, however, just is Nous.

Now, every *mereia* of an organism is entirely surrounded by Nous. The organism, consequently, is completely steeped, as it were, in the personality-element, and there is in the whole organism not a single *mereia* not cognized by Nous or not being the object of an intention of

[1] Whereas Erwin Rohde (*Psyche*, 4th ed., II, 196, n. 1) renders that ending sentence – which he isolates, not even mentioning the precedent part of the paragraph – in this way (literally translated!): "But (sc., as the body's so) also the soul's death consists in its severance (sc., from the body)." (?)

[2] Concerning the term "unfinished percept," τὸ ἀτελὲς (αἰσθητόν), cf. Arist. de anima III 7. 431a4–7.

Nous, etc. But – neither is there in the universe any molecule to which this would not likewise apply. Nous is the non-molecularized medium in which all the molecules in the world are embedded. Every molecule, or *mereia*, is encompassed on all sides by this "thinnest element."

This implies that there are no isolated Nous-individuals; that Nous is still one infinitely large being; that Nous is the only person in the whole universe.

But this does not conform with today's actual condition. *Today there is a plurality of persons.* No man knows what the other man is thinking or intending, and nobody knows how the cosmos has been put together, and even Anaxagoras himself has just conjectured it, but not remembered.

Should Anaxagoras not have seen these facts? Should he have made the same mistake in his construction as was made afterwards by Ibn Rushd (Averroës)? [1]

According to this Arabic philosopher's *monopsychism*, his theory that there is a oneness of *aql* [2] in the world, everybody would have to know everything, yea, there could not even be a plurality of persons. (His distinction between *active aql* and *passive aql*, between *aql* and *nafs*,[2] designed to get over this difficulty, is of no avail, strictly speaking.)

An Enigmatic Fragment

Among the Anaxagorean fragments, there is one that has not yet been mentioned here, a fragment strange and enigmatic indeed.

I shall try to pierce its shell and bring out the kernel of meaning. In this way, I may perhaps be enabled to demonstrate that *the problem implied in the plurality of consciousness-units has not escaped Anaxagoras' notice.*

The fragment runs as follows:

> In every [what?] a share [but it could also mean *moira* – the word is here somewhat iridescent] of every [what?] is contained, except for Nous, but there are some [what?] in which Nous, too, is contained.

ἐν παντὶ παντὸς μοῖρα ἔνεστι πλὴν νοῦ, ἔστιν οἶσι δὲ καὶ νοῦς ἔνι.

fr. 11 (Simpl. phys. 164, 22).

---

[1] 1126–1198 A.D.
[2] *Aql* is "mind," "intellect," *nous; nafs* is the same as the Greek *psyche.*

What the Riddle Consists in

The first part of this fragment is a pointed, brachylogical formulation of the Anaxagorean teaching about the interrelation of the elements.

The ancient reader had the whole context. For him it might not have been difficult to get the meaning by supplying the necessary complements. The words "in every" (ἐν παντί) and "of every" (παντός) make no sense by themselves alone, and it was no doubt easier for the ancient reader to add mentally the lacking terms than it is for the modern reader to whom only a few more or less incoherent fragments are available.

There are two possible ways of completion. One would be to tacitly add "element" (χρῆμα) in both cases. This could be quite appropriate to the obvious meaning of the sentence, but would be more satisfactory if the wording were, "In every *every* is contained" (ἐν παντὶ πᾶν ἔνεστι), instead of "In every *a share of every* is contained" (ἐν παντὶ παντὸς μοῖρα ἔνεστι). Therefore, the other possibility, likewise appropriate, is preferable:

> In every (sc., molecule) a share of every (sc., element) is contained, except for Nous.
>
> ἐν παντὶ (sc., συγκρινομένῳ) παντὸς (sc., χρήματος) μοῖρα ἔνεστι πλὴν νοῦ.

As has been shown in an earlier chapter, the "being in" (ἐνεῖναι) of the *moiras* in the molecule is meant as a true "in each other," a mutual penetration, of the spatialized qualities, and the molecules must be impenetrable to Nous because otherwise Nous would not be able to move them (cf. p. 196).

And then, suddenly, comes that strange supplement:

> But there are some (sc., molecules [this of course is the appropriate completion also here]) in which Nous, too, is contained.
>
> ἔστιν (sc., συγκρινόμενα) οἷσι δὲ καὶ νοῦς ἔνι.

At first glance, these additional words may look like a humdrum restriction of what had been stated just before, an inconsistency not very becoming for a philosopher.

If it were not for that reasoning of why Nous does not penetrate, one would be free to take those two contradictory assertions as applying to different fields. Then the one assertion would merely have to be given a formulation as specific as that of the other one. But that reasoning renders it difficult, or rather entirely unfeasible, to attempt a settlement in this way.

The decisive question, namely, is: *Do those molecules referred to in the one assertion remain unpenetrated by Nous because they are impenetrable to Nous or because Nous does not want to penetrate them?*

In the latter case, that reasoning makes no sense, and Nous will never be able to move even a single molecule. For if the molecules are not really impenetrable to Nous, and it wants to maintain their *de facto* not being penetrated, then it must not will to push them in any direction. Therefore, if Nous does not press, they will, of course, not move according to its will. But if Nous does press, it will just penetrate and pass through, and they will not move then, either.

If, however, those molecules remain unpenetrated by Nous because they are impenetrable to it, that is to say, because Nous would not be able to penetrate them even if it wanted to – of course, Nous would not want to, being a realist – then it certainly can move them as much as it likes. Now, a molecule – I mean: the Anaxagorean molecule, or *mereia*, as I prefer to call it – is nothing but a penetration district for elements *moiras*, and in every *mereia* all the elements are represented. Consequently, the general assertion, "In every *mereia* every element is represented, except for Nous," *would have to be valid for all the* mereias *without any exception.* (The number of the various *moiras* penetrating each other in a *mereia* could hardly make any difference in this respect.)

Hence, the restriction, "There are some *mereias* in which Nous, too, is contained," does still not make sense. One could almost feel inclined to take these words for a later supplement by a Peripatetic who perhaps wanted to perfect that (in his opinion) imperfect doctrine of Anaxagoras with the corresponding Aristotelian teaching. That is to say, one could feel like considering those concluding words a later polemic marginal note slipped into the context in the course of time. (Aristotle did teach that there were things containing also Nous: the human organisms.)

Attempts at Elucidation

However, let us continue our attempts at finding a solution.

The main passage on the impenetrableness for Nous of the elements reads:

> Nous ... *is mixed* with no element,
>
> νοῦς ... μέμεικται οὐδενὶ χρήματι,
>
> $\qquad\qquad\qquad$ *fr. 12 (Simpl. phys. 156, 14).*

while here it says:

99

There are some (*mereias*) *in which* Nous, too, *is*.

ἔστιν οἷσι δὲ καὶ νοῦς ἔνι.

Should perhaps some deeper meaning be hidden behind this phraseological difference?

One could try out the following distinction:

If a warm-*moira* and a moist-*moira* penetrate each other, then they are really *mixed* (μεμειγμέναι), for then the warm is moist and the moist is warm. But if a blood-*mereia*, for example, is penetrated by Nous – provided this were possible – then thinking becomes neither warm nor moist nor red, nor will blood begin to think: only Nous will be thinking in the blood as well as outside. Such relationship could then not be called a case of "being mixed" (μεμειγμένον εἶναι), but of "being in" (ἐνεῖναι).

Yet, this distinction does not work for three reasons:

In the first place, "to be in" (ἐνεῖναι) is often used by Anaxagoras with the same meaning as "to be mixed" (μεμειγμένον εἶναι), as can be learned right away from the first part of the fragment in question. True, this would not be of much consequence. For "to be in" could be the broader term, and one would be free to say "to be in" instead of "to be mixed," but not inversely.

Secondly, for the reasons explained above one could not understand how Nous should have been enabled to penetrate the blood-*mereia*.

And finally, there is no slightest difference, geometrically, between "to be mixed" and "to be in" when meaning "to be mutually in each other." For what is mixed with each other – in the Anaxagorean sense of the word (cf. p. 195) – as well as what is in each other is filling one and the same space. What should then account for such a difference? The only thing left would be reference to a divine will beyond possibility and impossibility. Which would not be very Anaxagorean. The fact in itself that one cannot say, "Blood is thinking," or "Thinking is red or warm," but only, "Nous is thinking," would have been bound to fortify Anaxagoras' belief in the absolute immiscibility of Nous.

'Conditio Pluralitatis Personarum'

Nevertheless, it does not seem to be without significance that in the one passage it says "is in" and in the other "is mixed":

"To be mixed" has certainly but one meaning. With "to be in," however, this is not so. Why should not Anaxagoras, too, have occasionally played upon words? Could he not have used the same word ἐνεῖναι ("to be in") *as a special term* with the meaning of μεμειγ-μένον εἶναι ("to be mixed") *in the first part* of that sharply pointed sentence, and *in the usual, commonly accepted meaning in the second part?* Archelaos is said [1] to have declared, obviously in conformity with his master, that the molecules are "so to speak, in Nous" (cf. p. 207). Could not as well a piece of Nous be *in a molecule – in the same sense as a fellow locked into a prison "is in"?*

Anaxagoras is said to have asserted that "the *mereias* have all kinds of shape" (τὰ ὁμοιομερῆ [2] πολυσχήμονα. [Aet. I 14, 4; A51.]). *Could he not have assumed that Nous formed also* mereias *which, like shells, contained Nous kernels?*

If the *mereias* have all kinds of shape, they should also be of *unequal sizes.* Consequently, in a sufficiently large *balloon mereia* a piece of Nous-medium, even together with any *mereias* embedded, can be locked in. Such isolated little pieces of Nous-medium can even be large enough to be perceptible macroscopically if Nous gives the shape of a balloon not to one single *mereia,* but forms a balloon out of several *mereias* welded together.

The very moment, however, when such a balloon has been shut on all sides, and the kernel has been completely wrapped up in that impenetrable shell, Nous has ceased to be a one and undivided being.

And – *impenetrableness has even turned out to be also the* principium individuationis.

Thus, then, in every organism whatsoever there is, severed from the World-Nous and isolated by an impenetrable tegument, a piece of Nous as the person, the self, of the organism.

Comparison with an Aristotelian Teaching

That those words, "There are some in which Nous, too, is contained," refer to the organisms in some way or other has been guessed by nearly all the interpreters. Not knowing the reason why Nous had to be unmixable with the other elements, they had no possibility nor desire to understand how any exception should be feasible. They accepted both assertions and reflected upon them as little as possible.

It is not easy to determine what gave the interpreters the idea that

---

[1] Hippol. refut. I 9, 1; 60 A4.

[2] The later authors are in the habit of confounding the terms ὁμοιομερές and ὁμοιομέρεια. Hence, it is certainly permissible to translate here ὁμοιομερῆ as "molecules" or "*mereias,*" although this term is likely to have meant something different to Anaxagoras himself (cf. p. 189).

the one of those statements was aimed at the organisms. Perhaps it was a more or less intentional assimilation to that known Aristotelian teaching that, whenever a human organism is formed, also Nous, "coming from outside" (θύραθεν), joins the mixture of substances and psyches, to leave it again at death.

Incidentally, as early as antiquity many a feature of Aristotelian doctrine was ascribed in retrospect to Anaxagoras. This can be learned from an assertion of Aetios', for instance, to the effect that Anaxagoras, too, teaches

Nous to join (sc., the human body) coming from outside,

θύραθεν εἰσκρίνεσθαι τὸν νοῦν,

(Aet. IV 5, 11; A93).

although according to Anaxagoras' doctrine this would have been unnecessary since

wherever all the other (elements) are,

ἵνα καὶ τὰ ἄλλα πάντα,

fr. 14 (Simpl. phys. 157, 5; cf. p. 207).

always also Nous is present.

On the basis of our attempt at elucidation, the conjecture that that sentence might aim at the organisms comes very close to being substantiated. At any rate, this interpretation relieves us from fathering upon Anaxagoras the fault of having been blind to the problem implied in the plurality of consciousness-units. If he did see this problem, he must have become aware of it only when observing, and reflecting on, organisms. Consequently, one may safely assume, the passage offering a solution of the problem will likewise refer to the organisms.

World-Nous and Separate Nous-Individuals

The inclosed piece of Nous is of the same nature as the World-Nous, having been a part of It before inclosure:

For the nous in every one of us is a god.

ὁ νοῦς γὰρ ἡμῶν ἐστιν ἐν ἑκάστῳ θεός.

Euripides, fragm. 1018; A48.

But compared with the World-Nous' infinite dimensions, this piece of Nous is so minute that of the World-Nous' omniscience no more than almost nothing has been left to the diminutive god of a diminutive world. Nearly all that it had known before, as World-Nous, has become hidden, unknown, in no direct way cognizable, ἄδηλον (*adelon*). The nous confined is dependent upon earning anew – *in the hard way of experience, of learning successively little by little* – a tiny portion only of its previous knowledge.

The World-Nous does not need experience. It knows whatever It is touching, and It is in touch with everything because It is the medium embedding.

Thus, touching (without penetrating) is a condition not only for Nous' moving the *mereias*, but also for knowing and cognizing. Aristotle's remark of comment, therefore, is correct:

> Hence Nous ... necessarily is unmixable, in order to *"rule,"* as says Anaxagoras, that is, in order to *know*.
>
> ἀνάγκη ἄρα . . . ἀμιγῆ εἶναι (sc., τὸν νοῦν), ὥσπερ φησὶν Ἀναξαγόρας ἵνα 'κρατῇ,' τοῦτο δ' ἔστι ἵνα γνωρίζῃ.
>
> *Arist. de anima III 4. 429a18; A100.*

It tells, however, but half the truth since it neglects the other Anaxagorean sense of that ' ruling," namely: "moving." [1]

The nous confined of an individual living being is in touch with the walls of its prison only. Therefore, it knows but little. It has to experience and infer from the reports transmitted by the body's senses, from the percepts, now for it the only way to get knowledge of the things that have become unknown:

> "For it is the percepts of the senses [2] that give percipience of the things unknown," as says Anaxagoras.
>
> "ὄψις γὰρ τῶν ἀδήλων τὰ φαινόμενα," [2] ὥς φησιν Ἀναξαγόρας.
>
> *fr. 21a (Sext. Emp. adv. math. VII, 140).*

Nous not only *moves* the things and *knows* the moved or touched, but also *perceives* and *discerns* all possibilities hidden therein and *resolves* accordingly.

---

[1] Elsewhere Aristotle appears fully cognizant of it, as, *e.g.*, when saying:
> But he (sc., Anaxagoras) attributes to the same principle *both cognition and motion* by declaring Nous to move the whole.
>
> ἀποδίδωσι δ'ἄμφω τῇ αὐτῇ ἀρχῇ, τό τε γινώσκειν καὶ τὸ κινεῖν, λέγων νοῦν κινῆσαι τὸ πᾶν. 　　　　*Arist. de anima I 2. 405a17; A100.*

[2] In this quotation by Sextus from Anaxagoras' work, I take τὰ φαινόμενα in the simple, common meaning "percepts of the senses," for good reasons avoiding translation as "phenomena." (τὰ φαινόμενα is the subject, ὄψις τῶν ἀδήλων, the predicate of the sentence.)

But only what the *World-Nous* decides upon is put into execution without hindrance. For the World-Nous perceives the total of all the possibilities contained in the total of all existing and can thus conform.

A *separate nous*, however, perceives only those possibilities which are in all that it has already experienced at a given time. But it does not perceive the conflicting, hindering possibilities in all that is still unknown to it.

Conflicting resolutions of *two nous-individuals* are but two components of an immensely manifold bundle of components, the resultant of which means realization of the World-Nous' resolution.

Sleep and Death – Psychologically

The World-Nous is free to open again the prison It has locked, as in (dreamless) *sleep* and *death. Then the nous-individual – although remaining in its place! – is immediately reunited with the World-Nous, and the organism has lost its separate consciousness.*

In this respect, sleep and death are exactly alike.

As demonstrated above (p. 263), the only difference between death and sleep is that in death the embedding World-Nous entirely ceases to exercise *psyche*, the working-functions, thereby abandoning the organism to decay; while sleep is conditional upon a temporary relaxation of those functions exercised by the embedding Nous.

But neither in sleep nor in death does the individual nous discontinue to think. It only discontinues to be separated and individual and tiny.[1]

Aetios, the epitomist, concluding that to Anaxagoras sleep was "a corporeal state, not a psychical one" (cf. p. 263), was right – except that he ought to have applied his remark to death as well. Nous never ceases to think, neither in sleep nor in death, and to think actually, and not potentially only,

for the (Anaxagorean) nous is (nous) *in actuality.*[2]

ὁ γὰρ νοῦς ἐνεργείᾳ.

Arist. Metaph. XI 6. 1072a5.

---

[1] This implies also the pattern of the relationship between the World-Nous and the nous-individuals. These individuals are no transformations of the God. Nor are they emanations from the God, strictly speaking. The basic pattern is rather Disjection with subsequent Reunion: The nous-individuals are splinters of the God, temporarily given separate existence by the God within the God.

[2] This recalls a striking analogy: the doctrine of Descartes that "mens semper *actu* cogitat."

The Site of the 'Soul'

Where in the organism is the place of personality supposed to be, in Anaxagoras' opinion?

There is a remark in Censorinus (6, 1; A108) that, according to the Clazomenian, in the development of the embryo the first thing to arise is "the brain from which all the organs of sense proceed" (cerebrum, unde omnes sunt sensus). This implies that Anaxagoras considers the brain the central organ of the organism. It is obvious, therefore, that he, just as Alkmaion of Croton, connects the brain with thinking and volition in some way or other.

On the basis of our findings, the nature of this connection is not difficult to guess. In Anaxagoras' opinion, as one may safely assume, *the separate nous, together with any embedded air-molecules, is located in the ventricles of the brain; and the brain, encircling those hollow spaces, is the shell which encases that precious kernel.*[1]

Conscious and 'Unconscious' Occurrences in the Organism

How is it that so many occurrences in the organism are never felt?

From those words, "The brain from which all the organs of sense proceed," one may infer Anaxagoras to have asked this question himself. For that very sentence implies the answer:

All the organs of sense, being outgrowths of the brain, are connected with the brain. The nous confined learns only what is transmitted by the senses. All the rest is imperceptible to it. And so are, consequently, all the occurrences taking place in those parts of the organism from where no nerve-conduction (as it would be called today) *leads to the brain. These happenings are activities of the World-Nous surrounding the molecules of the organism, and the World-Nous alone, therefore, knows them.*

On the whole, most of the proceedings in the organism are being operated by the World-Nous, and not by the separate nous, since it requires far too much wisdom for such a tiny morsel of nous to perform them correctly and with the necessary preciseness. The physiological processes of digestion, for instance, pertain to that big group of processes taking place "unconsciously," that is: *unconsciously for the separate consciousness.*

---

[1] This curious opinion that the hollow spaces in the brain are the site of the "soul" has proved enduring for a very long time. Vestiges of it can even be found in the teaching of Descartes that the hollow spaces in the brain are the thoroughfare and switching-place for the so-called *spiritus animales*, or *spiritus corporales*, mediating the reactions upon the percepts.

This group, however, is only one part of the operations performed in the organism by the World-Nous. To the other part belong all those occurrences which, although not enacted by the separate nous, become known to it because they happen in such parts of the organism as are, by means of a sense-conduction, connected with the brain, or rather with the separate nous inclosed in its hollow spaces. Yet, of these happenings the separate nous becomes aware not before, but only during their taking place or afterwards.

From a modern point of view, one might think that these two groups comprise all the occurrences in an organism. Yet, this is not likely to have been Anaxagoras' opinion. He may have taken into the second group not only the total of instinctive reactions, though. *But at least the deliberate movements performed on the basis of a resolution he may have reserved indeed for the separate nous.*

One could be tempted to say that that modern view is just too modern to be expected of Old Anaxagoras. But such objection would not be quite legitimate. One could very well imagine thousands of years passing until some master-minds may meet again with an idea which had arisen once before in the brains of a genius who was misunderstood by his own age and all later ages as well.

However, it is for another reason that Anaxagoras might have assumed that individual consciousness did effect movements. Is not the nature of the separate nous the same as that of the World-Nous? Consequently, the separate nous must likewise be able to produce movements. Or rather, to put it the other way round: *Had Anaxagoras not believed himself to be experiencing that his will* (or, more intellectualistically speaking: *his resolution) caused movement, he would not have imagined the World-Nous as a mechanical mover.* For

> Just as in the living beings, it is also in nature (generally).
>
> καθάπερ ἐν τοῖς ζῴοις, καὶ ἐν τῇ φύσει . . .
>
> *Cf. Arist. Metaph. I 3. 984b15; A58.*

Theory of Perception

Now we are finally in a position to attempt at hypothetically reconstructing what might have been Anaxagoras' teachings on perception.

The basic statement on this subject is implied in the report by Theophrastus on quite another man. That statement is almost hidden, and so it is no wonder that it has remained nearly unnoticed.

106

At the end of a short presentation of some teachings of Clidemus', who apparently belongs to the "men around Anaxagoras" (οἱ περὶ Ἀναξαγόραν [Theophr. de sensu 1]) and seems to be the first, or even "the only one" (μόνος), to point at *the relationship between the specialization of the structures of the various sense organs and the various, specifically different sensations*,[1] Theophrastus says:

> However, Clidemus maintains it is *only the ears* that by themselves discern nothing but transmit (all) to the nous, and does not make nous the principle of *all* (sc., sensations), *as does Anaxagoras.*

> μόνον δὲ τὰς ἀκοὰς (Κλείδημός φησι) αὐτὰς μὲν οὐδὲν κρίνειν, εἰς δὲ τὸν νοῦν διαπέμπειν, οὐχ ὥσπερ Ἀναξαγόρας ἀρχὴν ποιῶν πάντων (sc., αἰσθήσεων) τὸν νοῦν.

Theophr. de sensu 38; 62A2.

This appears to be perfectly the same as if Theophrastus had said:

> *Anaxagoras maintains that the senses by themselves discern nothing, but transmit (all) to the nous, as he makes nous the principle of all (sc., sensations).*

And this means that to Anaxagoras *the senses are mere messengers, incompetent to "discern and cognize"* (cf. p. 259, n. 1) *the messages they convey to the nous confined in the hollow spaces of the brain*, and that *these messages become sensations not until they are "discerned and cognized" by the little nous-individual.*

The messages conveyed, the "percepts that give percipience of the things unknown" (cf. p. 271) – of the things that have become unknown and hidden to the little nous by its being inclosed and surrounded with an impenetrable shell – these messages are the various specific qualities singly intercepted by the specific senses, the organs of interception and channels through which the messages are transmitted to the nous, to be combined and unified again.

---

[1] Thus, by this idea, Clidemus appears to be the solitary, ancient forerunner of those who, most recently, have abandoned the cortical theory concerning the site of sensation: Adolf Stöhr who has replaced it by his "sensorial" theory ("Gehirn und Vorstellungsreiz," in: *24. Jahresbericht der Philosophischen Gesellschaft in Wien.* Leipzig, 1912, and *Psychologie – Tatsachen, Probleme und Hypothesen,* 2nd ed., Vienna and Leipzig, 1922, pp. 77–90: "Die Bedeutung der Reizleitung von der Sinnesperipherie in das Zentralorgan"); and Bernhard Rensch who, independent of Stöhr, substitutes his "aesthetophysical" hypothesis for the ordinarily still dominant cortical theory (*Psychische Komponenten der Sinnesorgane,* Stuttgart, 1952).

These organs are weak and small, these channels, narrow.

True, there are differences. The organs of sense are not equally weak and small and narrow with the various organisms:

> (Anaxagoras says) that the bigger the living beings are, the more sense perception they get, and that, generally, perception is proportionate to the size of the organs of sense.

> αἰσθητικώτερα δὲ τὰ μείζω ζῷα καὶ ἁπλῶς εἶναι κατὰ τὸ μέγεθος ‹τῶν αἰσθητηρίων› τὴν αἴσθησιν.

> Theophr. de sensu 29; A92.

Yet, weak and small and narrow they are, all the same.

No Scepticism in Principle

This statement must not be taken for scepticism. The fact that the senses are small and narrow brings about a tremendous reduction of the amount of messages to be transmitted, and that they are weak means that their sharpness has limits. But whatever they do perceive and transmit is allright and adequate.

It is worth while taking up again that quotation in Sextus from Anaxagoras' work we have dealt with when discussing psyche (p. 251f.):

> In consequence of their weakness we cannot discern the real fact. For if we take two colors, black and white, and then pour, drop by drop, from the one into the other, the eye will not be able to distinguish the little by little changes, although they are actually taking place.

> ὑπ' ἀφαυρότητος αὐτῶν (sc., τῶν αἰσθήσεων) οὐ δυνατοί ἐσμεν κρίνειν τἀληθές. εἰ γὰρ δύο λάβοιμεν χρώματα, μέλαν καὶ λευκόν, εἶτα ἐκ θατέρου εἰς θάτερον κατὰ σταγόνα παρεκχέοιμεν, οὐ δυνήσεται ἡ ὄψις διακρίνειν τὰς παρὰ μικρὸν μεταβολάς, καίπερ πρὸς τὴν φύσιν ὑποκειμένας.

> fr. 21 (Sext. Emp. adv. math. VII 90).

It reads: "The eye will not be able to distinguish *the little by little changes*." But the human eye does have the ability of perceiving the one *big change* from the two colors in the beginning to the color at the end of that process, while it is one of the functions of the nous to *infer* that those little by little changes must have taken place. (Which, besides, shows that the later slogan, *nihil est in intellectu, quod non antea fuerit in sensibus*, would not have been accepted by Anaxagoras.)

It is not Anaxagoras, but Sextus Empiricus, the sceptic, who in his interpretation of Anaxagoras' statement on the weakness of the senses unawares replaces "weakness" by "treachery," saying (l.c.):

> Anaxagoras, the greatest natural philosopher, vituperating the senses as being weak, says: "In consequence of their weakness, we cannot discern the real fact," and adduces as a proof of their *treachery* the little by little change of the colors: "For if we take two colors, black and white," etc.

> ὁ μὲν φυσικώτατος 'Αναξαγόρας ὡς ἀσθενεῖς διαβάλλων τὰς αἰσθήσεις 'ὑπ' ἀφαυρότητος αὐτῶν,' φησίν, 'οὐ δυνατοί ἐσμεν κρίνειν τἀληθές,' τίθησί τε πίστιν αὐτῶν τῆς ἀπιστίας τὴν παρὰ μικρὸν τῶν χρωμάτων ἐξαλλαγήν. 'εἰ γὰρ δύο λάβοιμεν χρώματα, μέλαν καὶ λευκόν,' κτλ.

Yet, – "weakness" is not tantamount to "treachery," not even to "untrustworthiness" (the other possible meaning of ἀπιστία).

Anaxagoras' attitude toward the senses is faithful in principle, and so much so that he even has accepted their "messages," the qualities, as the ultimate "things" of the world, one must not forget.

Incidentally, with this faithful attitude toward the senses a report in Aristotle's *Metaphysics* on an utterance by Anaxagoras would seem to be well in keeping. The passage reads:

> But there is also handed down a remark by Anaxagoras to some of his friends (to the effect) that things will be for them such as they would perceive them.

> 'Αναξαγόρου δὲ καὶ ἀπόφθεγμα μνημονεύεται πρὸς τῶν ἑταίρων τινάς, ὅτι τοιαῦτ' αὐτοῖς ἔσται τὰ ὄντα οἷα ἂν ὑπολάβωσιν.[1]

> *Arist. Metaph. IV 5. 1009b25; A28.*

Physical Pain

The Anaxagorean "weakness" (ἀφαυρότης) of the senses has still another meaning: Not only the sharpness, but also the endurance and capacity of the senses are limited, due to their tenderness, narrowness, and smallness.

---

[1] Burnet renders that passage as "Things are as we suppose them to be," and, taking it for a sentence of scepticism, rejects this report as having "no value at all as evidence" (*Early Greek Philosophy*, 4th ed., p. 274). However, ὑπολαμβάνειν does not necessarily mean "suppose," it can mean as well "take up," "receive," "perceive." Furthermore, the integrant modification αὐτοῖς, "for them," implying "for every one of them," is omitted in Burnet's translation. And besides, the mere fact that Burnet says "we" instead of the "they" of the passage indicates that his words are not even meant as a translation, but just as a rough rendering of the approximate sense of the sentence as he understood it.

When the amount of a "message" is too great – because of one big amount storming in at once – or grows too great – by too many small amounts of the same, piling up through perseverance – the sense involved runs the risk of being hurt, damaged, or even destroyed, and *the message transmitted to the little nous-individual assumes the form of pain:*

> This, however, (says Anaxagoras) manifests itself in the length of duration (of the percepts) as well as in the excessive intensity of the percepts. For (he says) that the bright (dazzling) colors as well as the excessive noises cause pain, and that one cannot hold out dwelling on the same (percepts) for a long time.
>
> φανερὸν δὲ τοῦτο τῷ τε τοῦ χρόνου πλήθει καὶ τῇ τῶν αἰσθητῶν ὑπερβολῇ· τά τε γὰρ λαμπρὰ χρώματα καὶ τοὺς ὑπερβάλλοντας ψόφους λύπην ἐμποιεῖν καὶ οὐ πολὺν χρόνον δύνασθαι τοῖς αὐτοῖς ἐπιμένειν.
>
> *Theophr. de sensu 29; A92.*

This is true not only in the fields of sight and hearing. It applies to all the senses without exception:

> But (Anaxagoras says) that any perception whatsoever (can be) with pain.
>
> ἅπασαν δ' αἴσθησιν μετὰ λύπης.
>
> *(ibid.)*

And, to be strict, – for "with pain," μετὰ λύπης, could be taken ambiguously –:

> We experience pain in the manner of the perception itself.
>
> . . . λυπούμεθα κατ' αὐτὴν τὴν αἴσθησιν.
>
> *Theophr. de sensu 17; 31A86.*

This removes the possible misunderstanding as if to Anaxagoras pain were an independent perception *sui generis*, just combined with others.

Attempt at Reconstruction

How do these factual statements in Theophrastus on Anaxagoras' teachings about pain fit into this hypothetical reconstruction?

The World-Nous must undo the continual perturbations of the "normal," standard combining-ratios in the molecules of an organism by correcting deranged combining-ratios in the fields of the various specific pairs of opposites through opposite combining-ratios, or "through the opposites," as we have seen (cf. p. 261). And since in any molecule, or *mereia*, the normal combining-ratios can be different for each of the various fields (cf. p. 210), the *mereia* being not just a commixture of *moiras*, but a commixture of commixtures of *moiras*, the undoing of the perturbations has to be performed separately for the contrasting *moiras* of each quality. For only in this way can the previous combining-ratios be restored.

We remember, furthermore, that in the field of any quality equal numbers of *moiras* of the two opposites are being mutually compensated, and that always only the actual surplus, if there is any, of the one of the two contrasts is effective (cf. pp. 191 and 210).

The intensity of every quality, therefore, is a function of the quantity of the effective surplus-moiras in every field (cf. p. 187).

All this applies to all the mereias *of which an organism consists.*

But here we have only to deal with the undoing of those perturbations which occur in the various organs of sense of an organism. For these perturbations alone come to the knowledge of that organism's little nous, due to the connections of the senses with the brain (cf. p. 273).

There is a relationship not only between the quantity of the effective *moiras* of a quality and the intensity of that quality, but also between the sizes of the organs of sense of an organism and the intensities of the sensations resulting at the end of the whole process. Or to put it even more exactly: *The intensity of a sensation is conditional upon two factors: on the intensity of a quality to be perceived – which depends on the total amount of effective* moiras *of that quality – and on the size of the perceiving organ – which corresponds to the amount of the* mereias *that organ consists of.*

The amount of effective *moiras* can happen to be *too small* for the size of a sense organ of a certain living being, but just fitting to the size of the respective sense organ of another living being. That is to say: In relation to the total amount of the *mereias* of a sense organ of a certain living being, the amount of effective *moiras* can be so small that it is insufficient for "filling up again" (ἐπαναπληροῦν), for undoing in each of the *mereias* of the organ the continual, so to speak "physiological," perturbation of the normal combining-ratio in the field of the quality concerned. Yet, with the analogous sense organ of an accordingly smaller living being, the same amount may be sufficient. Thus, in the one case *the "message" passes unperceived, and there is no sensation at all,* while in the other case a normal sensation would result:

> (Anaxagoras says) that, generally, perception is proportionate to the size of the organs of sense. For (he says) that those living

beings which have large ... eyes see large (objects) as well as from far, but those having small ones, contrariwise (*i.e.*, small objects as well as from near). But (he says) that also with hearing it is the same. For (he says) that the large (living beings) hear the big (sounds) and the (sounds) from far, while *the smaller (sounds) remain hidden* (*i.e.*, unperceived), but the small (living beings), the small (sounds) and the (sounds) from near. And (he says) that it is the same also with smell ...

ἁπλῶς εἶναι κατὰ τὸ μέγεθος ‹τῶν αἰσθητηρίων› τὴν αἴσθησιν. ὅσα μὲν γὰρ μεγάλους ... ὀφθαλμοὺς ἔχει, μεγάλα τε καὶ πόρρωθεν ὁρᾶν, ὅσα δὲ μικρούς, ἐναντίως. ὁμοίως δὲ καὶ ἐπὶ τῆς ἀκοῆς. τὰ μὲν γὰρ μεγάλα τῶν μεγάλων καὶ τῶν πόρρωθεν ἀκούειν, τὰ δ' ἐλάττω λανθάνειν, τὰ δὲ μικρὰ τῶν μικρῶν καὶ τῶν ἐγγύς. καὶ ἐπὶ τῆς ὀσφρήσεως ὁμοίως, κτλ.

Theophr. de sensu 29 and 30; A92.

On the other hand, the total amount of effective *moiras* of a quality specific to a sense organ can be much *too great* for the size of that organ, that is to say, for the total amount of the *mereias* of the organ. The result will be that the amount of *moiras* spreading over the *mereias* of the organ surpasses the undoing of the previous perturbation and effects for every *mereia* an excessive derangement of its normal combining-ratio in the field of the quality in question far toward the opposite direction.

This can be brought about in two ways. Such an excessive derangement of the combining-ratio can occur at once, through an exceedingly intensive quality, that is: through an exceedingly great number of effective *moiras* storming in at once. And it can happen as well by way of a perturbation not superintensive as such, but becoming excessive through summing up, in other words, by a perception lasting for an exceedingly long time (cf. p. 278).

In these two cases, the resulting sensation will assume its form of pain.

Physical Delight

Pain is not a durable state. The excessive derangement ending in a combining-ratio exceedingly discrepant from the normal combining-ratio has to be ironed out. This the little nous does in the same way as the World-Nous when correcting perturbations: through "the opposites." The little nous makes the organism flee from dazzling light to shadow, from torturing noise to stillness, from unbearable heat to coolness, and so on, until normalcy is reached again, which means, until a percept is in perfect harmony, as to the mixture of the *moiras*, with the normal combining-ratio of the *moiras* of that quality in the *mereias* of the perceiving organ.

This *perfect harmony* – this ἐναρμόττειν (cf. Theophr. de sensu 7 and 9; 31A86 – is obviously *the condition for physical delight*.

For between "too little" (result: no sensation at all) and "too much" (result: painful sensation) there are many shades. Among these, there is a minimum, the point of "just enough" to make for a weak, indifferent sensation, and an optimum, the point of perfect harmony as described above, making for a strong but not too strong sensation, which is to say that the perception assumes its form of pleasure (cf. p. 186).

Thus, the condition for a percept to *be* pleasant is that harmony. And the condition for a percept to *become* pleasant is the process in itself of approaching to that state of vigorousness, be it a coming from the point of indifference or a coming back from the point of aching.

While physical pain excites a tumult in the organism, physical delight allays and pacifies. Yet, it is not durable, either, due to that "physiological" instability of the perceiving organs themselves, that continual perturbation beyond the power and control of the little nous.

Apparently, we have no authentic statement on what, in Anaxagoras' opinion, is the condition for physical delight. However, there is a sentence in Theophrastus that amazingly looks as if it could fill the gap:

> (He says,) however, that *delight comes about through those being alike as to the* moiras *and the mixture*, but pain, through the opposites (sc., as to the mixture of the *moiras*).
>
> ἥδεσθαι δὲ τοῖς ὁμοίοις κατά τε <τὰ> μόρια καὶ τὴν κρᾶσιν, λυπεῖσθαι δὲ τοῖς ἐναντίοις.
>
> *Theophr. de sensu 9; 31A86.*

True, this sentence is contained in Theophrastus' report on – Empedocles. But with regard to the new findings about the relationship between Anaxagoras and Empedocles (as presented p. 286 ff.), one could be tempted to apply this sentence to, if not to reclaim it even for, the Anaxagorean doctrine. And so I am taking the μόρια (*moria*) of the passage, which means "particles," in the sense of the Anaxagorean term μοῖραι (*moirai*), which means exactly the same.

No 'Pain-and-Delight'-Element

Anaxagoras, as we have seen, did not consider physical pain an independent perception *sui generis,* but a possible form of every perception. Nor did he take physical delight for a special kind of perception, we may safely assume. Pain and delight are not made of *moiras* of a specific pair of opposites. No λυπηρόν- and χαρίεν-*moiras* ("sore"- and "pleasant"-*moiras*) are mentioned anywhere in Anaxagoras' enumerations.[1]

Pain and delight, to all appearances, are ultimately conditional upon quantity: upon the quantities of the *moiras* of the various specific qualities and, on the other hand, upon the quantities of the *mereias* forming the various specific organs of sense (cf. pp. 187 and 279). Quantity, however, is not an ultimate "thing" in Anaxagoras' view, not an element, no more than are shape or surface. But the *moiras,* the "seeds," of the elements *have* shapes and surfaces and quantities, or, as Anaxagoras says, anticipating the result, "pleasures" (cf. p. 185), in that sentence about the

> seeds ... having all kinds of shapes as well as of surfaces and pleasures,
>
> σπέρματα ... καὶ ἰδέας παντοίας ἔχοντα καὶ χροιὰς καὶ ἡδονάς.
>
> *fr. 4 (Simpl. phys. 34, 28, and 157, 9).*

A Gross Misinterpretation

Anaxagoras' view that upon excessive intensity every perception becomes painful was given a meaning as if he had taught

> seeing and hearing ... to be painful,
>
> τὸ ὁρᾶν καὶ τὸ ἀκούειν ... εἶναι λυπηρόν,
>
> *cf. Arist. Eth. Nic. VII 15. 1154b7; A94.*

or

> every perception to be with pain,
>
> πᾶσαν αἴσθησιν μετὰ πόνου,
>
> *Aet. IV 9, 16; A94.*

or

> every perception whatsoever to be (actually connected) with pain,
>
> ἅπασαν αἴσθησιν μετὰ λύπης,
>
> *Theophr. de sensu 29; A92.*

---

[1] In the modern controversy about whether or not physical pain and delight are special "modalities," and whether or not there are separate pain-nerves or a specific pain-centre, Anaxagoras would have sided with William James (*Psychology,* I 143 ff.), Adolf Stöhr (*Psychologie,* 2nd ed., 165 ff.), Theodor Ziehen (*Leitfaden der physiologischen Psychologie,* 10th ed., 200 ff.) against Blix, Funke, von Frey, etc.

which is the way Theophrastus himself understood this sentence already quoted. And still more explicitly:

> However, frequently when having a perception we experience pain in the manner of the perception itself, (or, even, not frequently,) but, as says Anaxagoras, *always:* for (he says) every perception to be with pain.
>
> καίτοι πολλάκις αἰσθανόμενοι λυπούμεθα κατ' αὐτὴν τὴν αἴσθησιν, ὡς <δ'> 'Αναξαγόρας φησὶν ἀεί· πᾶσαν γὰρ αἴσθησιν εἶναι μετὰ λύπης.
>
> *Theophr. de sensu 17; 31A86.*

Only Aspasios, in a remark of comment upon the passage in Aristotle cited above, says:

> ... yet, it was not their (sc., the Natural Philosophers') opinion that the living being is in a condition of pain *continually.*
>
> ... οὐκ ἐδόκει γε αὐτοῖς (sc., τοῖς φυσιολόγοις) ἀεὶ ἐν πόνῳ εἶναι τὸ ζῷον.
>
> *Aspasios ad Arist. l.c., 156, 14; A94.*

That ostensibly Anaxagorean statement had to be considered nonsensical, of course. And as a matter of fact, Theophrastus was looking for a reason why Anaxagoras might have made such an assertion, and he came to say that

> this may seem to be conclusive from the presupposition (sc., that perception comes about through the opposites). For every unlike when touched effects pain,
>
> ὅπερ ἂν δόξειεν ἀκόλουθον εἶναι τῇ ὑποθέσει· πᾶν γὰρ τὸ ἀνόμοιον ἁπτόμενον πόνον παρέχει,
>
> *Theophr. de sensu 29; A92.*

as if Anaxagoras had come to his findings by means of Aristotelian syllogisms.

No doubt, this is a gross, a really bad misinterpretation of that Anaxagorean teaching. Theophrastus may have been influenced in this respect by Aristotle. But all the same, this palpable mistake should justify an attitude of reserve and cautiousness toward all of Theophrastus' reports on the Anaxagorean theory of perception.

Scanty Reports on Details

About details of Anaxagoras' research into the "psychophysiology" of the various senses, we can say very little beyond the basic ideas as delineated in the foregoing.

From the scanty reports by Theophrastus we learn only a few of these details, such as that Anaxagoras considered the image on the pupil of the eye the final condition for seeing; that he maintained that light, or as he himself would have put it: "the bright," must always be the concomitant cause if an image is to be formed on the pupil (so that, consequently, even a perception of black would not be possible without some light); that he knew some living beings see better by night, but most by day, and that he guessed this difference might be conditional upon the color of the eye; that he suspected hearing might have something to do with the fact that the bone surrounding the brain is hollow; and a few more.

And then there is also that passage in Vitruv (cf. p. 236, n. 1) alleging Anaxagoras to have dealt with optics to solve problems of scenography and perspective, following the example of Agatharchus who Vitruv says had been given advice by Aeschylus. This report seems to be considered unreliable by philologists. They ought to have cogent reasons, and it may be they really have. For otherwise the master of Euripides should not seem unlikely to have written also on this topic, making use of results from his analysis of sight which is said to have been one of his favorite subjects.

Strangely enough, Theophrastus when summing up calls the teachings of Anaxagoras on perception a "common and hoary doctrine." Yet, he admits that Anaxagoras has made original contributions of his own about all the senses and most in the analysis of sight because, obviously for its supreme degree of variegation and differentiation, this was to him the "great" sense, while the functioning of what Theophrastus calls the "more corporeal" senses was not made clear:

> Anaxagoras, then, ... upholds this somewhat common and hoary doctrine. Except that he says original things of his own about all the senses and particularly about sight because it is the great [1] sense, but he does not clarify the more corporeal senses.

> Ἀναξαγόρας μὲν οὖν ... κοινήν τινα ταύτην καὶ παλαιὰν δόξαν ἀναφέρει. πλὴν ἴδιον ἐπὶ πάσαις λέγει ταῖς αἰσθήσεσι καὶ μάλιστα ἐπὶ τῇ ὄψει διότι τὸ μέγα [1] αἰσθανόμενόν ἐστιν, οὐ δηλοῖ δὲ τὰς σωματικωτέρας αἰσθήσεις.
>
> *Theophr. de sensu 37; A92.*

---

[1] The replacement of the meaningless μέν of the text handed down by μέγα in the more recent editions seems well justified. In this way, the passage acquires a meaning similar to the idea of one of the first sentences in Aristotle's *Metaphysics* (980a26) where it says that, of all perceptions, we like most those through the

Plants, Too, Have Individual Consciousness

Nous, then, and not only World-Nous, but also separate nous, is present in every organism whatsoever:

> For Nous is in all the living beings whatsoever, in large ones as well as in small ones, in honored as in less distinguished ones.[1]

> ἐν ἅπασι γὰρ ὑπάρχειν αὐτὸν τοῖς ζῴοις καὶ μεγάλοις καὶ μικροῖς [1] καὶ τιμίοις καὶ ἀτιμοτέροις.

> *Arist. de anima I 2. 404b3; A100.*

This is true, even, of the plants, according to Anaxagoras:

> For the Platonists, the Anaxagoreans, and the Democriteans believe *the plant to be an animal stuck in the earth.*

> ζῷον γὰρ ἔγγειον τὸ φυτὸν εἶναι οἱ περὶ Πλάτωνα καὶ Ἀναξαγόραν καὶ Δημόκριτον οἴονται.

> *Plutarch. quaest. phys. I 911D; A116.*

Anaxagoras and Empedocles assert them (sc., the plants) to *be moved by desire* and positively declare that *they have sensations and feel pain and pleasure.*

> Ἀναξαγόρας μὲν οὖν καὶ Ἐμπεδοκλῆς ἐπιθυμίᾳ ταῦτα κινεῖσθαι λέγουσιν, αἰσθάνεσθαί τε καὶ λυπεῖσθαι καὶ ἥδεσθαι διαβεβαιοῦνται.

> *Nic. Damasc. [Arist.] de plant. I 1. 815a15; A117.*

Anaxagoras, however, and Democritus and Empedocles declared *the plants to have also mind and cognition.*

> ὁ δὲ Ἀναξαγόρας καὶ ὁ Δημόκριτος καὶ ὁ Ἐμπεδοκλῆς καὶ νοῦν καὶ γνῶσιν εἶπον ἔχειν τὰ φυτά.

> *Nic. Damasc. [Arist.] de plant. I 1. 815b16; A117.*

Thus, that also the plants have individual consciousness seems to have been taught first by Anaxagoras who, in this respect, was followed by Empedocles and Democritus.

eyes, "because among the perceptions this one makes us know a thing best and *shows (so) many distinctions*" (.. ὅτι μάλιστα ποιεῖ γνωρίζειν τι ἡμᾶς αὕτη τῶν αἰσθήσεων, καὶ πολλὰς δηλοῖ διαφοράς). – G. M. Stratton, in his *Theophrastus and the Greek Physiological Psychology before Aristotle*, renders the words διότι τὸ μέγα αἰσθανόμενόν ἐστιν as "*when he sets forth the part which size here plays in perception.*" One may doubt whether this can still be called a translation.

[1] This very Anaxagoras-like sentence makes quite an impression (despite the form μικροῖς instead of σμικροῖς) as if it were an outright quotation, though in indirect speech, from the work of Anaxagoras.

The same opinion was advanced by Albertus Magnus in the 13th century A.D., then again, in the beginning of the modern era, by Thomas Campanella [1] and, one century ago, by Gustav Theodor Fechner.[2]

An Ungrateful Disciple

Many a reader might have taken umbrage at the statement that Anaxagoras was followed by Empedocles in this respect. For it is customary to take the system of Anaxagoras for a further step in a direction previously inaugurated by Empedocles who, although the younger of the two, is commonly supposed to have influenced Anaxagoras.

However, I take the liberty of disagreeing. For I have taken to heart a precious sentence, written by A. E. Taylor in a remarkable essay on "The Date of the Trial of Anaxagoras" [3]:

> The history of scientific thought will never be rightly written, even in its main outlines, until we learn that a thing is none the more certain because it has been pronounced *allgemein bekannt* by a chorus of *Herren Professoren*.

It is not very difficult (though it would lead us too far here) to demonstrate that one can understand, and account for, all of Empedocles' natural philosophy if one presupposes Anaxagoras, but not inversely.

True, there is that well-known statement in Aristotle that Anaxagoras was to Empedocles.

anterior in age, but posterior as to their works.

τῇ μὲν ἡλικίᾳ πρότερος . . . τοῖς δὲ ἔργοις ὕστερος.

Arist. Metaph. I 3. 984a11; A43.

But this could mean that Anaxagoras began publishing later than did Empedocles who apparently was somewhat impatient in this respect and eager to become famous.

Besides, however, there have been handed down some reports that are just cut out for placing the whole relationship between Anaxagoras and Empedocles in quite a new and unexpected light.

Alkidamas of Elaia, a contemporary of Plato's, was a disciple of

---

[1] 1568–1639.
[2] 1801–1887.
[3] *The Classical Quarterly*, II (1917), 81–87.

Gorgias' who had been a disciple of Empedocles himself. This Alkidamas has related that *Empedocles attended lectures by Anaxagoras and later imitated his philosophy:*

> According to Alkidamas' report in the "Physics," at the same time Zenon and Empedocles attended lectures by Parmenides. Later they left, and then Zenon philosophized in his own way, but the other one (sc., *Empedocles*) *attended the complete courses* (διακοῦσαι) *of Anaxagoras' lectures and of Pythagoras'* [1]: *And of the one* (sc., *Pythagoras*) *he* (*then*) *imitated the dignified ceremoniousness in the habits of life as well as in outward appearance, but of the other* (sc., *Anaxagoras*) *the natural philosophy.*

> Ἀλκιδάμας δ' ἐν τῷ Φυσικῷ (*Orat. Att. II 156b6 Sauppe*) φησι κατὰ τοὺς αὐτοὺς χρόνους Ζήνωνα καὶ Ἐμπεδοκλέα ἀκοῦσαι Παρμενίδου, εἶθ' ὕστερον ἀποχωρῆσαι, καὶ τὸν μὲν Ζήνωνα κατ' ἰδίαν φιλοσοφῆσαι, τὸν δὲ Ἀναξαγόρου διακοῦσαι καὶ Πυθαγόρου [1] καὶ τοῦ μὲν τὴν σεμνότητα ζηλῶσαι τοῦ τε βίου καὶ τοῦ σχήματος, τοῦ δὲ τὴν φυσιολογίαν.

> *Diog. Laert. VIII 56; 31A1.*

This report by Alkidamas is well in keeping with the questionable character of a man tremendously gifted whose real motives were indulgence in his reckless vanity and a rage for affecting the multitude. It is quite in harmony with the way of a man covetous of fame, greedy of glory, who by reflecting people among his contemporaries was called an "impostor and charlatan," a γόης (*goes*):

According to Satyros (as relates Diogenes Laertius), Empedocles' own disciple

> Gorgias had reported that he himself witnessed Empedocles humbugging the public.

> Γοργίαν . . . λέγειν ὡς αὐτὸς παρείη τῷ Ἐμπεδοκλῆ γοητεύοντι.

> *Diog. Laert. VIII 59; 31A1.*

Which is readily understood when placed side by side with those of Empedocles' verses in which he boastfully promises to teach how to

---

[1] Burnet (*Early Greek Philosophy*, 4th ed., p. 202) remarks to this passage! "Alkidamas, who had good opportunities of knowing, made him (sc., Empedocles) a fellow-student of Zeno under Parmenides. Theophrastus too made him a follower and imitator of Parmenides. But the further statement that he had 'heard' Pythagoras cannot be right. No doubt Alkidamas said 'Pythagoreans'." Incidentally, it is a perfect enigma why neither here nor anywhere else in his book Burnet mentions with a word the momentous fact that Alkidamas, "*who had good opportunities of knowing,*" in that same sentence reports that Empedocles also "attended the complete course of Anaxagoras' lectures."

arouse or calm down a storm, how to make rain and sunshine, and how to revive the dead (fr. 111).[1]

But in addition, that report by Alkidamas joins well with another testimony of no less outstanding interest and importance:

Timaeus, the historiographer, in the ninth section of his work,[2] speaking of Empedocles as of a former hearer of Pythagoras, point blank relates

that he (sc., Empedocles), *having been found guilty of logoklopia*,[3] *was at that time denied (further) participation in the lectures (just as Plato [sc., recently])*.

ὅτι καταγνωσθεὶς ἐπὶ λογοκλοπίᾳ τότε (καθὰ καὶ Πλάτων) τῶν λόγων ἐκωλύθη μετέχειν.

Fr. Hist. Gr. I 211, fr. 81; 31A1.

This was the way the Pythagoreans were able to deal with people of that kind. Anaxagoras, however, did not have at his disposal an organization like the Pythagorean Union. Hence he was not in a position to punish a young, rich, vain Sicilian for exposing to the public in grandiloquent and bombastic verses [4] some of the basic ideas, diluted and popularized, of his master's philosophy at a time before the master himself had made up his mind to publish his own doctrine.[5] For Anaxagoras was by no means bent upon becoming famous. His way, concerning even the most brilliant of his teachings, was "to keep them dark and spread (them) step by step in a few words only and under precaution or in strict confidence" (cf. p. 223), since he taught in Athens and had to be on his guard ... The only thing Anaxagoras could do was to protect himself from similar experiences by being subsequently still more cautious in admitting new listeners to his lectures. And it may have been for reasons of this kind indeed that

[1] Cf. the very instructive essay by G. F. Unger, "Die Zeitverhältnisse des Anaxagoras und Empedokles." *Philologus*, Suppl. IV (1884), pp. 511–549.

[2] Cf., also, Diog. Laert. VIII 54; 31 A1.

[3] "Theft of the doctrine," meaning: publication without permission or even against interdiction.

[4] It is remarkable how disparagingly Aristotle speaks of Empedocles:

For if one ... takes it according to reason, and not according to what babbles Empedocles, one will find, etc.

εἰ γάρ τις ... λαμβάνοι πρὸς τὴν διάνοιαν καὶ μὴ πρὸς ἃ ψελλίζεται λέγων Ἐμπεδοκλῆς, εὑρήσει κτλ.

Metaph. I 4. 985a5; 31 A 39.

[5] It is understood, however, that Empedocles' philosophy does not consist of popularized Anaxagorean ideas alone.

Anaxagoras later on refused to admit as a hearer the young Democritus.

One almost feels inclined – although it is, of course, impossible to furnish any proof – to, also, interpret those lines of poetry by Euripides in praise of Anaxagoras (see p. 169) as an implicit repudiation of Empedocles. When reading of the man "who holds in his mind knowledge of science and *neither for damage of his fellow-men nor wrongful deeds intends to go*," and that "people of this kind *never are worried with grief over shameful commissions*," many a contemporary might perhaps have remembered Empedocles, of whom just the opposite was true. For in this man's life there were plenty of "wrongful deeds" and "shameful commissions." It might have been well known that in his native country he committed two downright judicial murders, not to mention other crimes, and that, at the urgent request of the sons and grandsons of those innocent victims, he alone was not permitted to come back to Akragas from exile (in 461 B.C.), although his fellow-exiles were allowed to return.[1]

An Overdue Vindication of Honor

Having mentioned that Democritus was not admitted to Anaxagoras' lectures, we cannot abstain from dwelling for a short while on this fact and seizing the opportunity for repudiating a vicious slander that has persisted through the ages up to this day.

Taking revenge for not having been accepted as a hearer, Democritus afterwards cast on Anaxagoras the slur of plagiarism:

> Favorinus, in his *Varia historia*, relates that Democritus says about Anaxagoras that his tenets on the sun and the moon are not his own but ancient ones, and that he stole them; and that he mocks at his cosmology and his teachings about Nous, *having a grudge against him because, as everybody knows, he had not admitted him.*

> Φαβωρῖνος δέ φησιν ἐν Παντοδαπῇ ἱστορίᾳ (FHG III 582 fr. 33) λέγειν Δημόκριτον περὶ 'Αναξαγόρου, ὡς οὐκ εἴησαν αὐτοῦ αἱ δόξαι αἵ τε περὶ ἡλίου καὶ σελήνης, ἀλλ' ἀρχαῖαι, τὸν δὲ ὑφῃρῆσθαι· διασύρειν τε αὐτοῦ τὰ περὶ τῆς διακοσμήσεως καὶ τοῦ νοῦ, ἐχθρῶς ἔχοντα πρὸς αὐτόν, ὅτι δὴ μὴ προσήκατο αὐτόν.

Diog. Laert. IX 34 and 35; A 5.

Diels has declared that by the "ancient" tenets "on the sun and the moon," allegedly "stolen" by Anaxagoras, Democritus meant doctrines

[1] Cf. G. F. Unger, *l.c.*, p. 530.

of Leucippus'. To bolster up his assertion, Diels adduces two passages, one from Diogenes Laertius, the other from Aetios.

In the first report, Leucippus is said to have taught

> the circle of the sun to be the outermost, the circle of the moon the nearest to the earth, the circles of the other (stars) to be between the two. And all the celestial bodies to be burning through the quickness of the movement, but the sun to be, additionally, set in flames by the stars; the moon, however, to get only a small share of the fire.

> εἶναι δὲ τὸν τοῦ ἡλίου κύκλον ἐξώτατον, τὸν δὲ τῆς σελήνης προσγειότα-τον, <τοὺς δὲ> τῶν ἄλλων μεταξὺ τούτων. καὶ πάντα μὲν τὰ ἄστρα πυροῦσθαι διὰ τὸ τάχος τῆς φορᾶς, τὸν δὲ ἥλιον καὶ ὑπὸ τῶν ἀστέρων ἐκπυροῦσθαι· τὴν δὲ σελήνην τοῦ πυρὸς ὀλίγον μεταλαμβάνειν.

> *Diog. Laert. IX 33; 67A1*

Yet, there does not seem to be much similarity between these opinions and the astrophysical teachings of Anaxagoras. Besides, it would have been an awkward way of expression if Democritus, who is said to have been younger than Anaxagoras by about forty years, had designated teachings of his own master, Leucippus, as "ancient." The marking, on the other hand, of the tenets in question as those "on the sun and the moon" could rather make us think of such as are really concerned with these two celestial bodies alone: the explanations of solar and lunar eclipses and, above all, the knowledge that moonlight is nothing but reflected sunlight. These were indeed teachings which Democritus could have justly called "ancient." But Anaxagoras, as we have seen (cf. pp. 236 and 238), never claimed as his own these ancient doctrines of which he just approved.

The second passage quoted by Diels in support of his assertion is quite a surprise: *It does not even refer to Leucippus, but to Democritus himself*, and consists of one short half-sentence indicating that

> Democritus (sc., said the sun to be) a glowing clod or stone.

> Δημόκριτος μύδρον ἢ πέτρον διάπυρον (sc., εἶναι τὸν ἥλιον).

> *Aet. II 20, 7; 68A87.*

Therefore, the one of the two passages pointed at by Diels collapses as an evidence.

That other passage, however, though not convincing to an unbiased reader, has been sufficient as a justification for Diels to contrive quite a story [1] about Leucippus of Abdera, the "nordic" scientist, who in 468 B.C. in the meteorite of Aigospotamoi (not far from Abdera) found masses of red-hot iron and, thereupon, made up the "amazing hypothesis that likewise all the other shining celestial bodies were glowing clods of metal." But in Athens people did not want to have anything to do with those "nordic" scientists of Abdera, says Diels, and so these teachings did not meet with response "until in Athens, the capital of the empire, they were soon afterwards presented as his own by the man from Klazomenai, Anaxagoras, whose story has been believed ever since up to this day, although Democritus, the pupil of Leucippus and no doubt a trustworthy witness, accused him of plagiarism."

Having read this "nordic" fantasy by Diels, one easily understands why he could not tolerate a pushing back of the life dates of Anaxagoras by 33 years (533–461, instead of 500–428, cf. p. 170), and why the Prussian *Herr Geheimrat* had to silence a scholar like G. F. Unger who, following the example of the great philologist K. F. Hermann, had dared to pronounce such a heresy.

The Actual Differences in Intelligence

In every organism whatsoever, then, Nous is of the same nature, Anaxagoras maintains.

But what about the differences in intelligence between man, animal, plant, and between the various species and individuals in these three realms? How may Anaxagoras have accounted for these differences? He has certainly not overlooked this obvious problem.

The difference in intelligence between any separate nous and the World-Nous was easily deduced from *the difference in their quantity.* The same explanation could also be applied to the differences between the miniature nous-individuals, although there is no knowing whether or not Anaxagoras took account of this point. But at any rate, if he did, then with the series (not sufficient alone, of course) of graded nous quantities he has combined another one, the series of *the different levels of organization:*

The World-Nous makes organisms of the most variegated structures, simple organisms and complicated ones, coarse ones and fine ones: Obviously, there is no accomplishing with a simple machine as much as with a highly complex one. Hence, *the more complex and the more subtile an organism's construction is, the more numerous and the more varied are the ways of acting available to Nous.*

[1] *Sitzungsberichte der Berliner Akademie der Wissenschaften,* 1908, p. 710.

Among animals, therefore, always that one is more intelligent which has a relatively larger skull or which is constructed in a relatively more complex and subtile way.

In the World-Nous, maximum quantity is combined with the highest level of the body's organization. For Its body is the sum total of the other elements.

This is not so strange as it may sound. True, Nous has spatial extensiveness [1] and, therefore, could be called a kind of body itself.[2] But just as the separate nous, filling the ventricles of the brain extensively, *is* a (fine) body and, besides, *has* a (coarse) body, the organism, so the World-Nous not only *is* a fine body, but also *has* a coarse body: the *sympan* of the other elements. If the World-Ghost is the world's ghost, then the world is that ghost's body, of course. If the organism is a micro-cosm, then the universe is a macro-organism. And only world-body and world-ghost together are a full world-personality.[3] The only difference is that the world-body, with all the organisms, is (embedded) in the world-ghost, whilst the separate little ghosts are (inclosed) in their bodies, according to Anaxagoras ...

It is quite certain that, to account for the differences in intelligence, Anaxagoras did make use of the differences in the levels of organization. Proof of it is his amazingly ingenious statement that

> it is because of his being armed with hands that man is the most intelligent animal.
>
> διὰ τὸ χεῖρας ἔχειν φρονιμώτατον εἶναι τῶν ζῴων ἄνθρωπον.
>
> *Arist. de partt. anim. I 10. 687a7; A102.*

The Aristotle Mystery

To this so astonishingly modern-looking statement, Aristotle reacts with the queer objection:

> But according to reason, (Anaxagoras ought to have said that) because of (man's) being most intelligent he has got hands.
>
> εὔλογον δὲ διὰ τὸ φρονιμώτατον εἶναι χεῖρας λαμβάνειν.
>
> *Arist. de partt. anim. I 10. 687a9; A102.*

No less queer is Aristotle's attitude in the face of the whole problem, Anaxagoras' solution of which he was not ready to appreciate. In Aristotle, as already mentioned, Anaxagoras' teaching is cited that

[1] Cf. p. 192.
[2] Cf., however, p. 320.
[3] Cf. p. 321 concerning panzoism, etc.

there is Nous *"in all the living beings whatsoever, in large ones as well as in small ones, in honored as well as in less distinguished ones."* This quotation is followed by Aristotle's polemic remark:

> But nous, if meant as intelligence, does not seem to be equally present in all the living beings, nay, not even in all the human beings.
>
> οὐ φαίνεται δ' ὅ γε κατὰ φρόνησιν λεγόμενος νοῦς πᾶσιν ὁμοίως ὑπάρχειν τοῖς ζῴοις, ἀλλ' οὐδὲ τοῖς ἀνθρώποις πᾶσιν.
>
> *Arist. de anima I 2. 404b5; A 100.*

On the whole, the Stagirite's way of presenting the doctrines of his predecessors does not seem to be quite appropriate. I cannot help having the impression that a great many of their constructions were understood too subjectively by Aristotle and have been distorted in his reproductions.[1]

[1] When in my small monograph of 1917 I wrote this and the subsequent sentences, I supported this opinion, considered heretic at that time, by the following annotation:

Allmählich hört man bereits auf, sich dieser Tatsache zu verschliessen. "Er (sc., Aristoteles) berichtet vorzugsweise als Kritiker, aber eben deshalb sind auch seine Angaben nicht überall unbedingt zuverlässig, besonders da er an fremde Lehren den Massstab seiner eigenen Grundbegriffe legt." (Ueberweg, *Grundriss der Geschichte der Philosophie*, I[10], herausg. v. Praechter, 1909, S. 13.) – "Denn so wenig skrupulös Aristoteles in historischen Dingen war, wo sein kritisch-polemisches Interesse ins Spiel kam, ..." (Heinrich Maier, *Sokrates. Sein Werk und seine geschichtliche Stellung.* Tübingen, 1913, S. 93.) – "Möchten die Plato-Interpreten doch endlich anfangen, wenn sie über Platos Ideenlehre etwas beweisen wollen, es aus Plato zu beweisen und nicht aus Aristoteles. Es wird ja eben bestritten, dass des Aristoteles Auffassung der Ideenlehre unvoreingenommen, objektiv historisch sei. Sie ist vielmehr, *wie übrigens seine ganze Darstellung und Beurteilung der älteren griechischen Philosophie*, durchaus diktiert von seinen eigentümlichen philosophischen Voraussetzungen. Wie darf man da immer wieder argumentieren: die Auffassung des Aristoteles ist die richtige, denn – Aristoteles sagt doch so und so!" (Paul Natorp, "Ueber Platos Ideenlehre," In: *Philosophische Vorträge, veröffentlicht von der Kantgesellschaft*, Nr. 5, Berlin, 1914, S. 20.)

Since then, the necessity of being cautions in using Aristotle's statements about his predecessors has been almost generally acknowledged and has become routine among philosophers as well as philologists, and so much so that today younger scholars are sometimes even inclined to disqualify a report merely because it is Aristotelian (Cf. p. 85). All the more gratifying is the objective, matter-of-fact attitude as expressed in the Foreword to *Aristotle's Criticism of Presocratic Philosophy* (Baltimore, 1935) by the American philologist H. Cherniss who, incidentally, has been familiar with that old monograph of mine. On pp. IX, X, XI, and XII of this meritorious book by Cherniss, we read the following brilliant sentences: "Aristotle was capable of setting down something other than

For centuries, this man was considered the unattainable model and pinnacle of human sagacity. And yet, the great Ephesian's construction, for instance, so bright and almost palpable, remained "obscure" (σκοτεινός) to him, and by his way of presenting the cardinal teachings of Anaxagoras he made it possible that, beginning from a millennium and a half later, every once in two or three centuries some scrap or other of Anaxagoras' doctrine was invented quite anew, as, e.g., by Ibn Rushd (Averroës), Nicolaus of Autrecourt, Leibniz, Berkeley, and Ernst Mach. What may have blinded Aristotle's eyes to such a degree, exactly when regarding those ancient philosophies? Are we to expect a thinker of his historical importance and authority simply to have been incapable of familiarizing himself with trains of thought different from his own, to have just had trouble in grasping those grand philosophies, and the doctrine of Heraclitus to have been obscure to him since he was dazzled by so much brightness?

Such an assumption would be considered almost blasphemy, I am sure, and the causes hinted at would hardly be accepted.

Therefore, this strange peculiarity of Aristotle has to remain a mystery beyond the reach of *luminis naturalis* cone of light, perhaps for ever . . .

Cosmogony has not yet come to an end, according to Anaxagoras.

Did he assume this process would endlessly go on spreading, in correspondence with the infinite extensiveness of the *pantahomou?*

One Cosmos or Many Cosmoi?

The answer to the question of whether Anaxagoras realized the process of cosmogony as endlessly spreading appears to be implied in the following sentences, as quoted in Simplikios:

---

the objective truth when he had occasion to write about his predecessors. . . . He was 'nearer' to them than are we, it may be objected; but nearer in time does not mean nearer in spirit, and it can be shown that Aristotle was so consumed with the ideology of Platonism and the new concepts he had himself discovered or developed that it was impossible for him to imagine a time when thinking men did not see the problems of philosophy in the same terms as did he. . . . the false impression that Aristotle was interested in preserving the doctrines of the Presocratics for their own sake. . . . Aristotle's belief that all previous theories were stammering attempts to express his own aids him in interpreting those theories out of all resemblance to their original form."

... and that (also there) human beings as well as all the other living beings having breath have been fit together (sc., out of the various *mereias*); and that (also there) men have common dwelling-places and tilled corn-fields, *just as with us*, and that they have also a sun and a moon and the other (stars), *just as with us*, and that the soil lets sprout forth for them many (plants) of every kind which they use for their living[1], gleaning the best. *By that I (wish to) have stated concerning differentiation that it may be taking place [2] not only with us, but elsewhere as well.*

... καὶ ἀνθρώπους τε συμπαγῆναι καὶ τὰ ἄλλα ζῷα ὅσα ψυχὴν ἔχει. καὶ τοῖς γε ἀνθρώποισιν εἶναι καὶ πόλεις συνῳκημένας καὶ ἔργα κατεσ-κευασμένα, ὥσπερ παρ' ἡμῖν, καὶ ἠέλιόν τε αὐτοῖσιν εἶναι καὶ σελήνην καὶ τὰ ἄλλα, ὥσπερ παρ' ἡμῖν, καὶ τὴν γῆν αὐτοῖσι φύειν πολλά τε καὶ παντοῖα, ὧν ἐκεῖνοι τὰ ὀνήιστα συνενεγκάμενοι εἰς τὴν οἴκησιν χρῶνται.[1] ταῦτα μὲν οὖν μοι λέλεκται περὶ τῆς ἀποκρίσιος, ὅτι οὐκ ἂν παρ' ἡμῖν μόνον ἀποκριθείη,[2] ἀλλὰ καὶ ἄλλῃ.

fr. 4 (Simpl. phys. 34, 28 [also 157, 9]).

[1] Literally: "of which the best they glean and use for living." The basic meaning of οἴκησις is "dwelling", "living", "household". Diels takes οἴκησις in its secondary meaning "house" and, taking εἰς τὴν οἴκησιν for a local determination of συνενεγκάμενοι, translates: "wovon sie das beste in ihr Haus zusammenbringen und davon (!) leben." (The faulty German of "und davon leben" has in Dr. Kranz' translation been replaced by "zu ihrem Gebrauch.") The rhythm of the sentence, however, does not seem to chime in with this interpretation, since to sever χρῶνται from εἰς τὴν οἴκησιν is rather violent. Besides, one should then expect the plural "into their houses" (εἰς τὰς οἰκήσεις).

[2] The optative with ἄν is the potential for the *present* tense, of course. Hence: "that differentiation may take place" (or "may be taking place") "not only with us." Diels' translation as *"stattgefunden hat,"* the *past* tense, is a double mistake since he neglects the meaning of an optative with ἄν (as a modest, conjecturing assertion) and, in addition, overlooks that in the past the potential would have to be expressed by the indicative with ἄν of an historical tense, according to an elementary rule of Greek grammar. I ruefully confess to have sinned against this rule myself when in my Anaxagoras publication of 1917, in opposition to Diels' *"stattgefunden hat,"* I wrote "stattgefunden haben dürfte" (p. 91). Only much later it came to my mind that this emendation still neglected the meaning of the optative with ἄν as the potential for the *present* tense. The adequate German translation would have been *"stattfinden dürfte."* This would have been also in keeping with the Anaxagorean view that cosmogony has not yet come to its end, and that differentiation of the *peri-echon* is still incessantly going on (cf. pp. 243 and 233). Alive to my translation of 1917, Dr. Kranz (in the 5th and 6th editions) has finally changed Diels' *"stattgefunden hat"* into *"stattgefunden haben dürfte."* Thus, he has corrected only one half of the mistake, I am sorry. (Incidentally, someone has pointed out [*Museum*, Sept.–Oct. 1949] that a modest assertion referring to the past has been expressed through the optative with ἄν allegedly somewhere in – Herodotus. But such exception does not invalidate the rule, of course.)

'With Us' and 'Elsewhere'

What do these sentences refer to? What is the meaning of "with us" and "elsewhere" in this context?

Is "elsewhere" supposed to mean any unknown regions of the earth? This is not probable. For then it would have to read "*the* sun and *the* moon" instead of "a sun and a moon," as already Simplikios has observed.[1]

Or should here ἄλλη ("elsewhere") have a temporal sense and refer to a past stage of the earth? This, too, is impossible. For Anaxagoras says, "they use" (χρῶνται), and not, "they used" (ἐχρῶντο), as likewise Simplikios has pointed out. And, besides, Anaxagoras says, οὐκ ἂν ἀποκριθείη, but not, οὐκ ἂν ἀπεκρίθη (or ἀπεκρίνετο).

One could perhaps also think that those sentences refer to inhabitants of some star. Yet, apart from the fact that in this case, too, "*the* sun" etc. would have been more appropriate – are not the stars glowing clods of stone? Only modern natural philosophers, now and then, believe that living beings can take birth, and survive, on a glowing (or having been glowing) celestial body ...

Is the Moon Inhabited?

However, what about the moon? According to Anaxagoras, its mass is mixed with particularly great quantities of the dark and the cold, so that, in contrast to the other celestial bodies, it is shady and cool (cf. p. 237f.). (In this way, Anaxagoras tried to account for the fact that the moon had to have its light from the sun and did not give off the slightest heat, although, as a glowing stone clod like the other stars, it should have been shining by itself and fiery.)

Yet, though second in size among the bodies in the sky, the moon is still quite a tiny thing in comparison with the earth, being smaller by far than the Peloponnesus peninsula. Why, then, should Anaxagoras have come to think the moon was inhabited? That the moon is "earth-like" means only that "it has high and flat and hollow parts" like the earth.[2]

True, Diogenes Laertius – and he alone – says [3] that, according to Anaxagoras,

the moon contains *homes* (οἰκήσεις), but also summits and gorges.

[1] Phys. 157, 9.
[2] Aet. II 30, 2; A77.
[3] Diog. Laert. II 8; A1; cf. p. 235, n. 1.

And it may be proper to assume that the source of this assertion are those sentences about "human and the other living beings ... having dwelling-places ... just as with us," all the more so since Diogenes employs the same word οἴκησις used by Anaxagoras, though not exactly in the same sense, in another part of that passage.

But such a view would be a misinterpretation due to some super-ficiality. It would certainly have been somewhat nonsensical to say that ostensible inhabitants of the moon have "also a sun *and a moon* and the other stars, just as with us" ...

And so Simplikios is obviously right when declaring that here Anaxagoras

> hints at some other cosmogony besides the one with us.
>
> ἑτέραν τινὰ διακόσμησιν παρὰ τὴν παρ' ἡμῖν αἰνίττεται.
>
> $\qquad$ *fr. 4 (Simpl. phys. 157, 9).*

Duration of Cosmogony and the Destiny of the Stars

Therefore, "*elsewhere*" *refers to other worlds*, existing or developing simultaneously with our own world system.

Nous started the differentiation of the pantahomou *simultaneously from infinitely numerous points probably equidistant* [1] *from each other.*

During the process of cosmogony, between the individual world systems there is present the *peri-echon*, consisting of *pantahomou*. Since this is invisible and impervious to light, the inhabitants of the one world system cannot become aware of the fact that their system is not the only one in existence. This fact can only be *conjectured* by the most sagacious minds among them, and that is what Anaxagoras does, saying *in a most modest way* [2]:

> ... that differentiation *might be taking place* not only with us ...
>
> ... ὅτι οὐκ ἂν παρ' ἡμῖν μόνον ἀποκριθείη ...

The growth of all these systems will come to its end when the

---

[1] This seems to me more appropriate to the way of Nous. Unless those starting-points were equidistant from one another, all of the *cosmoi* would not be finished within the same time.

[2] Theodor Gomperz (*Griechische Denker*, 2nd ed., I, pp. 181 and 182) pokes fun at the "orakelhafte Sicherheit, mit der er (sc., Anaxagoras) seine gesamten und darunter auch manche dem Menschenverstand grell widersprechenden Theorien verkündete," and particularly at the ostensible fact that he "mit der Zuversicht eines Offenbarungsgläubigen von anderen Welten erzählte, in denen es genau so zugehe, wie auf Erden." I have not been able to find any justification for this mockery.

pantahomou-stock of the *peri-echon* will have been consumed, as far as this is possible with the globularly undulating progress of differentiation.

The problem of whether or not the process of cosmogony requires infinite time has herewith been solved:

If the process began simultaneously from infinitely numerous points, equidistant from each other, of the infinitely extensive pantahomou, *then it must come to its end within a finite time.*

Its result will be: *an infinite number of finite* cosmoi.

This implies also the answer to the question of whether it is really the destiny of every star to fall down to the earth finally (cf. p. 234):

The pantahomou *once exhausted, there will be no* proskrithenta *any more nor, consequently, any further growing and becoming overweighty of the stars. And so they will remain henceforth in those spheres in which they will be at the end of evolution.*

'The Whole' and 'the Wholes'

The *primordial* period previous to this evolution, to sum up, was the period of the invisible *pantahomou*, of the *mereias* seemingly quality-less in consequence of the combining-ratio 1:1. In this period, there was nothing but one homogeneous, undifferentiated infinite multitude of molecules seemingly non-existing, embedded in the one infinite non-molecularized World-Nous.

The name for that is "the whole," "the universe," "the *sympan*" (τὸ σύμπαν) – *in the singular*. As a matter of fact, in that fragment which describes the truly primordial condition, characterized by its imperceptibility in consequence of "the *mixture* of all the elements," the word is used in this way, that is: in the singular.

Subsequently, Nous chooses an infinite number of infinitely small starting-districts, of "small somethings," of σμικρά τινα (*smikra tina*), equi-distant from each other, to be the centres of an infinite number of future worlds. By the globularly undulating progressions of the worlds forming activities of Nous, these worlds are steadily growing into a steadily decreasing *peri-echon* of *pantahomou*. And this *peri-echon* is incessantly being consumed by differentiation, διάκρισις (*diákrisis*), and by severance of the differentiated, ἀπόκρισις (*apókrisis*), in a constant stream of *proskrithenta*, augmenting these growing worlds.

Henceforth, there is no more one whole, no one *sympan* – in the singular –, but an infinity of wholes, an infinity of *sympanta* (σύμπαντα) – *in the plural* – each of them consisting of a growing cosmos and its *peri-echon*. And indeed, in that fragment which presents the condition immediately following the start of cosmogony – that condition in which the initial invisibility of the "things" already produced by differentiation is effected only by the initial *smallness* of their aggregations – in that other fragment, in a contradistinction distinct enough, Anaxagoras speaks of "the *sympanta*" (τὰ σύμπαντα), in the plural.

Today, the process of cosmogony is obviously still going on. For still

out of the clouds water is severed and out of the water earth,

ἐκ μὲν γὰρ τῶν νεφελῶν ὕδωρ ἀποκρίνεται, ἐκ δὲ τοῦ ὕδατος γῆ,

fr. 16 (Simpl. phys. 155, 21, and 179, 6).

and still no infinity of world systems is offered to the eyes of man, *still it seems as if the starry sky were the end of the universe.*

But when, *in times to come*, this evolution will have ended and, thereupon, the infinite embedding Nous' activity will but consist in preservation of the formedness, then *there will lie revealed an infinity of finite cosmoi*, beaming in the radiance of their shining suns and glittering starry skies, a heavenly beauty, marred not even by a rainfall ...

Witnesses – Contesting and Endorsing

There is a passage in Aetios (II 1, 2) according to which Anaxagoras would not have assumed a plurality of *cosmoi*. Anaxagoras is mentioned there as one of those teaching "the cosmos to be but one" (ἕνα τὸν κόσμον).

This report does not seem to be very reliable. The same Aetios relates that Archelaos, Anaxagoras' disciple, belongs to those assuming

infinitely numerous cosmoi in the infinite space ...

ἀπείρους κόσμους ἐν τῷ ἀπείρῳ ...

Aet. II 1, 3; 60A13.

The disciple, however, is not likely to have differed from his master in so essential a point. Either both taught the cosmos to be but one or both believed in infinitely numerous *cosmoi*. And I prefer that possibility which seems to me more probable with regard to the technique of composition.

True, there is one Anaxagorean fragment that, at a hasty glance, seems to tell against me:

The (elements) *in this one cosmos* are not separated from one another nor cut off with an axe from one another, neither the warm from the cold nor the cold from the warm.

οὐ κεχώρισται ἀλλήλων τὰ ἐν τῷ ἑνὶ κόσμῳ, οὐδὲ ἀποκέκοπται πελέκει οὔτε τὸ θερμὸν ἀπὸ τοῦ ψυχροῦ οὔτε τὸ ψυχρὸν ἀπὸ τοῦ θερμοῦ.

fr. 8 (Simpl. phys. 175, 11, and 176, 28).

But these words do not imply that there *is* only one cosmos. On the contrary, the meaning of the sentence apparently is: In this one cosmos, the one in which we ourselves are, in our cosmos, such and such a law is at work – that much I know. I cannot know whether the same law is valid also in the other *cosmoi*. But there, too, it might be "just as with us."

In addition, however, – what about the following passage in Simplikios?

Anaxagoras has placed Nous at the head as the cause of motion and origination, and the things being differentiated by Nous (*i.e.*, taking origin by this differentiation) have brought forth *the worlds* ...

τῆς δὲ κινήσεως καὶ τῆς γενέσεως αἴτιον ἐπέστησε τὸν νοῦν ὁ Ἀναξαγόρας, ὑφ' οὗ διακρινόμενα τοὺς ... κόσμους ... ἐγέννησαν.

Simpl. phys. 27, 2; A41.

(The plurality of cosmoi, of "worlds," as taught by Anaxagoras, has to be taken in the ancient sense and means no more, strictly speaking, than *a plurality of parts of space of the one and only world of the naive ametaphysical monism* of the Greeks. A true plurality of worlds – in the sense of the contrasts: "world appearing to me, or I-world," "thou-world, appearing to thee, metaphysical to me," and "external world, appearing to none of us" – was not yet conceived of by Hellenic antiquity.[1] Cf. also p. 164.)

The Ostensible Beginning in Time

Thus Anaxagoras might have restored the world fragment before his eyes to a complete world picture comprising all infinity, in the spatial sense. That in this picture the fathomless presents itself in an artistical-

---

[1] Allegedly, Protagoras and Aristippus of Cyrene the Elder did already have these contrasts. I do not agree. But it would lead too far afield to account for my reasons here.

ly symmetrical and harmonious arrangement is a trait genuinely Hellenic.

Has he with equal artistry moulded his world in the temporal sense?

First, *pantahomou*-stage lasting an infinitely long time; then, suddenly, a cosmogony taking a finitely long time; and, thereupon, everlasting duration of the finished formedness – this is not particularly artistic, to be sure. Such construction could be graphically symbolized by a straight line coming from the infinite; then, all of a sudden, being broken and mounting in an angle oblique to its previous direction; and, thereafter, running parallel with the former direction to the other side and again towards infinity. Such a picture appears to be primitive rather than artistic and of harmonious beauty.

Yet, this presentation fully responds to the interpretation accepted from times immemorial of the Anaxagorean doctrine:

> Anaxagoras says that the world after having originated from the mixture once and for all continues ever since being arranged and differentiated by the ruling Nous.

> τὸν 'Αναξαγόραν λέγειν ἅπαξ γενόμενον τὸν κόσμον ἐκ τοῦ μίγματος διαμένειν λοιπὸν ὑπὸ τοῦ νοῦ ἐφεστῶτος διοικούμενόν τε καὶ διακρινό-μενον.
>
> *Simpl. phys. 154, 29; A64.*

If Anaxagoras did construct in this way, then, in this respect, he was no artist, he alone, almost, among the philosophers of ancient Greece.

Eudemos' Reproach and Simplikios' Attempt at Refutation

Already Eudemos the Aristotelian considered Anaxagoras deserving of blame for operating with a cosmogony's beginning in time.

Simplikios by whom this is reported has tried to refute that reproach by asserting this whole origination of the world to be just a fiction, comprehensible from the requirements of didactic presentation. Xenocrates had declared Plato's cosmogony in the *Timaeus* to be meant as but virtual, that is to say, he had maintained one has to realize the Platonic cosmogony as placed back into eternity. Hence Simplikios believed himself to be justified, by the same right, in taking also Anaxagoras' doctrine in a way as if in his construction the world's simultaneous existence were drawn asunder into the succession of a genesis for reasons concerning style only:

> That the world took origin at the beginning of a (certain) time seems to be asserted by Anaxagoras, Archelaos, and Metrodoros of

Chios. They say, however, that also motion began (then). For, while all had been resting in the previous time, motion came in, they say, only by Nous, and in consequence of that motion the world took birth. *But they, too, seem to have assumed a beginning of cosmogony (merely) for the sake of a didactic arrangement of presentation.*

ἀπ' ἀρχῆς δὲ χρόνου δοκοῦσι λέγειν γεγονέναι τὸν κόσμον 'Αναξαγόρας τε καὶ 'Αρχέλαος καὶ Μητρόδωρος ὁ Χῖος. οὗτοι δὲ καὶ τὴν κίνησιν ἄρξασθαί φασιν. ἠρεμούντων γὰρ τὸν πρὸ τοῦ χρόνον τῶν ὄντων κίνησιν ἐγγενέσθαι φασὶν ὑπὸ τοῦ νοῦ ὑφ' ἧς γεγονέναι τὸν κόσμον. φαίνονται δὲ καὶ οὗτοι τάξεως ἕνεκα διδασκαλικῆς ἀρχὴν τῆς κοσμοποιίας ὑποθέμε-νοι.

Simpl. phys. 1121, 21; A64.

(Cf. also Simpl. de caelo 304, 5, and 305, 21.)

However, Simplikios' opinion cannot be accepted. For Anaxagoras expressly teaches the process of cosmogony has not yet come to its end. Consequently, the "beginning of cosmopoeia" (ἀρχὴ τῆς κοσμοποιίας) must have been meant as a true beginning in time.

Thus it looks as if Anaxagoras did deserve Eudemos' reproach.

Rehabilitation

In Eudemos' opinion, still other items of Anaxagoras' philosophy are deserving of blame. Let us have a look at these additional objections. It may be they will offer a handle for a – rehabilitation of Anaxagoras.

According to Simplikios' report,

Eudemos reproaches Anaxagoras not only because he maintains motion not having existed before to have arisen at some time, but also *because he has failed to make a statement as to whether it will last or will at some future time discontinue,* although it is not obvious (whether this will happen or that). "For what is there to prevent," he says, "that at some future time Nous will deem it right to bring the universe to a standstill, just as Nous has put it in motion, according to that man's assertion?" But in addition, Eudemos makes also the following animadversion upon Anaxagoras: "How is it possible that any privation should be prior to the positive condition contrary to it? Consequently, if rest is privation of motion, it could not exist before motion."

ὁ δὲ Εὔδημος μέμφεται τῷ 'Αναξαγόρᾳ οὐ μόνον, ὅτι μὴ πρότερον οὖσαν ἄρξασθαί ποτε λέγει τὴν κίνησιν, ἀλλ' ὅτι καὶ περὶ τοῦ διαμένειν ἢ λήξειν ποτὲ παρέλιπεν εἰπεῖν, καίπερ οὐκ ὄντος φανεροῦ. "τί γὰρ κωλύει, φησί, δόξαι ποτὲ τῷ νῷ στῆσαι πάντα χρήματα, καθάπερ ἐκεῖνος εἶπεν κινῆσαι;" καὶ τοῦτο δὲ αἰτιᾶται τοῦ Ἀναξαγόρου ὁ Εὔδημος· "πῶς ἐνδέχεται στέρησίν τινα προτέραν εἶναι τῆς ἀντικειμένης ἕξεως; εἰ οὖν ἡ ἠρεμία στέρησις κινήσεώς ἐστιν, οὐκ ἂν εἴη πρὸ τῆς κινήσεως."

Simpl. phys. 1185, 9; A59.

What is there to prevent, says Eudemos, that at some future time Nous will think it right to bring the world to a standstill, to undo cosmogony, to decompose the cosmos into the *pantahomou* again? Here Eudemos is quite right. The one assertion implies the other. If Nous is able to compose, Nous must also be able to decompose.

But why does Eudemos pronounce that statement in so reproachful a tone? According to Simplikios, Eudemos wanted to blame Anaxagoras for having failed to make a statement "as to whether it will last or will at some future time discontinue," although – in Simplikios' opinion! – this is not obvious. Eudemos himself, however, says, "What is there to prevent that ...?" This means exactly the same as, "There is nothing to prevent, it is evident, it is obvious that ..." And if it is obvious indeed that Nous being able to compose can decompose again as well, then it will no doubt have been obvious also to Anaxagoras. That he did not explicitly pronounce an obviousness is deserving of praise rather than of blame.

One could perhaps think there is some reason for another reproach: Even if Anaxagoras considered it self-evident that Nous will destroy the world again after a period of finishedness, he still should have offered a mechanics of that decomposition, just as he has constructed a mechanics of composition.

Yet, at second thought one easily understands that to explain the mechanics of decomposition would have been merely to say that decomposition would be the strict inversion of composition. In other words, not only the fact of decomposition but also its mechanism is an obviousness.

Eternal Periodicity

If, then, Anaxagoras assumed that upon the *pantahomou*-stage follows the stage of the world's formation, that this is succeeded by a period of finishedness, replaced, by turns, by a period of decomposition, until finally a return to the starting-condition, the condition of *pantahomou*, takes place – then it is obvious that he did not believe in this succession of phases as happening only once, but assumed *a beginning-less and endless periodicity of the cosmic occurrence.*

In this way, also the third reproach by Eudemos collapses. For now Eudemos is free to compose himself by imagining that prior to the *pantahomou*-stage, after which this actual cosmos is being formed, and even prior to any *pantahomou*-stage for that matter, there can always be placed another cosmos-stage.[1]

Does 'Pantahomou' Imply a Sleep of Nous?

According to Stöhr, the Anaxagorean construction might have been blamed also from another angle.

Diogenes of Apollonia, a contemporary of Anaxagoras', is quoted in Simplikios as saying:

> This, however, seems to me evident that (the divine being) is great as well as powerful and eternal and immortal and knowing many things.
>
> ἀλλὰ τοῦτό μοι δῆλον δοκεῖ εἶναι, ὅτι καὶ μέγα καὶ ἰσχυρὸν καὶ ἀίδιον καὶ ἀθάνατον καὶ πολλὰ εἰδός ἐστι.
>
> *64 fr. 8 (Simpl. phys. 153, 20).*

This sentence is allegedly a disapproval of Anaxagoras to the effect that the *pantahomou*-stage is an assumption below the dignity of Nous as a godhead since the *pantahomou* implies the conception of a sleep of Nous.[2]

Yet, there is no necessity to attribute such a meaning to that sentence. At any rate, however, such a censure would be unjustified. For never did Anaxagoras take Nous as sleeping during the *pantahomou:*

Always Nous knows all. But not always is Nous active, too. In the pantahomou-stages, Nous is merely resting, just like the Heraclitean Logos. The one time, it is the

Nous acting.

νοῦς ποιῶν.   *Hippol. refut. I 8, 1; A42.*

The other time, it is the

Nous resting,

νοῦς ἀναπαυόμενος.

---

[1] Incidentally, it is not by an incapacity of spontaneous motion that the *pantahomou* is unmoved. The pantahomou is without translatory motion merely due to the compensation of its own contrasting motion tendencies (cf. p. 201).

[2] A. Stöhr, *Der Begriff des Lebens* (Heidelberg, 1909), p. 34.

But any time, it is the

Nous having all knowledge about all.

νοῦς γνώμην γε περὶ παντὸς πᾶσαν ἴσχων.

cf. fr. 12 (Simpl. phys. 156, 20).

"Never He sleeps and never He slumbers."
Mens semper actu cogitat.

The Three Hellenic Attitudes Regarding Commencement

The doctrine of an eternal periodicity of the cosmic occurrence could be considered all the more obvious by Anaxagoras as it had already been propagated by the most distinguished among his predecessors and contemporaries, such as Anaximander and Heraclitus.

On the whole, there are among Greek philosophers but three types as to the attitude regarding these problems:

Those like Thales – provided one may give credence to the reports – or Aristotle simply offer *a description of the existent world* as it is and, in their opinion, has been from all eternity and will be forever. These are the inartistic ones.

The truly constructive natures among them, however, let the world originate from some starting-condition, and of these there are two groups. With those like Plato, *the origination's point of time has to be placed back into eternity*, and the whole construction has to be understood as meant but merely virtual. The others do mean an outright origination, but in return insert it into *a beginning-less and end-less periodicity*.

None has assumed a proper, true start in time happening but once. Anaxagoras would completely fall out of Greek ways had he done so.

With a Greek philosopher, the lack of an utterance about this point should rather imply that in this respect he agrees with his predecessors. One should not think of a Hellene as having assumed a true, Biblical beginning in time unless he affirms it expressly, unequivocally, and to the exclusion of the contrary.

A Weighty Endorsement

Besides, however, it is by no means so absolutely certain that Anaxagoras has not spoken about this point as one would expect with reference to Eudemos or Simplikios.

Not only is Anaxagoras mentioned by Aetios among those philosophers who have taught *the cosmos to be destructible.*

φθαρτὸν τὸν κόσμον.

Aet. II 4, 6; A65.

But, in addition, there is a very satisfactory and perfectly unequivocal endorsement. According to Aetios, Archelaos, Anaxagoras' disciple, has taught that

> *infinitely numerous worlds take origin and perish in the infinite space within every veering around.*

ἀπείρους κόσμους ἐν τῷ ἀπείρῳ κατὰ πᾶσαν περιαγωγήν (sc., γίνεσθαι καὶ φθείρεσθαι).

Aet. II 1, 3; 60A13.

To prove that in this fundamental point the disciple dissented from his master should be somewhat difficult ...

Remarkable Analogies

In the whole conception, there seems to be implied an intrinsic compulsion to construct in this way. For in philosophies positively unconnected with, and independent of, the Anaxagorean teachings there are quite astonishing analogies.

Exactly the same idea of an infinite number of world periods is in the Sâmkhya doctrine whence it has passed into Jainism and Buddhism.[1] Here, also, each world period consists of four phases. At first, there is the stage of *sâmyâ-'vasthâ*, the condition of *equilibrium* of the three *gunas*, those constituents of the "material" world.[2] Then follows a perturbation of the equilibrium of the three *gunas* and, as its consequence, the world's *evolution*.

> When the evolution of the world total (*sarga, srshti, samcara*) has come to its end, a period of *continuance* (*sthiti*) follows. ... When the time of continuance is over, the universe dissolves, in such a way that ... in retrograde motion the products become reabsorbed into the respective material causes from which they have originated. Through this process of *reabsorption* (*laya, pralaya, pratisarga, samhâra, pratisamcara*), the three *gunas* arrive finally at the state of *equilibrium again;* primordial matter is then in the

---

[1] See Richard Garbe, *Die Sâmkhya-Philosophie*, 2nd ed., 1917, p. 287.

[2] Also the *gunas*, just like the Anaxagorean elements, are absolute qualities, and the term *sâmyâ-'vasthâ* could even serve as an outright translation of *pantahomou*.

138

same condition again as in the time before evolution and perseveres in being so *until the dawn of a new cosmogony*.[1]

(Translated from the German original.)

Even Immanuel Kant, in his *Natural History of Heaven*, has not been able to escape from that compulsion to construct a periodicity. This is all the more significant as he was rather obliged not to offend Scriptural belief in a temporal beginning of the world.

Thus Anaxagoras, too, might have believed in a world built by Nous, upheld by Nous, destroyed by Nous, and built again, upheld again, destroyed again, in countless veerings of changes recurring again and again, from all eternity to all eternity.

ANAXAGORAS AND POSTERITY

From the very start, the philosophy of Anaxagoras seems to have been misunderstood in its fundamental and characteristic features: the doctrine of elements and the doctrine of Nous.

The Elements – Aristotelian And Otherwise

It has been demonstrated how confusing the reports in Aristotle are.

But the question still remains how Aristotle came at all to father upon Anaxagoras the queer teaching that parts of organisms, "such as bone and flesh and marrow," were the elements, and that air and ether were mixtures of these and other elements of that kind.

The Riddle of the Aristotelian Reports

According to Aristotle, Anaxagoras allegedly taught that

the *homoiomereses* are the elements,

τὰ ὁμοιομερῆ στοιχεῖα,

while, according to this hypothetical reconstruction, he could only have taught that

the "elements" are *homoiomereses*,

ὁμοιομερῆ τὰ στοιχεῖα.

One could very well imagine Anaxagoras as having said: "Those four principles of a former pupil of mine are no principles at all. They are *homoiomereses* only, as I call it, or masses of equal *mereias*. They are to

[1] R. Garbe, *l.c.*, pp. 284 and 285.

my really ultimate 'things' as roots are to seeds. And that is also why this unfaithful disciple has very wisely called them *roots of all* (πάντων ῥιζώματα [1]) and has not dared to call them *seeds of all* (πάντων σπέρματα)."

Now, *homoiomeres* is also a term in Aristotle's own phraseology, but with a considerably different meaning.[2] Aristotle, with his ever prevalent regard for verbal expression, was interested in when and when not the same name can be used for a part of a thing as for the whole thing,[3] and accordingly called a thing *homoiomeres*, "of equal parts," or *anhomoiomeres*, "of unequal parts."

Although, consequently, also the metals are *homoiomereses* to him,[4] he mainly applies this term to certain parts of organisms. Every bit of flesh can still be called flesh, and of marrow, marrow, etc., while a part of a face cannot be called a face any longer. Therefore, a face or a hand or a foot, etc., does not belong to the *homoiomereses*, but to the *anhomoiomereses*.

It could have been by the meaning of *homoiomeres* in his own terminology that Aristotle was lured into perverting what would have been correctly expressed as "The elements are *homoiomereses*" (ὁμοιομερῆ τὰ στοιχεῖα) into a "The *homoiomereses* are the elements" (τὰ ὁμοιομερῆ στοιχεῖα), which has no slightest resemblance to any Anaxagorean idea.

Confusion with Anaximander

There is another amazing performance of Aristotle's.

When discussing the philosophy of Anaximander, we have found that Aristotle takes the Apeiron, or "One," for a mixture and ascribes to Anaximander the teaching that "from the One *the contrasts* contained in it are secreted." And from Simplikios, the commentator, we have learned that by those contrasts are meant the well-known opposites: "warm, cold; dry, moist; and the others." [5]

[1] Empedocles, fr. 6. "Stoicheia," the word used by Aristotle, was since Plato the usual term for the four Empedoclean elements, earth, water, air, and ether.
[2] That "the word ὁμοιομερής, whether he (sc., Anaxagoras) actually used it himself or if others represent him as having done so, cannot have the same meaning as it has in Aristotle's system" has been found out also by A. L. Peck ("Anaxagoras: Predication as a Problem in Physics," in: *Classical Quarterly*, XXV [1931], p. 34).
[3] Cf. De gen. et corr. I 1. 314a18.
[4] Meteor. IV 8. 384b32, and 10. 388a13.
[5] Incidentally, the words "and *the* others" indicate that not just any opposites

We have come to understand (cf. p. 155) that to take the Apeiron of Anaximander for a mixture is not justified, that this is a confusion with the Anaxagorean doctrine,[1] and that such confusion may have arisen from the similarity of a mixture *containing* the opposites with a quasi-mixture: something unique, namely, that *changes* into opposites.

Yet – unless we want to impute to Aristotle a completely superficial, humdrum confusion of Anaximander with Anaxagoras –, from that none too exact report it would at least follow that Anaximander, and not Anaxagoras, would have been the first to arrive, in the analysis of the world, at those "opposites." And the decisive difference would then be that Anaximander still believed in a possibility of deriving the various pairs of opposites from one, unique, although undefinable, origin X, while Anaxagoras, for the first time alive to the naiveté of mutability, was also the first to understand that those various modalities of sensation, and the various pairs of "opposites," respectively, were really ultimate, irreducible constituents of the universe (cf. p. 177).

A Strange Criticism

It is worthwhile reading again, if only in translation, part of that passage in Simplikios and the passage in Aristotle, as mentioned just above and quoted at length in our discussion of the Apeiron of Anaximander (cf. p. 151f.):

> Yet, this man (sc., Anaximander) constructs the origination (sc., of the sensible stuffs) not so that the primordial stuff changes, but so that the opposites become separated in consequence of the eternal motion. That is also why Aristotle has put him into the group of the Anaxagoreans (!).
>
> *Simpl. phys. 24, 13; 12 A 9.*

And:

> ... The others, however, (teach) that from the One the contrasts contained (in it) are secreted, as says Anaximander and all those

are meant, but merely those of which each pair corresponds to one field of sensation (cf. p. 177). This is usually overlooked by all those interpreters, ancient as well as modern, for whom the problem implied in the irreducibleness of the so-called modalities of sensation is, and was respectively, too difficult to grasp.

[1] Cf. my Anaxagoras monograph of 1917, p. 103. – Abel Rey, likewise, (*La Jeunesse de la science grecque*, Paris, 1933, p. 59) considers the interpretation of Anaximander's "infinite" as a mixture a confusion with the theory of Anaxagoras.

saying that the One is also many, as do Empedocles and Anaxagoras. For these, too, have the other things be secreted from the mixture.

Arist. phys. I 4. 187a20; A 9.

The statement in Simplikios as well as Aristotle's own words show that Aristotle has attributed the opposites not only to Anaximander, but also to Anaxagoras and even Empedocles. May we, then, assume that Aristotle did have some occasional gleam of understanding of that the *homoiomereses* were not the ultimate Anaxagorean elements?

The answer is implied in the sentence following the quoted passage. Having stated that "these, too, (sc., Empedocles and Anaxagoras) let the other things be secreted from the mixture," Aristotle continues:

> But the difference between them is that the one (sc., Empedocles) constructs a recurrence of them, the other (sc., Anaxagoras), a happening but once, and that the latter (sc., Anaxagoras) assumes as infinite *the homoiomereses as well as the opposites*, but the former (sc., Empedocles), the so-called elements alone.[1]
>
> διαφέρουσι δ' ἀλλήλων τῷ τὸν μὲν περίοδον ποιεῖν τούτων, τὸν δ' ἅπαξ, καὶ τὸν μὲν ἄπειρα τά τε ὁμοιομερῆ καὶ τἀναντία, τὸν δὲ τὰ καλούμενα στοιχεῖα μόνον.[1]

Arist. phys. I 4. 187a23; 31 A 46.

Here the opposites and the *homoiomereses* are put side by side as if they were two co-ordinated things. And accordingly, after a few lines (187b5 [not quoted in Diels]) Aristotle, commenting on Anaxagoras, produces even a juxtaposition such as *"white or black or sweet or flesh or bone"*! This does not indicate that Aristotle grasped the proper meaning of Anaxagoras' idea.

(An Italian scholar, calling the opposites an "ancient Jonism," has managed – with reference to a' misinterpreted passage in fragment 12

---

[7] The last word of this sentence, "alone" (μόνον), has quite surreptitiously and without further ado been suppressed by Diels in his quotation of this Aristotelian passage among the reports on Empedocles (21 A 46). The purpose of this arbitrary proceeding is altogether incomprehensible. In later editions, Dr. Kranz has tried to offer something like a subdued justification. He reproduces the text as mutilated by Diels, though. But in a laconic footnote to 31 A 46, he states: "στοιχεῖα μόνον *Ar. Hss.:* μόνον fehlt Simpl. a. O." That is to say, he admits that in all the Aristotle manuscripts the last words of the sentence are στοιχεῖα μόνον, but points out that in Simplikios' quotation of that Aristotelian passage the word μόνον is lacking. Yet, this is at best an apology, but not a justification of Diels' high-handed suppression.

(cf. p. 202, n. 2) – to characterize the Anaxagorean opposites as "a not well digested and understood reminiscence of an ancient Jonism." [1] With regard to the appalling juxtaposition quoted above, it would have been more appropriate for that scholar to speak of a "reminiscence" of a fundamental Anaxagorean doctrine "not well digested and understood" by Aristotle ...)

Moreover, in another passage Aristotle criticises the Anaxagorean doctrine in a way manifesting beyond all doubt that he was indeed far from penetrating to the cardinal Anaxagorean conception. In his *Metaphysics*, some lines before that description of the (seemingly) quality-less Anaxagorean primordial mixture (cf. p. 204), we read:

> ... For although it is preposterous and wrong to maintain that all had been mixed in the beginning, first, because then it should be conclusive that still earlier (the constituents) would have had to be there unmixed; secondly, because by nature everything is not capable of being mixed with everything, and in addition to these reasons, *because the passions and accidentals would be severed from the substances* ...

> ... ἀτόπου γὰρ ὄντος καὶ ἄλλως τοῦ φάσκειν μεμῖχθαι τὴν ἀρχὴν πάντα, καὶ διὰ τὸ συμβαίνειν ἄμικτα δεῖν προϋπάρχειν, καὶ διὰ τὸ μὴ πεφυκέναι τῷ τυχόντι μίγνυσθαι τὸ τυχόν, πρὸς δὲ τούτοις ὅτι τὰ πάθη καὶ τὰ συμβεβηκότα χωρίζοιτ' ἂν τῶν οὐσιῶν, κτλ.

> *Arist. Metaph. I 8. 989a33–b3 (not in Diels)*.[2]

That is to say: *Exactly the very point of the whole construction is mistaken for a defect.*

A Dubious Evidence against Periodicity

Before leaving antiquity behind, we have still to dwell a little on that passage in Aristotle quoted above where he speaks of the differences between Anaxagoras and Empedocles. According to Aristotle, Anaxagoras "constructs a happening but once" of the world occurrence.

---

[1] ".. si tratta di una reminiscenza dell' antico jonismo non bene assimilata e dialettizzata." (D. Ciurnelli, *La Filosofia di Anassagora*. Padova, 1947, p. 54.)

[2] The highly important passage of 24 lines on Anaxagoras in Aristotle's Metaphysics I 8. 989a30–b19 has been suppressed by Diels and Kranz. Killing the very pith of that testimony, they quote, in A 61, only the first two lines, another two lines from the middle, and (incompletely) the last two lines, omitting everything in between. By this mutilation the whole testimony has been stultified. A full quotation would have shattered an "established" opinion about Anaxagoras' doctrine.

As in late antiquity, Aristotle's words τὸν δ' ἅπαξ are still commonly considered a corroboration of the opinion that Anaxagoras taught a true beginning of the world in time happening but once.

Yet, those words are no unambiguous proof of that, strictly speaking, any more than a lack of an utterance by Anaxagoras about this point is an unquestionable evidence (cf. p. 305). Aristotle merely says Anaxagoras has *constructed* (ποιεῖν) a happening once of the world's formation. This is correct as far as it goes. But Aristotle does not say belief in recurrence was rejected by Anaxagoras.

With Empedocles, however, it is quite a different story. In his natural philosophy, and there alone, he not only pronounces the dogma of recurrence, but is also forced to "construct" its mechanics. For he assumes two world powers fighting each other, and the mechanisms of their respective workings are by no means an obviousness (cf. p. 303).

It is extremely interesting that in his unsuccessful attempt at founding a new religion, in the *Katharmoi*, Empedocles craftily observes strict reticence about periodicity. In this work addressing himself to quite a different type of readers, he would have counteracted his own purposes if he had even slightly mentioned such a discouraging creed as the dogma that after Love's full victory there would be coming again an age of Hatred, and that all this would go on for ever, to and fro, in an eternal see-saw battle between the two powers. In his religious work, then, Empedocles' presentation makes, by implication, the reader believe that that cosmic battle is happening but once, and that the impending victory of Love is going to be final (cf. p. 389 f.).

Now, let us suppose hypothetically, just for the sake of the argument, that only the *Katharmoi* had been handed down, and that *Peri Physeos* had been lost. In this case, it would undoubtedly have been correct to say that Empedocles constructed a happening but once of the victorious battle of Love against Hatred. And nonetheless – any conclusion therefrom to the effect that Empedocles did not believe in periodicity would have been wrong.

Friedrich Nietzsche, Paul Tannery, John Burnet

The Aristotelian interpretation of the elements doctrine of Anaxagoras has been authoritative ever after and is still dominant even today. It has been contested but three times: by Friedrich Nietzsche, Paul Tannery, and John Burnet.

Friedrich Nietzsche, in *Die Philosophie im tragischen Zeitalter der Griechen* (1873), describes the primordial state of Anaxagorean "matter" as follows: [1]

> eine staubartige Masse von unendlich kleinen erfüllten Punkten, von denen jeder spezifisch einfach ist und nur *eine* Qualität besitzt, doch so, dass jede spezifische Qualität in unendlich vielen einzelnen Punkten repräsentiert wird.

The decisive words are, "von denen jeder spezifisch einfach ist und nur *eine* Qualität besitzt," implicitly abandoning the Aristotelian view.

Paul Tannery does not seem to have had any knowledge of that writing of Nietzsche's. His opinion on the elements doctrine of Anaxagoras, in a chapter of his book, *Pour l'histoire de la science hellène* (1887), likewise coincides to some degree with the interpretation this hypothetical reconstruction of the Anaxagorean system is based upon. He, too, – like Nietzsche, apparently, – had been struck by the palpable inconsistency of Aristotle's presentation with Anaxagoras' own words. He says (p. 286):

> ... Si l'on examine les fragments, on n'y voit rien de semblable: Anaxagore ne parle que de qualités, l'humide, le sec, le chaud, le froid, le lumineux, l'obscur, le dense, le ténu, et il énonce formellement ... que c'est par la concentration de ces qualités que se produit, d'une part, la terre, de l'autre, l'éther.

However, between the interpretations by Nietzsche and Tannery of Anaxagoras' words and this interpretation there is a veritable gulf, philosophically speaking:

As I conceive it, *Anaxagoras considers these "qualities" themselves the ultimate elements of the world. To him, so-called matter is not a carrier of the qualities, but these are themselves that "matter."*

This was not so understood by Nietzsche or Tannery. Nietzsche's words, "von denen jeder ... nur eine Qualität besitzt," imply that to him the filling of such a "filled point" was not a single quality itself, but a something that *carries* a quality. And Tannery says (p. 286):

> Le point capital est la question de savoir comment il (sc., Anax.) considérait ses éléments, soit comme des parties d'un mélange, soit comme des *qualités inhérentes à la matière*, mais variables en degré d'un corps à l'autre.

[1] Musarion edition, IV, 219.

In this way, however, all the ingenuity of the Anaxagorean idea is lost.

That Tannery does not get to the core of the Anaxagorean conception becomes particularly evident from the following passage (p. 288):

> ... Anaxagore se représente les choses comme si les qualités ne pouvaient varier que par un déplacement mécanique des *particules de la matière auxquelles il les a attachées.* C'est dire qu'il ignore toute la physique et toute la chimie modernes, que même *il n'a pas encore la notion complète de la qualité et qu'il n'établit pas une distinction parfaitement nette entre la qualité et la substance.*

This is almost exactly the same criticism as that uttered by Aristotle. Tannery, too, has interpreted as a defect what has been Anaxagoras' most ingenious and lasting idea.

John Burnet, the English philologist, seems to be the only one to prefer Tannery's interpretation to Aristotle's. (He, also, does not mention Nietzsche.) In his *Early Greek Philosophy* [1] he says:

> I still think that Tannery's interpretation is substantially right, though his statement of it requires some modification. It is, no doubt, difficult for us to think of the hot and cold, dry and wet as 'things' (χρήματα); but we must remember that, even when the notion of quality (ποιότης) had been defined, this way of thinking survived. Galen (De nat. fac. I, 2, 4) is still quite clear on the point that it is the *qualities* which are eternal. He says: οἱ δέ τινες εἶναι μὲν ἐν αὐτῇ (τῇ ὑποκειμένῃ οὐσίᾳ) βούλονται τὰς ποιότητας, ἀμετα-βλήτους δὲ καὶ ἀτρέπτους ἐξ αἰῶνος, καὶ τὰς φαινομένας ταύτας ἀλλοιώσεις τῇ διακρίσει τε καὶ συγκρίσει γίγνεσθαί φασιν ὡς Ἀναξα-γόρας. [1]

But then Burnet fails to specify that "some modification" which he justly says Tannery's statement requires. Besides, the words, "Even when the notion of quality (ποιότης) had been defined," etc., seem to indicate that Burnet took the designation of the qualities as "things" for a "way of thinking" that remained as a residue "surviving" from a more primitive state of mind, and that he might not have understood this way of thinking as an intentional substitution by Anaxagoras for

[1] 4th ed., p. 263, n. 1. Translation of the Galen passage quoted by Burnet: "The others, however, want the qualities to be in it (sc., in the underlying substance), though, but to be unchangeable and unalterable from eternity, and they say like Anaxagoras that these appearing alterations come into being by severing and mixing."

the common way of thinking. Burnet's quotation of the passage shows that he no more than Galen came to think Anaxagoras could have meant a cancellation of that "underlying substance," even though neither the notion of substance nor the notion of quality might have been already "defined" in Anaxagoras' time. One has to distinguish between having a notion and having a definition of a notion.

At any rate, however, the views of Nietzsche, Tannery, and Burnet come incomparably closer than the commonly accepted Aristotelian interpretation to that which, in my opinion, was really meant by Anaxagoras.

Eduard Zeller

Zeller refused to accept Tannery's opinion and retained Aristotle's.[1] To Tannery's interpretation he has dedicated the following annotation in his *Philosophie der Griechen* (5th ed., I, p. 980):

> Und an die Stelle dieser Stoffe mit Tannery, Science Hell. 286 f., "Qualitäten" zu setzen, durch deren Verbindung die einzelnen Stoffe entstehen, widerstreitet nicht bloss allen unseren Zeugen ohne Ausnahme, sondern es findet auch in den eigenen Aeusserungen des Philosophen keine Stütze. Tannery verweist auf f. 3, 6, 8. Allein, τὸ διερόν, τὸ θερμόν usw. heisst nicht: "die Feuchtigkeit, die Wärme" usw., sondern: "das Feuchte" usf., d.h. die mit diesen Eigenschaften versehenen Stoffe, und Anaxagoras selbst nennt das διερόν usf. fr. 6 χρήματα. Davon nicht zu reden, dass die Annahme für sich bestehender Qualitäten in jener Zeit eines unbefangenen Materialismus ohne Analogie wäre.

That Tannery's interpretation "is antagonistic to all of our witnesses without exception" – this does not matter too much.

But that τὸ θερμόν, "the warm," could not have – especially in a philosophic context – the meaning of θερμότης, "warmth," this is an opinion differing too much from lexical tradition for me to admit any foundation for it. There is nothing easier than to demonstrate that the use of τὸ θερμόν in the sense of θερμότης is not even sporadic. It may suffice to have a look into the *Thesaurus Graecus* by Henricus Stephanus. There one can read *sub verbo* θερμός, vol. IV, p. 331, column 2, sub lit. B:

---

[1] Also Clemens Baeumker (*Das Problem der Materie in der griechischen Philosophie*, 1890, pp. 73–79) follows the traditional Aristotelian view, but without any mention of Tannery.

Neutrum etiam pro θερμότης, calor (Plato Crat. p 413 C: τὸ θερμὸν τὸ ἐν τῷ πυρὶ ἐνόν). Theophr. C. Pl. (2, 6, 1), loquens de aquis frigidis: Πέψιν ποιεῖ μάλιστα διὰ τὴν ἀντιπερίστασιν τοῦ θερμοῦ καὶ κατάψυξιν, Propter cohibitum et coarctatum calorem a circumfuso frigore. 6 (7, 8): Πέττει γὰρ τὸ θερμὸν ἀντιπεριϊστάμενον, Concoquit enim calor intra terram compressus, et cohibitus coactusque ... Et ap. Alex. Aphr.: Τὸ ἔμφυτον θερμόν, Calor insitus (conf. I, 79); sicut Plut.: Τὸ οἰκεῖον καὶ τὸ σύμφυτον θερμὸν ἡμῶν, ᾧ τρέφεσθαι πεφύκαμεν.

However, supposing there were no parallel passages in other ancient authors to attest this usage of the word – this would still not be a logical argument against the possibility of Anaxagoras' having used the term in this way. For the very moment Anaxagoras carries out that spatialization of the "qualities," τὸ θερμόν not only can but must become to him equivalent to θερμότης. He would even have been compelled into a conflict with his mother-tongue, had it not been yielding enough anyway to comply with his idea. *Anaxagoras intentionally equates* τὸ θερμόν, *"the warm," and* θερμότης, *"warmth," just as Berkeley equated "esse" and "percipi,"* which can certainly not be justified lexicographically. But Berkeley happens to be supported by the broader context, that renders superfluous an interpreter.

As to "absolute qualities" – in Tannery's opinion, the Anaxagorean elements are by no means absolute qualities, as I have demonstrated above. For he speaks of "particules de la matière auxquelles il (sc., Anax.) les (sc., qualités) a attachées." Hence it is my interpretation, strictly speaking, that Zeller has anticipated, and when he alleges that "assuming absolute qualities would be without analogy in that period of unsophisticated materialism," it is incumbent upon me to apply this objection to myself and answer.

Let it be said, then, to begin with, that that period was neither the time of an unsophisticated nor of a sophisticated materialism, but of no materialism whatsoever.[1] Besides, it is never entire ages that philosophize, but always only individual men. Moreover, it is the very essence and token of a genuine philosopher that what he teaches is "without analogy," *i.e.*, original.

Finally, however, there is indeed (which Zeller seems to have forgotten) at least one very nice analogy in Indian philosophy. In the Sâmkhya system those three constituents of "matter," the three

[1] Cf. p. 321.

guṇas, Sattva, Rajas, and *Tamas,* are also nothing but independent "qualities," and they, too, just as the *chremata* of Anaxagoras, are not attached to a matter, but are that "matter" themselves.

Nous – Aristotelian And Otherwise

In later antiquity, it was taken for granted that the Anaxagorean Nous was a strange, "immaterial" power, opposed, in a dualistic sense, to the "material, unspiritual, unconscious" elements of the world. According to Simplikios,[1] Theophrastus following his master Aristotle [2] considered Anaxagoras' Nous the strict contrast of the "material principles," the ὑλικαὶ ἀρχαί.

Is Nous 'Pure Spirit'?

This interpretation does not seem to have been contested prior to the eighteenth century when interpreters were struck by the fact that in the extant fragments terms applied to the "material" elements are used also where Nous is characterized, particularly in that passage where Nous is called "the thinnest and purest of all the elements."

Hence, the question seemed to arise: Was Nous indeed "pure spirit," an immaterial divine principle, or was the alleged "spirit" of Anaxagoras to be understood rather as something like a kind of matter?

Modern Interpretations

These are some of the answers given so far:

Schaubach (*Anax. Clazom. fragm.,* 1827, p. 103) says: Quaeritur, num haec epitheta (sc., the "thinnest" and "purest") tropice an proprie intelligenda sint. Praeferenda esse videtur prior ratio, quandoquidem alioquin aperte sibi repugnaret etc. ("The question is whether these epithets are to be comprehended figuratively or literally. The first interpretation seems to be preferable since otherwise he would obviously contradict himself, of course.") And with reference to Carus, Tenneman, Hemsen, and Ritter, he maintains that that expression is used *de mentis acumine omnia penetrante* ("of the sharpness of Mind penetrating all things").

Similarly Breier (*Die Philosophie des Anaxagoras von Klazomenae nach Aristoteles,* 1840, p. 63 ff.) assumes Anaxagoras to have conceived

[1] Phys. 27, 2; A41.
[2] Cf. Arist. Metaph. I 8. 989a31, and elsewhere.

of Nous as certainly immaterial, but to have expressed this idea in a defective, popular way.

Heinze first maintained the doctrine of Anaxagoras to be a dualism not yet perfect and aware of itself. Later he changed his mind and tried to prove that Anaxagoras meant quite consciously a genuine dualism. For this purpose, he translated, following Schaubach, λεπτός ("thin") as *scharfsinnig* ("sagacious") and gave the word χρῆμα the meaning of the indefinite *etwas* ("something"), in this way allegedly removing the philological difficulties. (*Ueber den Nus des Anaxagoras.* Berichte über die Verhandlungen der kgl. sächsischen Gesellschaft der Wissenschaften zu Leipzig, philologisch-historische Klasse, 1890.)

No less decidedly does J. Freudenthal stand up for the immateriality of Nous (*Ueber die Theologie des Xenophanes*, 1886, p. 46).

In E. Rohde's opinion, also, Anaxagoras is "der erste entschiedene und bewusste Dualist unter den griechischen Denkern." For his "*Geist* ... wird mit solchen Beiwörtern beschrieben, dass man das Bestreben des Anaxagoras, ihn von allem Materiellen verschieden, selbst immateriell und unkörperlich zu denken, nicht verkennen kann." (*Psyche*, 4th ed., II, 192.)

On the other hand, already Brucker (*Historia critica philosophiae a mundi incunabulis ad nostram usque aetatem deducta*, 1742–1744, 2nd ed. 1766–1767, I, 513 [1]) considered Nous corporeal and attributed to it an aeriform nature. Similarly Tiedemann (*Geist der spekulativen Philosophie*, 1791–1797, I, 329 ff.[1]) interpreted the Nous of Anaxagoras as an ethereal or fiery being.

Fr. Kern (*Ueber Xenophanes von Kolophon*, 1874, p. 24, n. 69) declared it impossible to demonstrate, on the basis of the fragments and the reports of reliable witnesses, that Anaxagoras taught anything immaterial, anything not extended in space.

Windelband (*Lehrbuch der Geschichte der Philosophie*, 5th ed., 1910, p. 35) says outright that Anaxagoras' Nous is a stuff, a material element, the power element, the motion stuff, the thinking-stuff.

Theodor Gomperz, likewise, considers Nous *ein vernunftbegabtes Fluidum.* (*Griechische Denker*, 2nd ed., I, 175.)

The same line is followed by Werner Jaeger (*The Theology of the Early Greek Philosophers*, 1947, pp. 166 and 167). Also in Jaeger's opinion was Anaxagoras "not yet aware of a real opposition between

---

[1] Quoted from E. Arleth, *Die Lehre des Anaxagoras vom Geist und der Seele* (*Archiv für Geschichte der Philosophie*, VIII [1894], nos. 1 and 2). Arleth himself maintains the immateriality of Nous.

matter and mind" and "still conceived" of Nous "as something material, endowed with the power of thought."

According to B. A. G. Fuller (*A History of Philosophy*, 1936, pp. 34 and 35), the Anaxagorean Nous is not an "immaterial, divine intelligence, planning and directing the universe," but merely "the one self-moving stuff in a universe otherwise composed of inert elements," or (as he puts it in his *History of Greek Philosophy*, 1923, p. 219) merely "the cosmic brain-matter."

A third group stands between the two antagonistic interpretations.

Zeller (*Die Philosophie der Griechen*, 5th ed. I, 993) believes Anaxagoras to have really thought of an incorporeal being by which matter had been moved and put in order;

> und mag es auch nicht bloss der Unbeholfenheit seines Ausdrucks zur Last fallen, wenn der Begriff des Unkörperlichen in seiner Beschreibung nicht rein heraustritt, mag er sich vielmehr den Geist wirklich wie einen feineren, auf räumliche Weise in die Dinge eingehenden Stoff vorgestellt haben, so tut dies doch jener Absicht keinen Eintrag.

According to Dilthey (*Einleitung in die Geisteswissenschaften*, 1883, I, 207, n. 2), Nous is *ein verfeinertes Stoffliches* ("a refined material thing"), or, at least, *an der Grenze von Stofflichkeit* [sic!] *noch befindlich* ("still being at the borderline of materiality").

Salvatore Fimiani ("Alcune osservazioni su la relazione tra il νοῦς e la ψυχή nella dottrina filosofica di Anassagora," *Rivista italiana di filosofia*, 1889, p. 67) says:

> Il noo di Anassagora, di fatti, sta in mezzo, tra il concetto d'una intelligenza pensante, umana, incorporea, distribuita tra gli esseri viventi, e quello d'una forza impersonale, motrice; tra il concetto d'una divinità radicalmente distinta da ogni elemento corporeo, e quello d'una forza della natura, i cui attributi non potrebbero riferirsi ad un essere schiettamente spirituale.[1]

Likewise, Albert Rivaud in his presentation of Anaxagoras' doctrine (*Le Problème du devenir et la notion de la matière et de l'esprit dans la philosophie grecque depuis les origines jusqu'à Théophraste*, 1906, p. 199)

---

[1] "In fact, the Nous of Anaxagoras stands in the middle between the conception of an intelligence, thinking, human, incorporeal, distributed among the living beings, and that of an impersonal, moving force; between the conception of a deity altogether different from any corporeal element and that of a natural force, the attributes of which could not refer to a purely spiritual being."

holds that "sans doute il n'y a point là encore une distinction claire de la matière et de l'esprit."

v. Arnim, in his presentation of ancient European philosophy (*Kultur der Gegenwart*, I/5, 1909), takes the "spirit" of Anaxagoras for *eine vom Stoff verschiedene Bewegungsursache* ("a motive cause different from matter").

In *Friedrich Ueberwegs Grundriss der Geschichte der Philosophie* (vol. I, ed. by Praechter, 12th ed., 1926, p. 100) there is the following statement:

> *Diese letztere Stelle* (sc., that the Nous is "the thinnest and purest of all the elements") zeigt zugleich, dass es Anaxagoras nicht gelungen ist, in seiner Auffassung des Geistigen den prinzipiellen Gegensatz zwischen Geistigem und Körperlichem voll zur Geltung zu bringen: Es genügt ihm, den Geist als feinsten und reinsten Stoff den gröberen, zusammengesetzten Stoffen entgegenzusetzen.

Similarly John Burnet (*Greek Philosophy*, vol. I, p. 79):

> He (sc., Anaxagoras) did not, however, succeed in forming the conception of an incorporeal force ...

An overwhelming majority of authors, then, maintain the immateriality of Nous. The only difference is that some suppose Anaxagoras to have conceived the idea of dualism with perfect clarity, while in the opinion of others he had but a vague notion of it. And only a few scholars hold Anaxagoras to have taught a materialistic monism, to have conceived of Nous as a sort of matter.

New Answer by Counter-Question

Are these the only possible interpretations?

The main source of these troubles is no doubt that opinion about the Anaxagorean elements doctrine which since Aristotle has been commonly accepted. On the basis of that Aristotelian interpretation, there would be a fundamental contrast indeed, in a truly dualistic sense, between the "material" elements and Nous, and any matter-like attribute given to Nous would justly be considered an inconsistency of Anaxagoras, stemming from his alleged failure to carry the idea of dualism to its extreme consequences.

The Aristotelian interpretation, however, does not correspond to the genuine teaching of Anaxagoras who – unless we refuse to give credence to his own words – has assumed elements like those described in this reconstruction. Now, if we bear in mind this new interpretation, then *to the question: Is Anaxagoras' Nous "pure spirit"?, the obvious answer is a counterquestion: Are his moiras "pure matter"?*

It has been overlooked that Anaxagoras, too, is a *panzoist, i.e.,* one to whom *body and consciousness are still a unity not yet analysed.* In this respect, he is not different from his predecessors, the Ionian Transformists, who had believed in a divine person, one and boundless, a living divine primary substance, one and homogeneous. This "principle," this ἀρχή, was the unseparate "together" of a body-component and a consciousness-component. But it probably did not even enter the heads of those thinkers not to take an identity of body and consciousness for self-evident. The notions of a "matter without consciousness" and a "consciousness without body" do not yet exist for these men.[1]

Anaxagoras, however, makes two unprecedented discoveries.

The one: *Within a principle homogeneous throughout* – that is to say, within a body uniform throughout and a consciousness uniform throughout – *nothing distinguishable can happen,* in an outright physical and mechanical sense, *and no cosmos could arise from it. If a world is to result there must be dissimilarities.*[2] (This in itself would have been another reason for assuming a plurality of different, unequal elements [cf. p. 203, n. 1].)

The other discovery: *The principles of the predecessors are not uniform, anyway. For the deity's body, be it water or air or whatever else, is but seemingly homogeneous. Strictly speaking, it is a complex: a complex of an irreducible plurality of "things" really simplest and specific, the proper "seeds in no way resembling each other."*

Only these would be homogeneous – if they could be isolated. Each of them, if such isolation were feasible, would then be as homogeneous in itself as is that one purest and thinnest of all "things," the medium in which the others are embedded: the deity's spirit.

But *neither is this a "pure spirit," nor are the constituents of the deity's body "pure matter."*

There is no such gap between the purest and thinnest thing and the other things as between "spirit" and "matter." Or rather, the gap of dissimilarity is not greater than between the other things themselves, between a color and a temperature, for instance, or between any of the "seeds in no way resembling each other." But all the "things" alike are

---

[1] That is why I am avoiding the usual term "hylozoism." It seems to me misleading and inadequate.

[2] Cf. A. Stöhr, *Der Begriff des Lebens* (Heidelberg, 1909), pp. 69 and 340.

of spatial extensiveness, all of them have aseity, all of them are equally eternal, and also in power there is only a difference of quantity, just as between a ruler and his subjects. And while Nous is extensive like "matter," the "material" elements are never outside "consciousness," because at any time they are embedded in Nous and touched by Nous and thereby known by Nous who is always present *"wherever all the others are."* [1]

It is highly significant that as a designation for all the ultimate constituents of the world, for all the "elements," for Nous as well as the others, Anaxagoras employs the term "thing" (*chrema*). This is no doubt one of the most general and most neutral expressions one can imagine, an expression as neutral as, or even more neutral than, the term "neutral stuff" of certain great epistemologists of our day.[2]

All this is built up consistently throughout. It is along the same clue that Anaxagoras has arrived at the assumption of a Nous and of the other constituents of the universe. He could not construct a full world-personality without a Nous. For him the other elements alone would not have constituted, in a monistic sense, a complete set, but a truncation.

Anaxagoras, the Monist, the Dualist, the Pluralist

And here we are again. "In a monistic sense," I have said. We have returned, then, to that topic usually given such outstanding importance: the question of attaching a number-label. Is Anaxagoras to be called a "dualist"? Or a "monist"? Or what?

As already mentioned, Anaxagoras has from times immemorial been labelled "the first dualist." Only a small minority of scholars prefer to consider him a monist, and even a materialistic one.

If there is any sense at all to this custom of labelling, one has to ask first: What is it that is supposed to be counted? Then, however, one and the same thing would obviously have to be given various labels, according to the different classifications possible:

[1] fr. 14 (Simpl. phys. 157, 5). (Cf. pp. 207 and 271).
[2] There are striking similarities between Anaxagoras' pre-dualistic theory and the post-dualistic views of William James (*Essays in Radical Empiricism*) and E. B. Holt (*Concept of Consciousness*). The term *neutral stuff* is indeed less neutral than Anaxagoras' plain "thing," the word *stuff* still implying something like matter, after all, and *neutral* admittedly (cf. Holt, p. 124, annot., and p. 136) being a substitution for "conceptual."

For if classified according to the assumed number of constituents not reducible to one another, Anaxagoras is even a *pluralist*.

But if the oneness of the clue and the deeper meaning of the whole construction is considered, then Anaxagoras is a *monist*, though certainly not a materialistic, but at any rate an immaterialistic monist.

If, however, one is absolutely bent on keeping the old label, – well, then this is likewise feasible, though not in the traditional sense. For Anaxagoras is indeed a *dualist*, too, in so far as he accepts the disunion into sense and intellect, into αἴσθησις and νόησις.

A Heretic Digression

When speaking of Anaxagoras' fundamental discovery that if a world is to result there must be dissimilarities, I have added in parenthesis: "This in itself would have been another reason for assuming a plurality of different, unequal elements." (p. 321)

It would justly be called neglect, or even cowardice, if I failed to make use of this opportunity for frankly discussing a sacred dogma of the historians of philosophy: the alleged dependence of Anaxagoras on Parmenides.

One may, I daresay, at least leave open the question as to whether or not Anaxagoras' assumption of a plurality of unchangeable elements was also dependent, historically, on the doctrine of Parmenides, and whether or not that assumption was also conditioned by any regard for ostensible immanent contradictions in the notion of becoming. At any rate, for an understanding of the inner development of the Anaxagorean system it would not be necessary to presuppose such relationship.

There are, even, momentous reasons telling against a probability of such relationship. In fact, namely, Anaxagoras' construction betrays no regard at all for the prohibitions issued by Parmenides. In the world of Anaxagoras there is plenty of locomotion, of change of place, while according to Parmenides one must not take for true any changing of place (τόπον ἀλλάσσειν). There is also plenty of qualitative change, in flagrant contradiction of the Parmenidean denial of any changing of color (χρόα ἀμείβειν). And when Anaxagoras explains (not: "explains away"!) qualitative changes by changes of combining-ratios, he just explains one sort of change by another sort of change – in perfect disregard for Parmenides' banishment from the realm of Truth of any change whatsoever.

Those alleging that Anaxagoras was intent on strictly observing a Parmenidean "canon of No Becoming" and that he nonetheless could "postulate motion in space" because this is "the only change that does not involve 'becoming'" (F. M. Cornford, A. L. Peck, O. Gigon, G. Vlastos, etc.) ought to have had one more look at Parmenides' own words. They would have learned that the primordial law of Parmenidean philosophy is not any "canon of No Becoming," but the warning, "There is no μὴ εἶναι, no not-being." And they would have found that Parmenides' rejection of γίγνεσθαι (becoming), ὄλλυσθαι (perishing), τόπον ἀλλάσσειν (change of place), χρόα ἀμείβειν (change of color and, of course, of any quality for that matter), of ἦν (past), and of ἔσται (future) is simply consecutive to his "canon of No Not-Being," since to him all these are just as many instances of Not-Being and, therefore, nothing but "(empty) words." (Cf. p. 541).

For Parmenides, then, there is not any becoming or perishing or any change whatsoever, and all that our senses tell us to the contrary is untrue. Anaxagoras, however, merely maintains (cf. p. 183) that there is no coming into existence out of nothing nor any literal annihilation. Which is something utterly different.

Also, the reason for Anaxagoras' assumption of a plurality of unchangeable elements is not given by, nor can be derived from, his reprehension that the words γίνεσθαι and ἀπόλλυσθαι are "wrongly used by the Hellenes." It is exactly the other way round. Just because he has assumed – for quite other reasons, as we have seen – a plurality of eternal, unchangeable elements, he finds that it would be correct to replace those expressions by "to become mixed together" and "to become severed," respectively.

It has been overlooked that the same remark about the inadequacy of those words could have been made by Anaxagoras if he had assumed only one, and changeable, element. Then, too, he could have said: "'To come into existence' and 'to be annihilated' are wrongly used by the Hellenes." Only the argumentation would have been different. He would have continued: "For no one thing comes into existence or is annihilated, but all things are merely as many different transformations of the one principle that eternally exists. And thus it might be correct for the Hellenes to replace both of those terms alike by 'to be changed'."

Is Anaxagoras an Inconsistent Teleologist?

Today as in antiquity, Nous is considered a deity setting purposes. Anaxagoras is still taken for the first teleologist. And it is still thought right to accuse him, as did Plato, of inconsistency therein.

When Socrates – according to that well-known passage in Plato's *Phaedo* – had learned of Anaxagoras introducing Nous as the world's "arranging principle" (διακοσμῶν) and "originator of all things" (πάντων αἴτιος), he read the writings of the Clazomenian with great zeal and, as he says,

> in order to obtain *knowledge of the best and the lesser* the speediest possible.

> ἵν' ὡς τάχιστα εἰδείην τὸ βέλτιστον καὶ τὸ χεῖρον.

And with gross mockery he complains:

> Yet, my friend, I have most rapidly dropped such wonderful hope. For when going on reading I see a man not making use of "intelligence" at all *nor assigning any reasons for arranging affairs*, but adducing as "reasons" airs and ethers and waters and a lot of other preposterous rubbish.

> ἀπὸ δὴ θαυμαστῆς ἐλπίδος, ὦ ἑταῖρε, ᾠχόμην φερόμενος, ἐπειδὴ προϊὼν καὶ ἀναγιγνώσκων ὁρῶ ἄνδρα τῷ μὲν νῷ οὐδὲν χρώμενον οὐδέ τινας αἰτίας ἐπαιτιώμενον εἰς τὸ διακοσμεῖν τὰ πράγματα, ἀέρας δὲ καὶ αἰθέρας καὶ ὕδατα αἰτιώμενον καὶ ἄλλα πολλὰ καὶ ἄτοπα.

> Plato, Phaedo, 98B; A47

However, as has been demontrated (cf. p. 198), teleology in its exact meaning is out of the question with Anaxagoras, since Nous, the divine mechanician, the construction engineer of the world, is not "setting purposes." Hence, it does not seem quite justified to blame Anaxagoras for not having sufficiently availed himself of the (supposedly) teleological principle of a Nous.

Is Nous Really But a Stop-Gap?

With this reproach by Plato, an Aristotelian animadversion is commonly confused, although it does not coincide with the Platonic criticism nor would be affected by its confutation.

In his *Metaphysics*, Aristotle blames Anaxagoras because allegedly

> *he makes use of Nous for cosmogony in the way of a theatre-machine and drags it in only when in a dilemma as to the cause by which anything happens necessarily*, whilst otherwise he alleges as causes of the occurrences all things rather than Nous.

> μηχανῇ χρῆται τῷ νῷ πρὸς τὴν κοσμοποιίαν καὶ ὅταν ἀπορήσῃ διὰ τίν'

157

αἰτίαν ἐξ ἀνάγκης ἐστί, τότε παρέλκει αὐτόν, ἐν δὲ τοῖς ἄλλοις πάντα
μᾶλλον αἰτιᾶται τῶν γιγνομένων ἢ νοῦν.

Arist. Metaph. I 4. 985a18; A47.

That is to say, in Aristotle's opinion Anaxagoras employed Nous but
as a stop-gap, a make-shift, having Nous intervene in those cases only
in which he had not managed to uncover the natural, necessary
mechanics.

Should this criticism be justified, then Aristotle would have pointed
indeed at a badly amateurish insufficiency in Anaxagoras' construction.
(Today, of course, one would not blame Anaxagoras, as did Aristotle,
for having used the working of Nous as an explanation in those few
cases only, but for not having left everything to the same natural
lawfulness.) For then Anaxagoras, instead of singly admitting his
inability to uncover the mechanics, would have had the limit of
natural lawfulness coincide with the limit of his knowledge of it. Thus,
in this respect, Anaxagoras would be modern in a way not very
favorable to him. He would acquire some resemblance to certain
biologists who likewise let the actual shore of their knowledge of the
mechanics of things be bound by an ocean of new, different, un-
mechanical lawfulness, without paying heed to the fact that year after
year fresh soil emerges from the supposedly bottomless.

Was Anaxagoras really so "modern" as to contrive a new agent, only
to stop with it the gaps of his insight? Is it true that only when being
unable to indicate "by what cause a thing occurs necessarily" does he
have Nous intervene? Are the δῖνοι ("whirls") in Anaxagoras' world
really ἀνόητοι ("irrational"; the word means also: "nous-less"), and do
they really occur "without action and cognition by Nous" (σὺν τῇ τοῦ
νοῦ ἀπραξίᾳ τε καὶ ἀνοίᾳ), as Clement of Alexandria says,[1] following
Plato and Aristotle?

All these critics did apparently not understand that *to Anaxagoras
the very mechanics, seemingly blind, of the world occurrence was so full of
genius, so fraught with meaning, so beauteous and grand, that he could
comprehend it but from the conscious working of an intellect, an intellect
ingenious like a god's.*

His critics did not pay enough attention to the fact

that Anaxagoras had been *the first to put on the head of the world
systems as principle of arrangement not hazard nor (blind) necessity,
but Nous,*

[1] Strom. II 14 p. 435 P; A57.

ὅτι τοῖς ὅλοις πρῶτος οὐ τύχην οὐδ' ἀνάγκην διακοσμήσεως ἀρχήν, ἀλλὰ νοῦν ἐπέστησε,

Plutarch. Pericl. 4; A15.

and that

> he says that
>
>> "none of all occurrences occurs by (a blind) fate, but this very word is void of sense."
>
> λέγει γὰρ οὗτος (sc., 'Αναξαγόρας) μηδὲν τῶν γινομένων γίνεσθαι καθ' εἱμαρμένην, ἀλλ' εἶναι κενὸν τοῦτο τοὔνομα.

Alex. de fato 2 (II 165, 22 Bruns); A66.

And neither Plato nor Aristotle has noticed that *precisely all those ostensibly preposterous and senseless things, those* ἄτοπα καὶ ἀνόητα, *are original and own performances of Nous, that all this* perichoresis *continues only as long as Nous Itself keeps on rotating, and that no organism can stay alive unless Nous keeps it going.*

To blame Anaxagoras for allegedly having used Nous as a stop-gap betrays some superficiality on the part of the critics:

Anaxagoras taught that *the whole world course was being operated by Nous,*

> All has been arranged by Nous,
>
> πάντα διεκόσμησε νοῦς,

and

> All is ruled (*i.e.*, moved as well as known) by Nous.
>
> πάντων νοῦς κρατεῖ.

Besides, however, Anaxagoras *tried to uncover the mechanics* applied to it by Nous, to find out

> *in what way* God brings about each of the occurrences in the sky,
>
> τῶν οὐρανίων ᾗ ἕκαστα θεὸς μηχανᾶται.

Xenoph. Mem. IV 7, 6; A 73.

That is to say, consequently:

In all those cases in which, in his opinion, Anaxagoras had succeeded in solving the riddle, he has of course *not repeated* again and again what he had stated once and for all: *that it is Nous who performs all this* in the way described. Only when Anaxagoras had not been able to find out the mechanism of an occurrence, he will have marked it *expressly* as a work of Nous. By so doing, however, he meant to indicate: *In this occurrence, the same lawfulness is at work as in all the other occurrences; this, too, is done by Nous; but I am not yet able to explain how.*

Thus, Aristotle does not seem to have done justice to Anaxagoras in this point, either.

Plato, however, – even if in every instance Anaxagoras had expressly mentioned Nous as the principle at work in the mechanics – Plato, from his standpoint, could still have said: "Well, this certainly is a deification of the world mechanics. But – what, in all that, is supposed to be considered 'the best' and what 'the lesser' (τὸ βέλτιστον καὶ τὸ χεῖρον) is known to me no better now than heretofore."

EPILOGUE

To comprehend the structure of the world and reproduce it in a philosophic mould – this was the task Anaxagoras had undertaken. His philosophizing's deepest root had been a bent for moulding like an artist's.

His speculation's way was worked upon neither by hidden wishing nor by hankering after comfort or desire for hope. He may not have at all put to himself the question of how defectiveness and pain could come into a world ruled by a Nous. He never may have felt an impetus to interpreting the world, to looking for a meaning of the sufferings of life. The mere theorist just is not very sensitive to life's essential tragedy.

This Nous, Lord of the World, is neither a kind-hearted father nor a spiteful demon, but an ingenious mathematician and physicist entirely devoid of sentiment.

Nous is "Originator of All Things" (πάντων αἴτιος [Plato, Phaedo 97B]) and "The Cause of 'Beautifully' and 'Correctly'" (τὸ αἴτιον τοῦ καλῶς καὶ ὀρθῶς [Arist. de anima I 2. 404b2]). That means together:

In this universe, there is no one occurrence whatsoever not passing off in beauteous, divine exactness. It is in beauty and correctness that the world is running on, phase by phase, and veering after veering, without beginning and without an end, a magic pastime of the World-Nous for the sake of beauty.

INDEX OF PASSAGES

The numbers in bold type refer to pages in this work. The statements in parenthesis refer to places in the 6th edition of Diels' *Die Fragmente der Vorsokratiker*, ,,A''meaning reports, ,,B'' meaning literal quotations. Lack of such parentheses indicates that those passages are not contained in the Diels collection.

INDEX OF NAMES